Final Choices

Making End-of-Life Decisions

Final Choices
Making End-of-Life Decisions

Lee E. Norrgard

Senior Investigative Analyst
Consumer Affairs Section
American Association of Retired Persons

Jo DeMars

Consumer Affairs Consultant and President,
DeMars and Associates, Ltd.

Choices and Challenges: An Older Adult Reference Series
Elizabeth Vierck, Series Editor

ABC-CLIO
Santa Barbara, California
Denver, Colorado
Oxford, England

Library of Congress Cataloging-in-Publication Data

Norrgard, Lee E.
　　Final choices : making end-of-life decisions / Lee E. Norrgard,
　Jo DeMars.
　　　　p.　cm.—(Choices and challenges)
　　Includes bibliographical references and index.
　　1. Death—Social aspects—United States.　2. Decision-making—
United States.　3. Right to die—United States.　4. Funeral rites
and ceremonies—United States.　5. Bereavement.　6. Aged—United
States—Life skills guides.　I. DeMars, Jo.　II. Title
III. Series.
　　HQ1073.5.U6N67　1992　　306.9—dc20　　92-28781

ISBN 0-87436-613-5

99 98 97 96 95 94 93 92　　10 9 8 7 6 5 4 3 2 1

ABC-CLIO, Inc.
130 Cremona Drive, P.O. Box 1911
Santa Barbara, California 93116-1911

This book is printed on acid-free paper ∞
Manufactured in the United States of America

Contents

Chapter 6: Directory of Organizations, 115

Chapter 7: Reference Materials, 149

List of Figures

Preface

To every thing there is a season, and a time to every purpose under the heaven: a time to be born, a time to die; a time to plant, and a time to pluck up that which is planted. . . .

Eccles. 4:1–2

End of life, dying, death. These words are hard for most people to read, to think about, and especially to speak. Loss, especially the loss of someone who is dear, is among the most tragic and traumatic experiences human beings have.

Therefore, simply picking up a book titled *Final Choices: Making End-of-Life Decisions* is an act of courage and acknowledgment. It takes courage to admit the mortality of loved ones and of oneself. Most of us prefer to think of our lives as never-ending and our deaths as far off in the future, an event hardly worth a scant thought. As people grow and learn, they come to terms with the facts of life and death. Most people come to realize that death is one fact of life that everyone will experience.

Recognizing the reality of death enables people to acknowledge the importance of making conscious, thoughtful, and responsible decisions about how one will die, how to handle final disposition of the body, and how to pay for the services and merchandise selected in a funeral or other disposition. These are all important decisions that reflect the individual's values and attitudes. Whether making the choices for oneself or for another, these items deserve careful thought, consideration, and attention.

These decisions may involve planning a funeral, memorial, or other service. One may have to decide about medical and health care procedures that one wishes to decline or use. There are many details to decide in finalizing a plan. A sample checklist of final decisions might include:

___   A Living Will or other Advance Medical Directive is prepared.

___   The will is in order.

___   A complete and up-to-date Letter of Instruction is prepared.

___   All individuals who need to have access to these documents know where they are located.

___   A representative has been designated to make the necessary final decisions if one becomes unable to act on one's own behalf.

___   Any additional steps needed to provide the representative with appropriate legal authority to make these decisions are completed.

___   The decisions are made about how and where the body will be handled.

___   If a service or funeral is desired, the instructions are complete.

___   Choices have been made about using a casket, an outer burial container, or a container for cremated remains.

___   A monument or memorial stone, if desired, has been selected.

___   The cemetery or other place for final disposition is identified.

___   The total anticipated cost has been calculated.

___   The advantages and disadvantages of preplanning and prepayment have been considered.

___   It has been determined who will handle filing the death certificate and any other necessary legal forms.

___   The means for paying the bills has been identified.

___   All available death benefits are specified, including life insurance and Social Security.

___   Individuals who need to know of these wishes have been informed and know where to locate any necessary forms or other information.

How This Book Is Organized

Final Choices: Making End-of-Life Decisions has been written primarily for older adults and their children. However, many other people, young or middle-aged, may find the book useful as well. This book is designed to introduce basic information about the many available options. It is divided into two parts: the first a narrative section organized by topic and the second a collection of resources.

Part One

In Part One, basic information is provided on death, dying, and funeral services from three perspectives: financial, legal, and emotional. These subjects are arranged as follows.

CHAPTER 1: THE RIGHT TO DIE

Detailed information on Living Wills and Advance Medical Directives can be found in this chapter. Recent medical advances have enabled health care professionals to maintain the vital functions of many patients who previously would have died. This chapter explains these changes and offers suggestions that may help readers decide what options to exercise. It also provides suggestions about points to consider when making health care decisions, whether for oneself or another. People who want to ensure that their medical care decisions are carried out will find background information in this chapter.

Decisions To Make

1. Is an Advance Medical Directive desired or necessary?

2. Will a Living Will provide appropriate guidance?

3. Is a comprehensive Advance Medical Directive desired or necessary?

4. Is a Durable Power of Attorney for Health Care desirable or necessary?

5. If so, what types of treatment might be used or declined?

   nutrition and/or hydration

   resuscitation

dialysis

ventilation

blood pressure support

antibiotics

pain relief

6. Is a health care agent desirable or necessary?

7. If so, on what factors will one choose the agent?

trust

location

assertiveness and intelligence

kindness

family relationship

8. What kinds of decisions are inappropriate?

9. What guidelines will a health care agent use when making decisions?

substitute judgment

best interest

10. How can the health care agent make decisions when there is no clear Advance Directive?

This information may also be useful to those who serve as guardians for a loved one or a ward. Specific suggestions are included to assist in making difficult decisions when no clear instructions have been provided by the ward.

CHAPTER 2: COPING WITH DEATH

This chapter focuses primarily on the emotional aspects that accompany death and dying. It includes simple explanations of grief and mourning as well as suggestions for finding and giving help during the grieving process. Research has supplied information to help bereaved people understand that what they are feeling is normal and necessary. This chapter provides a listing of the stages of grief that often serve as signposts for those who are grieving.

Decisions To Make

1. Will accepting death as a natural part of living be difficult?

2. What previous experiences have prepared one for loss? For this particular loss?

3. How are each of the stages of grief apparent in this loss?

   denial

   hostility or anger

   bargaining or negotiation

   depression

   acceptance

4. Has mourning been apparent?

5. Is it comfortable to allow the grief to take its natural, necessary course? If not, where can support be obtained?

6. Are personal skills available to assist others in their grief?

   listening

   offering empathy

   utilizing tolerance

   learning about individual characteristics

   staying alert for warning signs

7. Can normal grief be differentiated from depression?

8. Is professional help needed?

9. If professional help is chosen, how will the counselor be selected?

Those individuals who are coping with the intense emotional work of letting go of a loved one will find this chapter a resource and a starting point. Suggestions for helping others and for locating support groups are included.

CHAPTER 3: ARRANGING OR PREARRANGING A FUNERAL

This chapter presents descriptions of traditional funerals, alternative funerals, the various costs of services and merchandise, and basic consumer-protection information. Readers may be unaware of the many options that are available and the relative costs of different types of merchandise and services. Detailed information defines various items that may be used and explains when some of these items are not necessary. Additionally, some typical prices are provided, which may be helpful when making preliminary choices. This chapter is useful to individuals who are selecting services and merchandise either for an immediate need or for a future need.

Decisions To Make

1. What kind of ceremony will be held—traditional funeral or alternative?

2. What merchandise will be needed?

   casket

   outer burial container

   urn or other container for cremated remains

   monument or marker

3. Will there be a wake or viewing?

4. What kind of flowers, music, and service, if any, are preferred?

5. Will the body be buried above ground or in the ground, donated, or cremated?

6. Will a funeral director be involved? If yes, which one?

7. Who will file the legal documents such as the death certificate?

8. Will there be an embalming?

9. Who will preside at the ceremony, if one is held?

10. If needed, what cemetery will be used?

11. What kinds of service and merchandise will fit the available budget?

12. What is the total cost for merchandise, services, and the cemetery, including opening and closing fees?

Information is supplied about how to gather comparison prices in the area. And basic consumer protection suggestions are included.

CHAPTER 4: PAYING OR PREPAYING FOR A FUNERAL

Information about the resources that may be available to pay for a funeral are listed in this chapter. The question of whether to prepay for one's funeral is discussed, along with detailed information about various methods of prepaying. Additionally, this chapter offers points to consider when making these financial decisions. Basic consumer-protection measures that regulate the sale of pre-need funeral plans are outlined.

Decisions To Make

1. What financial resources are available to help pay for the funeral?

   Social Security, veterans', or other benefits

   life insurance

   savings

2. Should money be set aside for funeral expenses if the individual is a Supplemental Security Income or Medicaid recipient?

3. Will prepaying be an advantage or a disadvantage?

4. How might funds for prepaying be invested?

   personal trust, revocable or irrevocable

   state-regulated trust

   insurance

5. What earnings and safety factors will affect the type of investment chosen?

6. If prepaying is selected, will the plan continue to fit the consumer's needs in the event of a move or other change?

This information, in conjunction with that in Chapters 3 and 5, will answer the readers' basic questions about how to plan and pay for the final disposition, whether it be a traditional service or a simpler version.

CHAPTER 5: SORTING OUT THE FINAL DETAILS

This chapter features a comprehensive listing of the items one needs to remember when taking care of the estate of someone who dies. It includes a checklist of final details, descriptions of possible sources of death benefits, and instructions about how to deal with property and possessions. This chapter will be particularly useful to people who are not certain what assets are available or where information about the assets can be located.

Decisions To Make

1. Has a Letter of Instruction been prepared?

2. Are all of the legal documents organized?

   death certificate

   marriage certificate

   birth certificate

   certificates of honorable discharge, adoption, etc.

3. Has a will been prepared? If not, is one desired or necessary?

4. Has a personal representative or executor been named?

5. Do the individuals who need access to these documents and a safe deposit box know where they are located?

6. What documents are needed in order to file federal and state income tax forms?

7. What documents are needed in order to file federal and state estate and inheritance tax forms?

8. What are the person's debts and assets, and how will they be distributed?

   real estate

   motor vehicle(s)

   bank accounts

   employee benefits

   life insurance (including mortgage and credit life)

   Social Security

   investments

   other assets

9. Is probate necessary? If yes, what level of court involvement is required?

10. Will an attorney be needed?

11. Will names or addresses have to be changed on utility bills, credit cards, and other accounts to facilitate the transfer of credit records and prompt payment?

12. Have documents been filed to transfer the titles of real estate, motor vehicles, bank accounts, and so forth?

13. What other steps should be taken to reduce the tax liability and the financial uncertainty for loved ones?

This chapter is particularly important if topics such as insurance, death benefits, wills, and estates are new to the reader. It also describes how to track down information about the location of safe deposit boxes or life insurance policies.

Part Two

Part Two offers resource information and is divided into two chapters, a glossary, and two appendixes.

CHAPTER 6: DIRECTORY OF ORGANIZATIONS

This chapter contains three parts. The first lists organizations and agencies associated with death and dying or funeral service. This directory provides background and referral information for the reader who is interested in a specific topic or who needs consumer-education/protection information.

The second part lists groups that provide information or services on other subjects of interest to older adults or people who are terminally ill. This listing of allied industries and organizations provides supplemental information.

The third section lists the addresses and telephone numbers of state and local chapters of the Continental Association of Funeral and Memorial Societies, Inc.

CHAPTER 7: REFERENCE MATERIALS

The listings in this chapter include books, pamphlets, brochures, articles, films, videotapes, audiotapes, and computer-based information available on death, dying, and funeral service.

GLOSSARY

The glossary provides concise definitions for several terms that are relevant to the subjects covered in this book.

APPENDIXES

Appendix A: Letter of Instruction is a sample personal inventory form. Appendix B: Funeral and Cemetery Regulatory Agencies,

Right-To-Die Laws, and Schools for Body Donations is a state-by-state listing of death-related information. Included are the consumer-protection agencies for funeral directors and cemeteries, the latest right-to-die statutes, and institutions that accept body donations.

Conclusion

Making end-of-life decisions is a complex matter that involves handling legal requirements such as Living Wills and death certificates, dealing with financial obligations including estate taxes and funeral expenses, and facing emotional issues such as guilt, grief, and sorrow.

For many people, making these final choices represents the last opportunity to give time, attention, and talents to a loved one. Many people have expressed a deep appreciation for the opportunity to take care of a loved one's final needs. Some find comfort in "being able to give back," and others say it just helps to "have something to do." Others simply handle the job out of a sense of duty.

Regardless of the individual's feelings, every person requires someone else to perform these tasks. The dignity with which these tasks are undertaken and carried out speaks of the respect one holds for all life and for humanity.

The very nature of grief and mourning often causes people to become self-focused and less aware of those around them. It's important to remember that others share one's grief and loss. As Howard Raether, former executive director of the National Funeral Directors Association, says, "A funeral is the only formal occasion for which no invitations are sent, but at which all are welcome." It's helpful to keep in mind that others may welcome an opportunity to participate in the process of finalizing details, and in remembering the life.

We hope that this book lightens the load, simplifies the task, and eases the heart. And we hope that, in time, it will be the season to laugh and the time to dance.

Acknowledgments

The authors wish to express their gratitude for the technical input of the National Funeral Directors Association, Service Corporation International Inc., the American Cemetery Association, the Center for Public Representation, Hillenbrand Industries, Inc., and the U.S. Department of Veterans Affairs.

In addition, the authors would like to thank the following individuals: Laurel Beedon, Helen Marks Dicks, Judy Fink, Lori Flemming, Karen P. Goebel, Charles Harrington, Sandra Hering, William V. Hocker, Judy Husbeck, Diane L. Kauffman, Michael J. Klug, Katherine LaTour, Tom Nelson, Howard Raether, and Robin Talbert. Without the careful review and comments of these individuals, this book would never have been written. Any oversights, however, belong to us.

Our thanks also go to our families, whose patience made the job easier.

How To Use This Book

Each book in the Choices and Challenges series provides a convenient, easy-access reference tool on a specific topic of interest to older adults and those involved with them, including caregivers, spouses, adult children, and gerontology professionals. The books are designed for ease of use, with a generous typeface, ample use of headings and subheadings, and a detailed index.

Each book consists of two parts, which may be used together or independently:

A narrative section providing an informative and comprehensive overview of the topic, written for a lay audience. The narrative can be read straight through or consulted on an as-needed basis by using the headings and subheadings and/or the index.

An annotated resource section that includes a directory of relevant organizations; recommended books, pamphlets, and articles; and software and videos. Where appropriate, the resource section may include additional information relevant to the topic. This section can be used in conjunction with or separately from the narrative to locate sources of additional information, assistance, or support.

A glossary defines important terms and concepts, and the index provides additional access to the material. For easy reference, entries in the resource section are indexed by both topic and title or name.

Final Choices

Chapter 1

The Right To Die

John Brady sat in the kitchen with his son and two daughters. It had been a long discussion; the second pot of coffee was half-empty.

John's 84-year-old wife, Marie, was in a nursing home across town. John had called each of the children six months ago to tell the news: Marie had collapsed in the backyard and the paramedics were on the way. It had seemed like hours before the ambulance arrived, even though John knew it was only minutes. That was just the start of the endless waiting.

After spending days in the hospital's critical care unit, Marie had been moved to a semiprivate room, and then to the nursing home. The life-support equipment kept up a steady hum in the small room. John and the kids visited Marie every day, but they couldn't tell if she even knew they were there.

The doctor has said that things don't look good. It wasn't just the stroke; Marie's cigarette smoking had affected her lungs, and the doctor was also worried about her kidneys. He couldn't tell if Marie would ever wake up.

Now, John and the kids must decide, "Do we let Mom die?"

KEY FACTS

- Ten thousand people in the United States are in a chronic or persistent vegetative state, that is, the individual is in a coma with little or no hope of recovery.

- Fewer than 5 percent of Americans have completed a Living Will.

- Six out of ten Americans agree that someone with an incurable disease has the right to end his or her life.

- In a recent survey, 72 percent of the respondents approved of doctors ending the life of the hopelessly ill at the patient's request.

- Some 88 percent viewed stopping of treatment as a family matter when the person has no hope of recovering.

- In the survey, 8 percent said the doctor should decide when to terminate treatment; 1 percent said the matter should be handled by a judge.

- Some 11 percent of Americans have written instructions regarding their wishes for medical treatment.

In western movies, when a cowboy was mortally wounded, his compatriots gathered around in tense sadness and witnessed the death. Then one of the survivors would bend over and place an ear on the dead man's chest to listen for a heartbeat or a flutter of breath. "Jake's dead," he'd say solemnly. And Jake's friends would sadly shake their heads as they acknowledged death's finality.

In hospitals today, the procedure for determining when a patient has died is quite different. Modern technology provides medical science with machines that can continuously monitor the patient's heart, respiration, and brain waves. Doctors use the electronic feedback from this equipment to decide when death occurs.

The idea that an individual might be kept alive by "tubes" or machines alarms and concerns many people. Some have discussed with their friends and families the concepts of death with dignity and quality of life. Many of these people have made specific decisions about the type of medical treatment they approve and don't approve for themselves. These decisions are usually spelled out in a formal document such as a Living Will or an Advance Medical Directive to be followed by medical personnel. Sometimes these decisions are not recorded in writing but have been expressed as opinions about "medical heroics" or organ donations during a conversation with a friend or family member.

This chapter provides information that individuals and family members will find useful in determining what type of medical treatment they want or don't want. It explains what documents can be used to ensure that one's wishes will be carried out. It presents facts for the reader who wants to make informed decisions about "right-to-die" and medical treatment issues. This chapter also offers suggestions about factors to consider when deciding about medical treatment and the termination of treatment for oneself or another person.

In the 1970s, news articles publicized the court cases concerning Karen Quinlan, a young woman in a persistent vegetative state. Her parents petitioned the courts for permission to remove her life-support system and allow her to "die in dignity." More recently, the U.S. Supreme Court ruled on the issue of Nancy Cruzan, another comatose woman whose family asked that she be allowed to die.

These dramatic court battles focused attention on the issues of the right to die, dying with dignity, and the quality of life. These are emotional issues that divide families, the medical community, and even the courts. Families are forced to make painful decisions without a clear right-or-wrong answer. The questions most often asked are, When does death occur? and When do we turn off the machines?

Life-support systems such as ventilators and feeding by tubes can keep a permanently unconscious person alive for several years. Even though machines are able to reproduce the functions of the heart electronically and to provide oxygen to the body, there is no machine that can replace even the simplest brain activity. It has been argued that brain death is the appropriate criterion for determining when a patient is legally dead.

Therefore, 41 states have adopted brain death as the standard of death. This means that a person who is certified to have absolutely no electrical activity in the brain, by clinical observation and measurement by an electroencephalogram, is defined as dead. In the same way, a person who has no spontaneous heartbeat or respiration is defined as dead. In this situation no one needs to give permission to stop medical treatment, because the person is legally dead.

But a patient in a persistent or chronic vegetative state, without consciousness but with at least some brain activity, does not fit this definition. Many people believe a person should be declared dead when further medical treatment will not benefit him or her, especially if the person's organs could be transplanted for the benefit of another gravely ill person. In these cases, the determination of death is legally and medically more controversial. Therefore, many people choose to record or express their wishes about being kept alive if they're ever in an untreatable, unconscious medical state.

The statutory definition of brain death is typically similar to the language used by the state of New Mexico, as shown in Figure 1.1.

---

(1) Based on ordinary standards of medical practice, there is the absence of spontaneous respiratory and cardiac function and, because of the disease or condition which caused, directly or indirectly, these functions to cease, or because of the passage of time since these functions ceased, there is no reasonable possibility of restoring respiratory or cardiac functions; in this event death occurs at the time respiratory or cardiac functions ceased; or

(2) in the opinion of a physician, based on ordinary standard of medical practice:

   (a) because of a known disease or condition there is the absence of spontaneous brain function; and

   (b) after reasonable attempts to either maintain or restore spontaneous circulatory or respiratory functions in the absence of spontaneous brain functions, it appears that further attempts at resuscitation . . . and supportive maintenance have no reasonable possibility of restoring spontaneous brain function; in this event death will have occurred at the time when the absence of spontaneous brain function first occurred. Death is to be pronounced pursuant to this paragraph before artificial means of supporting respiratory or circulatory functions are terminated and before any vital organ is removed for purpose of transplantation in compliance with the Uniform Anatomical Gift Act.

Figure 1.1   Definition of Brain Death. New Mexico Annotated Stat., Section 12-2-4.

Advance Medical Directives

Many experts advocate preparing Advance Medical Directives to make individual preferences known. These documents ease the weight of the decisions about medical treatment and the termination of treatment for family members or others.

Living Wills

The most common form of an Advance Medical Directive is the Living Will. Most jurisdictions (40 states and the District of Columbia) have Living Will statutes, commonly titled the "Natural Death Act" or "Death with Dignity Act." A state-by-state listing of these statutes is included in Appendix B.

Living Wills vary from state to state because the language is written to reflect the specific laws of the state. To be sure a Living Will is enforceable, it is important to verify that it provides adequate guidance for each of the decisions that might be faced and conforms with the laws of the state in which the person lives.

A typical Living Will may be similar to the one prepared for residents of New York, shown in Figure 1.2.

Since Living Wills are legal documents under state laws, it is important that individuals seek information regarding the specific requirements in the state in which they live. Generic forms supplied by national organizations may or may not be legally binding in certain states. Therefore, it is important to get up-to-date information before making plans for Advance Medical Directives. This information is available from the state or Area Agency on Aging. The phone number is listed in the local telephone directory. The Society for the Right to Die, listed in Chapter 6, also has information.

Hospitals, nursing homes, and hospices are also good sources of information about how to protect health care interests. Hospitals and nursing homes that accept Medicare and Medicaid are required to furnish information about Advance Medical

8

I, _____, being of sound mind, make this statement as a directive to be followed if I become permanently unable to participate in decisions regarding my medical care. These binding instructions reflect my firm and settled commitment to decline medical treatment under the circumstances below:

I direct my attending physician to withhold or withdraw treatment that serves only to prolong the process of my dying, if I should be in an incurable or irreversible mental or physical condition with no reasonable expectation of recovery.

These instructions apply if I am:
    (a) in a terminal condition;
    (b) permanently unconscious; or
    (c) if I am conscious but have irreversible brain damage and will never regain the ability to make decisions and express my wishes.

I direct that treatment be limited to measures to keep me comfortable and to relieve pain, including any pain that might occur by withholding or withdrawing treatment.

While I understand that I am not legally required to be specific about future treatments, if I am in the condition(s) described above I feel especially strong about the following forms of treatment (check those items which apply to your wishes):

_____ I do not want cardiac resuscitation.

_____ I do not want mechanical respiration.

_____ I do not want tube feeding.

_____ I do not want antibiotics.

_____ I do not want maximum pain relief.

Other directions (insert personal instructions).

These directions express my legal right to refuse treatment, under the law of New York. I intend my instructions to be carried out, unless I have rescinded them in a new writing or by clearly indicating that I have changed my mind.

Signed _____ Date _____

Witness _____ Witness _____

Figure 1.2   State of New York Living Will

Directives. In addition, these institutions are required to ask about Advance Directives at the time of admission.

Copies of the Living Will or any other Advance Medical Directive should be given to all health care providers and any family members who may be called on to make decisions. They should also be filed with important papers such as the will.

While a Living Will can be an important tool for managing medical treatment, it also has shortcomings. For example, as in the sample shown in Figure 1.2, Living Wills may be valid only in the event of a terminal condition. And they typically are silent on the issues of nutrition and hydration. Nutrition and hydration are the medical terms that refer to the use of tubes to supply food and water to a comatose patient.

For example, Nancy Cruzan suffered irreversible brain damage as the result of a car accident when she was 27 years old. Since she did not have a terminal condition, a Living Will would not apply. For seven years she was kept alive in a semi-comatose state by tubes that supplied nutrition and hydration. Cruzan's parents petitioned all the way to the U.S. Supreme Court to allow Nancy to die. In their 1990 decision, the justices said the states have broad power to keep patients on life-support systems when the patients have not made their exact wishes known.

This means that states have the right to forbid the withdrawal of support systems if the patient has not clearly stated the wish to refuse this treatment. Therefore, individuals who have not expressed an opinion on life-support measures have decisions made for them in accordance with state law. It's best to have personal opinions in written form, prepared according to the individual state requirements.

Durable Power of Attorney for Health Care

Many advocates suggest that people thoughtfully consider their opinions about the kind of medical care they want and record those decisions in a comprehensive Advance Medical Directive. In addition, they advise that a surrogate decision maker be appointed. The directive should:

appoint an agent

apply to terminal and nonterminal conditions

include any specific information about treatment(s)

Legally, this is accomplished through a Durable Power of Attorney for Health Care. "Durable" means that the document will be recognized in a court of law; a power of attorney is a legal document that allows the authorized person to act on behalf of the person named in the document, in designated areas. With this document, the authorized person would be able to decide about medical care, and those decisions would be upheld by a court of law in the event of any lawsuit. In some states all powers of attorney for health care are durable.

Because a clear understanding of the individual's desires can be vitally important for management of that person's dying, thoughtful care should be taken when people consider their choices about treatment and choose a surrogate decision maker.

Deciding on Medical Treatment Options

When thinking about medical care options, Dr. Charles Culver of Dartmouth Medical College recommends answering the following questions.

1. *If you were terminally ill and permanently incompetent, would you want any life-sustaining treatment to be continued?* This question applies to the common situation of a terminally ill patient who is no longer able to make decisions and who is expected to have no chance of recovering mental competence in the future. The person may have some degree of consciousness, but is clearly unable to make treatment decisions. In this situation, to continue using a life-support system is to prolong dying.

    Most people probably would choose not to be kept alive in this condition. But it is helpful to the doctors and the family if the individual's wishes have been recorded in an Advance Medical Directive.

2. *Whether terminally ill or not, if you were permanently unconscious would you want any life-sustaining treatment to be continued?* This question is important when patients have suffered such total or near-total destruction of the cerebral cortex that they are unconscious and have no chance of recovering consciousness. With careful medical care, many people in this condition can be kept alive for years. It is estimated that there are 5,000 to 10,000 people living in this condition in the United States. It's rational to expect that someone who is competent to make decisions would choose not to be kept alive indefinitely in this condition.

3. *Whether terminally ill or not, would you want to be kept alive if you were unconscious, had very little chance of ever recovering consciousness, and would almost certainly be very brain-damaged if you did recover consciousness?* This question applies to patients who have suffered serious brain damage from a severe stroke or an accident, and are presently unconscious. The best estimates indicate an 80 to 90 percent chance of never recovering consciousness and, if they do, it is almost certain they will be brain-damaged. On rare occasions, less than one in 1,000, these patients recover fully or almost fully. It may be necessary to continue life-support systems for months before ruling out the chance of some recovery of consciousness.

   Family members of these patients experience great difficulty in advising physicians whether to continue life-support systems and for how long. It can be anguishing to consider discontinuing treatment when a slight chance of recovery exists. However, many people (especially the elderly), when asked about these situations, indicate they would want their families to discontinue treatment. Most are unimpressed with the slight chance of recovering, particularly if their quality of life would be affected by physical and intellectual handicaps.

People who wish to have full treatment continued should make their wishes clearly known.

4. *Whether terminally ill or not, would you want to be kept alive if you were gravely ill, had only a 5 percent or less chance of recovery, and would probably require weeks or months of further treatment before it was clear whether or not you would recover?* This question applies to many patients in critical care units. Usually they have serious conditions involving one or more vital organs, and their prognosis is bleak. If taken separately, each of their disorders is theoretically reversible, but when combined, the chance that all the conditions will be reversed is highly unlikely. Statistics don't clearly indicate the patient's chance of recovery. It's possible that they might recover, but no one realistically expects it.

It would be rational for some people to say yes to this question and no to all the rest. It would be just as rational to say no.

Many older adults, especially those already in frail health, often say they don't want to subject themselves or a loved one to this type of long, almost always fruitless, course of treatment. Some older adults are afraid of being admitted to a hospital because they have seen friends with only a slight chance of recovery kept alive "on tubes" for lengthy periods of time, only to die anyway.

Everyone, young and old alike, should have the option of ruling out long, aggressive treatment when the odds of recovery are poor at best.

5. *If you choose to have life support discontinued in any of the above conditions, would you desire, in addition to discontinuing any other life-support measures, that fluids and nutrition be discontinued?* This question applies to one specific type of life support. People who have firm opinions on this type of treatment should make their wishes known. Deciding whether or not to allow someone to die by discontinuing fluids and

nutrition can be one of the most agonizing questions in medical care. It causes tremendous conflict between family members and health care professionals, and has been a frequent subject of articles on medical ethics.

Medical ethics experts agree that any life-support measure should be withheld only when the patient would not experience significant discomfort. Most people agree that if a competent, terminally ill patient makes a rational decision to refuse fluids and nutrition, the decision should be honored. If incompetent patients have previously made it clear, when they were competent, that they would not wish nutrition and hydration administered if they were permanently incompetent and terminally ill, that desire should also be honored, say medical ethicists.

Several recent court cases in a number of states have ruled on the question of the removal of nutrition and hydration. Usually the court inquires whether the patient has ever explicitly indicated a wish to have fluids and nutrition withdrawn under the circumstances that now exist. If the person has not specifically addressed this issue, but only expressed a more general opinion of "no life support," then the courts generally are willing to consider fluids and nutrition as forms of life support.

For both moral and legal reasons, it is important for people to indicate if they wish distinctions to be made among various types of treatment. An individual's attitudes, age, medical history, and religious convictions may all play a part in these decisions. People should consider under what circumstances they would choose to refuse:

cardiopulmonary resuscitation

dialysis

nutrition and hydration

ventilation

blood pressure support

antibiotics

pain relief

A Durable Power of Attorney for Health Care does everything that a Living Will can do, and also does more. With this document, there is no need to have a Living Will. If a person has both a Living Will and a Durable Power of Attorney for Health Care, the Living Will predominates.

There are four primary advantages to completing a Durable Power of Attorney for Health Care rather than a Living Will.

1. If a person is temporarily incompetent, as in the case of an accident victim, or is incapacitated but doesn't have a terminal condition, as in a stroke, the Living Will does not authorize withdrawal of life-support systems.

2. The Living Will lacks enforcement power. If the physician decides not to honor the form, there is no appointed person who can talk with the physician and confirm the patient's wishes.

3. The Living Will in some states specifically eliminates fluid and nutrition tubes from its definition of life-support procedures. In this case, even if a patient has a strong belief against being kept alive on tubes, the Living Will doesn't allow the withdrawal of this treatment.

4. Living Wills don't cover nonterminal conditions or situations where death is not imminent.

A Durable Power of Attorney for Health Care can be fashioned to overcome these limitations. It can apply to any and all health care situations, not simply terminal ones. It names an agent to make decisions for the patient, if he or she becomes incompetent, including when to withhold or withdraw life-support systems. This agent is authorized to act on the patient's behalf and ensure that the patient's wishes are carried out. The agent can advocate for the patient and act in his or her best interests. The individual can also give the agent authority to admit him or her to a nursing home, community-based residential facility, or hospice facility.

How To Choose a Surrogate Decision Maker

An individual who is competent, or of sound mind, makes decisions about his or her own affairs, including health care. When people become incapacitated, temporarily or permanently, someone must make decisions for them.

Generally, these decisions are made by the next of kin, but sometimes no one is available or able to take this responsibility. In these situations the court appoints a guardian to represent the individual. In a Durable Power of Attorney for Health Care, the competent individual has named an agent to represent the patient's interests.

In her book, *Power of Attorney for Health Care*, Wisconsin attorney Helen Marks Dicks lists several points to take into consideration when choosing a surrogate decision maker or agent.

TRUST

The agent should be someone the individual feels confident will make health care choices that the individual would want. It is advisable that individuals discuss their preferences in detail. All of the answers to the questions listed above should be reviewed.

It's not possible to record all the information in a written document, so the individual should trust the agent to understand. In some cases it may be necessary for the two people to negotiate a compromise between what the individual wants and what the agent is comfortable doing.

The agent may also be called upon to make smaller decisions, which may or may not be medical. There may be times when other parties aren't available or interested in making some of these decisions. Some family members may be uncomfortable with having to go into court against other family members. It's important that the person who accepts the role of agent is both trustworthy and willing to take on the responsibility of carrying out the individual's wishes for managing dying.

LOCATION

It's best if the agent lives in the same area as the individual. Ideally, the agent should be able to visit the patient on a convenient and regular basis.

If the patient is receiving long-term care, as in a nursing home, the agent ought to make both regular and unscheduled visits to verify that the patient is receiving adequate care. It's difficult to determine whether the patient is being neglected by telephone or infrequent visits. The agent needs to be able to determine if regular, day-to-day care is being provided. This would include comfortable clothes, lotions, entertainment, and any special foods.

The agent must participate in meetings to help identify how to meet the patient's needs. During a long-term illness, meetings are held to discuss decisions regarding future health care. The patient's interests are better served if the agent actively participates in these meetings.

Sometimes no family member lives in close proximity. Then the individual must choose between a distant family member and a friend who lives close by to be the health care agent. Generally speaking, the better choice for the individual is the agent with whom he or she feels more comfortable. If the agent lives far away, a patient needing long-term care may be moved to a facility closer to the agent.

If there is a possibility that the individual will be moved to a different state, one should also look at the other state's laws. Most states recognize a Durable Power of Attorney, and these laws are changing rapidly. It's important to get up-to-date information and to review the decisions periodically.

ASSERTIVENESS AND INTELLIGENCE

When choosing between two equally qualified people as potential agents, evaluating their assertiveness may help make the decision. An assertive agent will advocate on behalf of the patient and make certain the patient gets the needed care and treatment. An assertive agent will more likely question physicians, rather than passively accept their recommendations, especially if they don't follow the patient's wishes.

The agent should also be intelligent enough to do basic research on the patient's disease, illness, or condition. In the case of a major illness, organizations or support groups can help the agent make sound decisions. The agent should be prepared to seek second opinions when surgery or extreme procedures are recommended. Being able to evaluate conflicting information before making a decision is very important. In many instances the agent needs to evaluate several courses of treatment. The decision making will require more than simply saying yes or no.

KINDNESS

Often the agent is the patient's only link with the outside world. A spirit of compassion and kindness is very important. Patients who are incapacitated do not have the mental ability to remember their birthdays, arrange to attend religious services, purchase incidental items, or make plans for special events to provide a break from the routine. The agent should be able to care about the patient in little everyday ways as well as in major decisions.

CHOOSING AMONG CHILDREN

Many people find it difficult to decide between two or more children as a health care agent. The Durable Power of Attorney for Health Care provides an opportunity to name a primary agent and an alternate agent. This can help ease the problem.

If there is more than one child, the individual can appoint one child as the agent and then require that the agent advise the other children of any decisions made. This can be accomplished by adding the line, "I would like (agent's name) to advise my other children about the health care decisions being made." In this way the other children are kept informed, yet one person is the legal and final authority on decisions.

It is not necessary to include all children, and in some situations the individual may feel that simply naming one child as agent is a better option. For example, a parent might feel it would be difficult or impossible for one child to handle the emotional responsibility. In that situation the parent may choose to leave that child off the list of additional agents.

COAGENTS

It is not advisable to appoint coagents. Disagreements, confusion, and indecision can result from having diffused authority. It is best to appoint a single individual who will have final legal authority to make decisions. In this way the health care providers understand exactly whom to contact. A single agent is also preferable when a quick decision is necessary.

PROHIBITED DECISIONS

There are several instances in which an individual would probably be well advised not to give decision-making authority to someone else. These include:

   authority to admit or commit the individual to a mental health institution, an immediate care facility for the mentally retarded, or a state or other treatment facility

   authority to consent to experimental mental health research, psychosurgery, electroconvulsive (shock) treatment, or other drastic mental health treatment procedures.

   If an individual has had a history of mental health disorders, extreme care should be taken in preparing a Durable Power of Attorney for Health Care. These individuals may be vulnerable and questions may arise about whether or not they were pressured to sign. In addition, state laws regarding involuntary and voluntary commitment procedures need to be taken into consideration.

Making Decisions

In most situations an agent and the patient have discussed the individual's wishes and the agent is making informed, considered decisions to carry out those wishes. This is a legal standard called substitute judgment. In these types of decisions, the agent, based on knowledge of the patient's wishes, makes choices that simply enact the expressed desires of the patient. In other words, the agent is standing in as proxy for the patient.

In other cases the agent is called upon to use his or her own judgment. For example, if there was no prior discussion on the health care choice the agent is being asked to make, then the agent must act in the best interests of the patient. The best interests legal standard requires the agent only to make the decision that would be in the best interest of the patient, based on standard views and practices in the medical community. Most medical decisions based on these views favor prolonging life.

SUGGESTED GUIDELINES FOR MAKING DECISIONS

Making decisions, especially in best-interest situations, can be difficult and morally challenging for agents. Some suggestions come from the Florida court case *In re Browning*. The court held that agents or surrogate decision makers must obtain current information on the following four issues in the event they wish to discontinue life-sustaining treatment.

1. Is the patient suffering from a medical condition that would permit the patient, if competent, to forgo life-sustaining medical treatment?

2. Is there any reasonable probability that the patient will regain competency and be able to decide?

3. Is the patient's personal decision on this subject sufficiently clear that the guardian can make a substitute decision?

4. Is the patient's right to forgo medical treatment outweighed by state interests? The patient's right to refuse medical treatment is based on the constitutional right of privacy and the common law right of bodily integrity, and must be balanced against the countervailing state interests in the preservation of life, the protection of third parties, the prevention of suicide, and the maintenance of the ethical integrity of the medical profession.

In Wisconsin, the courts were asked to rule on the situation of an individual who had never been competent and was a ward of the state. The court suggested 12 guidelines through a document titled *In the Guardianship of L. W.* These questions may also be helpful to the agent who is making best-interest decisions. The guardian was asked to look at:

1. Whether or not the ward at the time expressed his or her wishes in these circumstances.

2. What are the wishes of the family?

3. What information can the guardian glean from an independent medical opinion?

4. If the institution has a biomedical ethics committee, what recommendations has that committee made in this case?

5. What is the physical capability of the person to recover from the condition he or she is in?

6. What is the likelihood of the person recovering brain function, and to what extent?

7. What is the likelihood of physical, psychological, or emotional injury as a result of providing or not providing treatment?

8. What is the likelihood of the person surviving without treatment, and for what duration?

9. What are the physical effects to the person of continued life, with and without treatment?

10. What are the benefits to the person from continued life, with and without treatment?

11. To what extent are proponents of withdrawing or withholding treatment acting in their own interests or the public's interests, as opposed to the incompetent person's best interests?

12. Are there any other factors that may seem important in the particular case, as bearing on the best interests of the ward?

Active and Passive Euthanasia

Euthanasia is the most controversial topic among the many issues concerning the right to die. Everyone has strongly held, emotional opinions on the ethics of actively aiding another to die.

Recent news stories have polarized the medical, religious, and other communities as people wrestle with the basic notions that frame the subject. The apparent increase in these stories indicates that this area challenges traditional thoughts and demands contemporary review.

While some countries have adopted permissive policies toward euthanasia, in the United States physicians and family members who aid in another's death are subject to prosecution. Recent public-policy questions are being addressed in some states, including:

1. Is euthanasia ethical?

2. Are passive and active euthanasia equally acceptable?

3. Should euthanasia be legalized?

4. Should doctors support or oppose euthanasia decisions?

5. What criteria should be used when euthanasia is considered?

   quality of life

   age

   individual or societal economic factors

6. Who should make euthanasia decisions?

   patients

   doctors

   families

   communities

It appears that this debate will continue and expand as individuals and communities struggle to develop policies that fit current needs and attitudes. It's important that individuals express their opinions about euthanasia to their health care agents. If wishes are clearly spelled out and identified, the agent can make the appropriate decision, if needed, within the bounds of the law.

Conclusion

The choices involved in the management of one's health care and dying reflect very personal opinions. These decisions are medical and legal. It's vitally important that anyone with an opinion about the right to die express and record those opinions in order to make certain his or her wishes are honored.

The best way to ensure that one's wishes will be carried out is to prepare an Advance Medical Directive and to name a surrogate decision maker. State laws vary and are subject to frequent change. It's important to research the specific state requirements before preparing these legal documents and to review the documents periodically to see if any changes need to be made.

Serving as a surrogate decision maker means being involved in the simple day-to-day choices, as well as the complicated medical care decisions. Careful thought must be given when choosing a health care agent. The agent must be equally thoughtful when considering the legal and moral responsibilities involved in selecting the course of treatment and the withholding of treatment.

THINGS TO REMEMBER

People who want to make sure their wishes for medical treatment are honored should prepare an Advance Medical Directive.

A Living Will can provide guidance to loved ones and medical care providers. However, a Durable Power of Attorney for Health Care provides guidance under more situations and with more clarity.

It's important to give careful thought when deciding what type of treatment to use or refuse.

The selection of a health care agent requires careful planning.

The health care agent may need to research the patient's condition or disease and get several opinions before being able to make sound decisions.

Chapter 2

Coping with Death

Ruth honestly didn't know where the last few months had gone. Since David's death in March, it seemed as if every day had arrived with a particular set of problems to be solved. First there were all of the funeral plans, then the notes to be written, and the seemingly endless details of settling the estate.

But now the days stretched in front of her as an endless, empty wasteland. Her friends were busy with "couple" activities, and her children had their own young families and careers. Ruth found the television set was her only companion, and, on some days, even getting dressed felt like a chore. Cooking for one seemed pointless and sometimes she just skipped eating entirely. She couldn't shake the nagging feeling that no one needed her any more. The grief and emptiness filled every corner of her life and her mind.

KEY FACTS

- The average age at which Americans are widowed is 67.9 years.

- 77.9 percent of black women over 65 are widows.

- 67.6 percent of white women over 55 are widows.

- 20.6 percent of white men over 55 are widowers.

- Grief can last from three weeks to three years.

- There are various stages and necessary tasks in grieving.

- Unacknowledged grief can emotionally cripple the individual.

- Suicide rates are higher among people who are recently widowed.

- Experts recommend postponing, if possible, significant life changes after experiencing a major loss.

As penance has the power of undoing the past, grief has the power of perpetuating the past.

Dr. Viktor Frankl

Several years ago, each episode of "Ben Casey, M.D.," a popular television series, began with a dramatic scene from a medical lecture. An eminent older doctor drew symbols on a chalkboard while intoning, "Man, woman, birth, death, infinity!" The message was clear: All these symbols were part of the cycle of life.

The science of biology teaches several signs of life: movement, growth, and change. Biology also teaches that change is to be expected in people's lives and that, as a result of change, life ultimately will end. But even with knowledge of this certainty, most Americans find it emotionally difficult to accept and believe that changes are a normal, necessary part of life and that death itself is a condition of life.

This chapter discusses the emotional aspects of the end of life. It explains that death is a natural part of being alive and represents only one of the many losses people experience during their lifetimes. This chapter will describe the stages of grief, or the internal, emotional reaction to loss; it will describe how mourning, the external expression of grief, is experienced; and it will describe how to be helpful to someone who is grieving.

Necessary Losses, a best-seller by Judith Viorst, discusses the various losses everyone experiences during the course of a lifetime. Viorst says it is important to experience losses, because they provide opportunities for renewal and growth. She begins by describing the loss an infant experiences when it perceives itself as separate from its mother. Losses occur throughout everyone's life, Viorst explains.

For example, the loss of high school experiences—the teachers, the friends, the familiar schedule, and the comfort of having known relationships and a known identity—provides an opportunity to move on and explore work experiences or higher educational experiences. The loss of the high school way of life is necessary, and people understand that it's impractical to stay stuck in their high school identities (although some folks may try).

Most people recognize the importance of moving on, of losing familiar patterns of living in order to gain new levels of achievement. Giving up a home to move into a different house and changing jobs or careers are usually opportunities to experience loss that people accept and often welcome. This pattern is familiar to parents, who watch their children give up crawling as they learn to walk, give up drinking from a bottle as they learn to drink from a cup, and give up the comfort of home as they start school.

These examples of loss are comfortable for most people to accept because they signal growth and progress. But many people find it infinitely more difficult to accept the loss of a loved one. The losses of companionship, some level of economic security, emotional security, along with many other factors, can combine to make acceptance of death a long process. In fact, in some ways the process never ends because, since change is a part of life, we are perpetually experiencing loss throughout life, and the feelings of grieving over a loss can be triggered again and again. However, grieving becomes more bearable when the process is understood and when individuals recognize that grief is experienced many times in every lifetime.

Grief

Elisabeth Kübler-Ross is widely recognized for her description of five distinct phases of dying. In her book *On Death and Dying* (1969), Dr. Kübler-Ross first identified the five phases, which have also been used to explain the process of grief.

Kübler-Ross identified these phases as a result of her work with dying patients. She became curious when she started to recognize a pattern among patients who faced eminent death. Later, as she observed more and more people behaving in the same way, she realized the significance of this pattern.

Since Kübler-Ross's findings were first published, many other researchers have expanded on her work. Some argue that there are more than five phases and some have relabeled the phases, but there seems to be nearly universal agreement that people experience five general emotional stages when dealing with loss, and that these can be used as signposts in the grief process.

It's important to remember that the nature of grief is very individualized, which means that different people handle their grief in different ways. Many people find they do not proceed through the stages of grief in a straight line; rather, they move back and forth among the phases.

Kübler-Ross described these phases as:

1. Denial

2. Hostility (Anger)

3. Bargaining/Negotiation

4. Depression

5. Acceptance

Denial

With every loss the first reaction is denial, or thoughts such as, This never happened, My husband isn't dead, That isn't my child, my mother, etc. These are normal reactions that family members and loved ones experience when someone dies.

Denial is a defense that acts as a mechanism to protect people from the cruel, hard, shocking fact that they have experienced a tremendous loss, a change that may very well affect every facet of their emotional, physical, and spiritual lives. Because the loss of a loved one in death is so enormous and the potential results of the loss are so staggering, the mind sets up a temporary detour. This detour shelters the person from the horrifying reality and finality of death.

Hostility or Anger

As the grieving process moves to the next stage, the denial occurs less frequently. During the course of this process, the full knowledge of the loss is realized and the individual reacts to that knowledge.

Any time someone loses something of value, he or she feels anger. This is a normal human reaction, but it is especially troublesome when people are dealing with the loss of a loved one. Instinctively they feel it isn't acceptable to be angry with someone who is dead. So they may focus the anger on God, on themselves, or on others. Anger and guilt often become hopelessly intertwined as people experiencing grief look for someone or something to blame.

One widow may blame herself by saying, "If only I hadn't left to go shopping that afternoon," or another may say, "I should have insisted he take better care of himself and start walking regularly." Still others may blame health care providers: "I can't believe the doctor didn't recommend surgery earlier. We counted on them to advise us and by the time Mary had surgery she was so weak," or "Why did it take so long for the ambulance to get here? There must be some way we can hold them accountable!"

Bargaining or Negotiation

At this stage in the grieving process many people, even those who previously were nonbelievers, find themselves bargaining with God. They search for a meaning, for some greater context in which to fit their loss. They try to make the pain bearable by explaining the loss in terms of a greater good. Some people say, "I can accept it if I could just know that she didn't suffer." They feel it would be easier to accept their own pain if they were assured their loved one didn't feel pain.

Others ask God for a sign, or go back over their memories again and again to reassure themselves that the bargain they are seeking to make has actually occurred. In this stage they remember each event, analyzing it carefully for each detail that may support the notion they want to reinforce. Stories may be compared with the memories of others, either to reinforce the strength of the bargaining terms or to persuade others, and themselves, of the reality that the bargain has been struck.

In some situations, people attempt to make sense out of the death by taking some positive, concrete action. Many people have joined Mothers Against Drunk Driving, the American Cancer Society, and other groups related to the cause of death as a way of proving the death of their loved one wasn't "in vain." For some, belonging to a support group and working to help ease another's pain becomes their cause. Grievers in the bargaining stage find they have a real need to prove to themselves, to the larger community, and perhaps to God that the loss meant something. They may say, "If I could just know that one other life had been saved, or that someone else benefited, then all this work would be worth it."

Depression

As the reality of the loss is understood as an undeniable, unchangeable fact of life, the griever moves into the phase of depression. The full realization hits with a powerful punch. The very pervasiveness of the loss becomes painfully clear.

One widower said, "I woke up one morning and realized I was never going to hear her voice again. Her touch was gone, her laughter and her shining eyes, even the little, peeved sigh. She wasn't going to fix my breakfast, or wax the floor, or walk in the afternoon with me ever again."

A widow recalled, "When Bob died there were all sorts of offers to help. Someone came in and plowed the driveway, another took me grocery shopping. But I guess after a couple of weeks they lost interest, or they just wanted me to 'get over it.' But anyway, there I was, in that big house, just rattling around with no one to talk to, no one who needed me, and nowhere to go."

At this stage, grievers may feel pressure, real or imagined, from others to pull themselves together and get on with their lives. Some people try to put on a mask of "being OK" for the world. But somehow the mask doesn't fit, and the depression is a nagging, aching presence that simply sits, stubbornly affecting their thoughts and actions. In this phase they may even find the task of getting out of the house more than they can manage.

Acceptance

When people move into acceptance, the final stage of grief, they find the lessons learned from the previous phases help them to form resolution. They discover that the acknowledgment of the loss is integrated in their lives. Many people use the term *unity* to define their feelings of resolution. While they may still think of the deceased person as if he or she is in the next room, they realize it is the memory of the loved one, and not the actual person, that is alive to them.

Someone grieving from a loss still experiences anger or wants to bargain from time to time, as the full knowledge of the loss is realized. But at this stage the knowledge is tempered with the realization that change has occurred, as a necessary part of living. The new life the griever builds combines many positive aspects of the life shared with the loved one with new activities and elements that make life today fuller and richer.

People still find that depression crops up at unexpected intervals and they recall the loss. But as acceptance grows, the fullness they've built into their present lives continues to reassure them that life and loss, as Viorst writes, mean growth and change. And each individual is responsible for the direction of the growth and change in his or her own life. The acknowledgment of this responsibility also brings with it reassurance and trust.

One widow said, "I knew I'd finally told Paul goodbye when I visited his grave on our anniversary. There are many good memories, and I'll always feel he is with me. But I really enjoy the new interests in my life. The classes I'm taking and the friends I've met during the last few months have given me some new ideas about what I want to do with my time. Don't get me wrong, I was happy with my life with Paul. But it's fun to learn and do new things. I feel as if I have a second life now!"

Grieving is a very individual process. For some losses an individual may work through the process in three weeks, or for another loss it may take several years. No one can predict how long an individual may grieve or how the grief may be manifested. There is no "normal" period of grief.

Some cultures are less comfortable with grief and mourning, and therefore put pressure on the individual to get on with life or to hide tears and feelings. This tendency to rush through or hide grief may explain why some people ask, How long does it take? or When should I be done with it? It is important to remember that grief is a process, not a thing with tangible dimensions that designate the start, middle, and end.

Grief consists of the thoughts and feelings about a loss that are experienced *within* the individual. Mourning, by contrast, is the *external* expression of the grief experience.

Mourning

Dr. John Bowlby also identified phases that describe the grief and mourning processes. Although they correspond in some ways with those spelled out in Kübler-Ross's work, these phases are different and their description may provide helpful information. The following description of mourning uses Bowlby's phases and examples of how grief may be externally manifested as mourning.

The four phases are:

1. Numbing

2. Yearning

3. Disorganization and Despair

4. Degrees of Reorganization

Numbing

Closely associated with denial, the numbing phase is a natural reaction to the overwhelming task of accepting a major loss. Many people find they are unable to recall the details of the funeral or the first few days following the death. "I was so surprised to see you had signed the guest book. I'm so sorry, but I didn't even remember seeing you at the funeral. I just felt as if I was in a haze!" one mourner told a friend.

Yearning

As people begin to comprehend the meaning of the loss, they look with nostalgia at the relationship and the way their lives were structured before the loss. It's common to have only fond memories, glossing over any reminders of the less perfect aspects of the times or people. These pleasant memories may be recalled again and again. Grievers find it comforting to repeat these happy stories to the people around them and to themselves. In some ways this may help them admit the loss, by simply remembering those special, precious times.

A widower would recount, "I met Betty at a USO dance. I knew right away she was really special. All my buddies noticed her right off, and they all wanted to dance with her. So I knew I had to catch her eye real fast. That night I said, 'She's the girl for me!' And you know, we were as happy as two people have ever been."

Yearning may also involve an overwhelming desire to change things, either to put them back the way they were or to remake reality into a wished-for ideal. Distortions of reality normally fade over time.

Disorganization and Despair

The equilibrium of an individual's life is affected by a major loss. One may lose the car keys or be unable to remember if the doctor's appointment is today or next week, and starting the most minor project may seem too difficult to think about. Even a simple decision about what to do with time can leave one mired in indecision. Sleep patterns become erratic, eating may be completely forgotten, and not only may a griever forget what day it is, an entire season may pass by unnoticed.

Some people who have lost loved ones say they felt as if they were going quietly, or not so quietly, insane. After being widowed, actress Helen Hayes said, "For two years I was just as crazy as you can be and still be at large. It was total confusion. How did I come out of it? I don't know, because I didn't know when I was in it that I was in it."

For some people, irrational, but very real, fears crop up. For example, the basement stairs suddenly look sinister. Many people who have lost their mates say they continue to see, hear, or even feel their partners. While this may be disconcerting, the feeling of being temporarily insane is a natural and normal reaction while one is adjusting to major changes in life.

People in grief learn that as they regain balance, the various aspects of life stabilize. Sometimes the disorganization persists and the despair may be overwhelming. In situations when the despair becomes disabling, it is important to find professional help.

Degrees of Reorganization

As people begin to restructure their lives and to adjust to new economic and emotional realities, they move into the reorganization phase. Balancing the checkbook becomes a normal activity instead of an afternoon of fear and dread. Gradually, they are delighted to discover they still enjoy life and find new ways to spend time and organize their lives. Some say they are surprised at the new activities they've discovered, or how much they appreciate the chance to spend more time on an enjoyable hobby. Many people find that the prospect of spending time alone isn't terrifying; in fact, sometimes it's just what they want!

As grievers feel more comfortable with their new life order, they begin to focus more outside themselves and their emotions. After spending this period of time working through grief, which by its very nature is necessarily self-centered, they begin to notice that the rest of the world is still around.

An unexpected call from an old friend, a notice in the newspaper about a support group, a neighbor who pauses to chat, may surprise the grieving widower. He is surprised to look up and see there are other people out there. The reorganization phase completes the cycle and brings the griever back into the community with an active, enjoyable life.

Grief Is Cumulative

Working through grief is a cumulative process. This means that each phase needs to be completed before the individual can move on to the next part of the process. It is very common for people in grief to feel as if they are "skipping around" through the stages. Many people enter a new phase, only to find they are suddenly back in the anger stage. This is normal and should not be seen as a cause for alarm.

Similarly, some individuals may start in the middle, for example, by bargaining. They may say, "God, just give me the money to pay these bills and I won't ever complain about losing Mike." This, too, is a very normal way of getting on with the grieving. Each person works through grief in his or her own way and time. It's important to allow each person to get through each phase.

Getting Stuck

Often, someone becomes stuck in a particular stage of grief. One woman who has been widowed for 40 years continues to recount her day to her deceased husband each evening. Her inability to move beyond the yearning stage has kept her socially isolated and emotionally alone most of her life.

Others get stuck in denial, structuring their lives around the deceased spouse's schedule: Dinner is at 5:30 P.M. because Dad was always hungry when he came in from the fields. Even though she's lived alone for many years, a widow may hang on to old patterns and behaviors, perhaps for the rest of her life.

For most people these leftover behaviors are comforting and don't get in the way of their lives.

Finding Help

But occasionally the griever needs help in rebuilding life. At the extreme, the individual becomes despondent or even suicidal. An intervention by caring family members and friends, with the assistance of a professional, is critical when serious warning signs are seen. (Some suggestions of how friends and others can help a grieving person are given later in this chapter.) Other in-dividuals decide on their own that they want some support and guidance in working through their grieving process.

Many communities, churches, community colleges, and funeral homes sponsor support groups that are free of charge. Often the groups offer specialized self-help for those dealing with a specific type of loss, e.g., widowers, parents dealing with the death of a child, or family or friends of cancer or AIDS patients.

Research conducted by Phyllis Silverman indicates that wid-ows and widowers find it most helpful to relate to individuals with whom they have many issues in common. For example, the study found that people who had experienced a similar loss, were of the same sex, and had similar education and income levels had more credibility and proved to be more helpful to the widow or widower. It's a good idea to shop around for the most appropriate support group.

The American Association of Retired Persons (AARP) operates a Widowed Persons Service; Catholic Social Services, as well as many hospitals, cemeteries, hospices, and other organizations, also provide support groups. Local newspapers often list these groups as a public service. These self-help groups provide several functions, including support, information, and social interaction.

Sometimes people who are stuck seek the assistance of a credentialed therapist, minister, priest, or rabbi.

Assessing Professional Help

Individuals who are thinking about therapy should consider several factors as they make decisions about treatment.

What are the counselor's credentials?

Is the therapist certified or licensed?

Does the person have experience in the area in which assistance is needed?

What are the charges, and how are they determined: by the hour, by the session, etc.?

Can one contact people who know this counselor and his or her work for references?

How long is the expected term of therapy? Weeks, months, etc.?

Who will determine when the treatment is completed? How will that determination be made?

What types of therapy will be employed, i.e., group, individual, drug, art, etc.?

Before deciding to commit to a particular course of treatment, the individual should meet with the therapist to discuss these questions. Counseling involves building a trusting relationship.

If the situation doesn't appear to encourage or foster the development of that trust, the client should consider ending the relationship and locating a different counselor.

Suggestions for Helping

Some people are in the profession of helping people deal constructively with their grief; others simply want to be helpful because of a personal relationship with someone who is grieving. The following suggestions for being helpful are universal; they apply to anyone who wishes to be of assistance to someone who has experienced a major loss.

1. *Listen.* Active listening is a skill. It means listening not only to the words but also to the ideas, attitudes, and assumptions beneath the words. Active listening involves using feedback to confirm that one understands the verbal and nonverbal meanings the individual is attempting to communicate.

   Being an active listener is of primary importance for the helper. Someone once said the greatest gift we can give someone is rapt attention. It's important to remember that people want to talk about their losses. They find it helpful to express their thoughts and feelings and reveal their grief to another person.

2. *Offer empathy.* While no one can really understand the pain of another, the expression of empathy is welcome and helpful. Empathy can be shown by saying such things as, How can I help?, Tell me how you are feeling, It must be very hard to accept, and I'm sorry.

   It's important to practice patience. Especially in the early stages, the griever may need to repeat the same story over and over.

3. *Be tolerant.* Almost any reaction can be expected when someone is mourning. Some people find it difficult to be with others when they are angry, especially if the anger is directed toward God or a well-respected person. It's important to remember that emotions are often irrational and that those who are

grieving often experience explosive emotions. A helper who can remain with the individual without being judgmental during these difficult times is tremendously supportive.

It's also important to tolerate the individual's grieving process. Setting deadlines or commenting on the appropriateness of another's feelings is rarely helpful.

4. *Learn about individual characteristics.* Every person is unique. Assisting someone in grief means understanding the various personal factors that have an impact on the process.

For example, the nature of the death, the closeness of the relationship, whether the individual has experienced a previous or similar loss, and the reaction to the funeral, if any, all affect a person's grieving. Similarly, the religious or cultural aspects of the griever's life, the availability of a support system, and the presence of other stressful factors can also influence the grieving process.

5. *Stay alert for warning signs.* It's important to remember that the experience of mourning can and does vary widely, from individual to individual and between various losses. Recognizing warning signs of more serious depression or other problems in adjusting can therefore be difficult. Generally speaking, when grief takes on the signs of clinical depression, the helper should take note.

Alan D. Wolfelt, director of the Center for Loss and Life Transition in Fort Collins, Colorado, makes distinctions between normal and more stressful grief and suggests asking these questions:

Does the individual respond to and appreciate support? The depressed individual often does not accept support.

Is the individual often openly angry? A depressed person complains and shows irritation but doesn't directly express anger.

Does the individual explain the depressive factors in his or her life as being related to the death? Someone who is clinically depressed often cannot relate the depression to any life event.

Does the individual still experience moments of joy or other feelings? Depression usually involves a pervasive sense of doom.

Do those around the individual sense feelings of sadness and emptiness? Depressed people project a sense of hopelessness and emptiness.

Does the individual appear to have passing physical complaints? Depressed people often have chronic physical complaints.

Does the individual often express feelings of guilt over some specific aspect of the loss? Depression often includes generalized feelings of guilt.

Does the individual's self-esteem seem to be temporarily affected? Those who are depressed often exhibit a deeper loss of esteem.

Differentiating between normal grief and unusual grief experiences is difficult. Helpers who are unsure of whether or not the warning signs are present should seek assistance. Obviously, assessments should be conducted by a credentialed professional.

Conclusion

The very fact of being alive means that life will change and loss will occur. Just as forest fires are sometimes needed for renewal and new life, the experience of handling individual losses provides an opportunity to learn and to grow.

While the process of grieving losses is highly individualized, there are recognized phases that define the process. By understanding the internal process of grief and the external manifestations of grief, or mourning, people can increase their acceptance and become more comfortable with the experience of loss.

Individuals who wish to help others who are grieving need to listen and be empathic, tolerant, and aware of warning signs of more serious problems. Many resources are available to assist those who are grieving, such as support groups, counseling, and educational programs. Many of these programs are free of charge.

THINGS TO REMEMBER

Grief is an individual process that varies with each person and each situation.

Grief is the internal reaction to loss, and mourning is the external manifestation of the grief.

People should delay making major changes in their lives after suffering a major loss.

Friends or family members who want to help a person who is grieving should focus on being compassionate, understanding, and a good listener.

Chapter 3

Arranging or Prearranging a Funeral

"A place for everything and everything in its place."

Mary Wilson, an older woman living alone, likes to prepare for everything, including what will happen at her death. She has a will on file with an attorney, along with deeds to her house and cemetery lot, records of investments, and insurance policies. Everything's in place.

A woman in her 70s has experienced enough of life to know the pressures a sudden or unexpected death thrusts upon survivors, Mary believes. Just a few years ago, a neighbor died suddenly. No advance arrangements had been made and the neighbor's son had only hours to struggle with funeral arrangements.

At the funeral, the son sought reassurance for every decision made during that emotional time. Over and over he asked, "It's a nice casket, isn't it? It's the same one Dad had, only this one's blue instead of gray."

For her own peace of mind and to know that her daughter and son-in-law, living halfway across the country, won't be troubled, Mary Wilson has made arrangements for her own funeral. Family members won't have to quarrel over whether to get a gray or blue casket or whether too much or too little money is spent. Everything's arranged, and the funds to pay for the funeral are set aside in a payable-on-death (P.O.D.) bank account.

Preplanning her funeral required only some phone calls to several mortuaries to ask about prices and services. Later, Mary scheduled appointments to select a casket and plan a service. Once these decisions were made, she filed copies of the prearrangement agreement with the funeral home, her children, and the family attorney.

For Mary Wilson, everything is in place for what is to come.

KEY FACTS

- The cost of a traditional funeral and in-ground burial is between $5,000 and $6,000.

- Of final dispositions, 17 percent are cremations, and this rate is expected to increase to 25 percent by the year 2000.

- The Federal Trade Commission's (FTC) Funeral Rule is a national regulation requiring funeral directors to provide price information over the phone and in person.

- Funeral directors are required to have three separate price lists, for caskets, outer burial containers, and a general price list for services.

- There are 22,000 funeral homes across the country. A large number of them perform fewer than 100 funerals a year.

- There are more than 10,000 cemeteries and 1,000 crematories in the country.

- Funeral directors and embalmers are regulated and licensed in 49 states.

- Cemeteries are regulated by state agencies in 37 states.

Few Americans who were alive in 1963 have forgotten the solemnity and pageantry of President John F. Kennedy's funeral. The nation's television sets glowed with the sad beauty of the riderless horse, the sentiment of the president's young son saluting the passing cortege, and images of the world's leaders paying homage. The funeral drew the largest U.S. television audience in history. Millions of Americans were personally touched and saw this funeral as a way to say good-bye to a charismatic president.

All funeral services are rituals held to honor the deceased, whether a head of state or your own loved one. They celebrate his or her life, acknowledge the reality of death, and seek to find meaning in the loss. The ceremony also benefits the living people who must endure the loss.

Funerals vary according to personal finances and individual and religious preferences. Some are elaborate, costing thousands of dollars. Other people prefer no ceremony at all.

When a nation loses its leader, the resources of government are marshaled to plan and execute the ritual. Funeral planning for everyone else has traditionally fallen to the closest survivors. But whether the honored dead is a president or a mother, father, husband, or wife, arranging a funeral involves the same three essential groups of questions.

What kind of ceremony is to be conducted? Should it be a traditional funeral with the body present or a memorial service? Will there be a wake or viewing? Who should be told? What kind of flowers and music are best? Where should the service be held?

What will be the final disposition of the body? Should there be an in-ground burial? Cremation? Donation of the body?

Who will handle the arrangements? Which funeral director, if any, will take care of the body? How will legal requirements, such as completing a death certificate, be met? Where will the body be cremated or buried? Who will lead the ceremony?

Traditionally, survivors must answer these questions while still grieving the loss of a loved one. The decision-making process can lead to family conflict over the kind of service to hold and the amount of money to spend. An adult child who no longer follows a parent's religion may not want the kind of service a faithful aunt does.

In many states, freedom-of-choice laws specify who makes funeral arrangements. Generally, the first priority is given to surviving spouses. If there is no surviving spouse, in descending order of priority, adult children, parents, adult siblings, and guardians have legal responsibility. However, few lawsuits are ever filed under these laws. It's best for families to work out their differences themselves. Courts are reluctant, for example, to exhume a body because certain rituals weren't performed.

But survivors need not be saddled with this burden. Like Mary Wilson, more and more older people are deciding to arrange their own funerals. Contemplating one's own mortality is never easy, but with the luxury of time and laws requiring full disclosure of costs by funeral homes, preplanning has become easier.

To assist anyone in arranging or prearranging a funeral, this chapter discusses funeral planning, whether for a traditional or an alternative arrangement. It outlines the elements and costs of a funeral, based on the price lists used by all funeral homes, and burial or other disposition. It describes legal requirements, suggests how to select a funeral home and cemetery, and summarizes federal and state consumer-protection laws. This chapter also stresses that while a funeral is a religious or spiritual ceremony, it's also a major consumer purchase costing from $700 to more than $5,000.

A Traditional Funeral

Older adults grew up with what has come to be known as a traditional funeral. Most wish to continue this ritual for themselves and their spouses. While there are regional and religious variations, such a ritual usually involves the following.

Transporting the remains, usually in a hearse (also called a funeral coach), to a funeral home at first, later to a church or synagogue, and then to a cemetery.

Preparing the body, which may include embalming, and placing it in a casket.

Conducting a wake or viewing of the body, with open or closed casket, at the funeral home with family and friends present. This may include a Rosary or other religious ceremony.

Holding a religious service at a church, synagogue, or funeral home with the body present. The casket can be open or closed depending on religious beliefs and personal preferences. There may be music and flowers with spoken words.

Processing to the cemetery where a committal service is held as the body is placed in a grave or crypt (a burial space in a tomb).

Installing a marker or monument with the deceased's name (memorialization).

Many personal and religious variations in these elements are possible. For example, instead of an in-ground burial, the final means of disposition may be cremation with the ashes (cremated remains or cremains) scattered or placed in a columbarium (a vaultlike structure holding cremains). In some faiths such as Judaism, the body is never embalmed. It is cleansed and placed in a wooden casket. The Jewish and other religions also have strictures on cremation.

Alternative Arrangements

A growing number of people cannot afford to, or prefer not to, pay a $5,000 funeral bill. Others object to the conventional rituals of the traditional funeral. Instead, they select an alternative arrangement coupled with a memorial service in which the body is not present, or a committal ritual to say good-bye and honor the memory of the deceased. Alternative arrangements include immediate burial, direct cremation, personally burying family members, or donation of the body for medical education.

Immediate Burial

In this arrangement, the body is interred, or buried directly in a cemetery, without embalming or any funeral service with the body present. A funeral director or, in some metropolitan areas, a direct disposal firm makes the arrangements. Direct disposal firms are listed in the yellow pages of the telephone directory under the heading of funeral director.

Usually, the deceased is buried in an alternative container, that is, one of particle board, hard cardboard, or pine costing about $150, much less than a casket. Caskets are also used. The simplicity of this disposition keeps the price at a minimum. Although it's called an immediate burial, interment likely will not occur until after a waiting period of at least 24 hours.

Immediate burial is often sold as a package by funeral directors and can range from $700 to $1,800 excluding the cost of a container or casket. Note that the prices cited in this chapter reflect 1990 averages. Higher or lower prices for the same item or service can be found, and prices will most likely increase over time.

Storing the body for more than a day may add a charge for refrigeration. Some states require embalming if the body is stored for more than 24 or 48 hours.

Cremation

Nationwide, 17 percent of all bodies are disposed of by cremation, or burning the remains, and this percentage continues to grow. There are about 1,000 crematories nationwide. In other countries, like Japan and Great Britain, where land is scarce, the cremation rate is much higher.

A direct cremation is like an immediate burial. It takes place without a funeral service at which the body is present. The funeral director usually transports the body to the crematory. Some crematories, however, work with survivors directly, and a funeral director's involvement isn't required. Direct cremations are also sold as a package which include the cost of cremation and the services of a funeral director, averaging $700 to $1,000.

In many instances, the crematory or funeral director requires an alternative container to transport the body. This container normally isn't included in the package price. A casket isn't required by law for cremations, and saying that one is may violate the FTC's Funeral Rule (the Funeral Rule is discussed in detail later in this chapter.)

Disposition by cremation isn't limited to direct cremations, however. A traditional funeral can be followed by a cremation.

A casket can be rented for $400 to $600 or purchased for a higher price; a few states prohibit casket rentals. After the service, the body is transported in a casket or an alternative container and cremated. After any cremation, the remains are returned to survivors for final arrangements, which may include spreading the ashes, saving them in an urn, placing them in a columbarium, or burying them.

Burial by Family Members

Some people choose to bypass the funeral director completely and make all arrangements themselves. This requires careful planning and attention to detail because the survivor is responsible for meeting state and local legal requirements. These may include securing a death certificate, transportation and disposition permits (sometimes called burial transit permits), and other legal papers. Transporting the body to a crematory or burying the deceased at home is legal in most states but may not always be possible.

A helpful book on this subject is *Caring for Your Own Dead* by Lisa Carlson. It describes state requirements in addition to providing practical advice.

Body Donation

Donating one's body after death can be a generous contribution to medical research and education. Medical and dental schools rely almost exclusively on voluntary donations for their cadavers. A body donation can also be the least expensive form of final disposition, usually involving only transportation costs. Be aware, however, that some states, such as Illinois, require the services of a funeral director at a cost of $500 to $700.

In some instances, the body or, more likely, the cremated remains can be returned to the family after the body has been used by the educational institution. This may not occur for several years, however. Be sure to ask when and how a body or the remains might be returned. The medical school can also make arrangements for final disposition, usually by cremation and burial. Many institutions conduct memorial services honoring the individuals who donated their bodies.

But sometimes a body is not accepted at the time of death. For instance, a medical school may not accept a body that has been mutilated in an accident or autopsied, or where death has occurred from an infectious disease like AIDS or meningitis. At times, a school can't accommodate any more bodies. Another means of disposition must be planned just in case. Contact one of the medical schools listed in Appendix B for more details.

The National Anatomical Service in New York and St. Louis may also be contacted. This for-profit organization is in the business of transporting cadavers to medical schools that are in short supply. The service can be particularly helpful for those who live in states where no medical schools exist, like Alaska and Delaware. The service has 24-hour telephone coverage and makes arrangements for refrigerating and transporting bodies. This firm can also help locate a low-cost cremation. (See listing in Chapter 6.)

Discuss your wishes to donate your body or organs with family members. By law, final decisions surrounding body disposition rest with survivors. In most instances, they honor the wishes of the deceased. A uniform donor card should also be completed; see Figure 3.1 for an example. They're available from memorial societies, tissue banks, and, in some states, on the back of drivers' licenses. It's best to have the next of kin sign as a witness; otherwise, this document may not be binding.

Organ Donations

Instead of a total body donation, some people want to provide their organs, tissues, and other body parts for medical use. For example, cornea transplants can endow sight and a kidney or skin graft could be a gift of life for someone else. At any given time, more than 20,000 individuals in the United States await donated organs or tissues to restore their health or save their lives.

There are age limitations for donors of some organs, such as hearts and lungs. However, tissues from even 80-year-olds are used, and a cornea from a 107-year-old has been successfully transplanted. Unlike the case with body donations, a traditional open-casket funeral can still be conducted in almost every

UNIFORM DONOR CARD OF _____

(print or type name of donor)

In the hope that I may help others, I hereby make this anatomical gift, if medically acceptable, to take effect upon my death. The words and marks below indicate my desires.

I give:

(a) any needed organs or parts

(b) only the following organs or parts

_____

(specify the organ(s) or part(s))

for the purpose of transportation, therapy, medical research, or education

(c) my body for anatomical study if needed

Limitations or special wishes, if any _____

_____   _____

Signature of Donor   Date of Birth of Donor

_____   _____

Date Signed   City and State

_____   _____

Witness   Witness

This is a legal document under the Anatomical Gift Act or similar laws.

[ ] Yes, I have discussed my wishes with my family.

Figure 3.1   Sample Uniform Donor Card

instance after organs and tissues have been removed. The body isn't disfigured.

Nationwide, there are 72 organ and tissue registries. Two of these are the Living Bank and the National Kidney Foundation (see Chapter 6 for the addresses and phone information and organizations). Contact either agency for information and placement on their computer registries. In most instances, there is no charge for a donation, but be sure to ask.

Some religious faiths object to body donations, as well as embalming, on religious grounds. They consider such an act to be a desecration of the body. However, most faiths don't object to organ and tissue donations.

Memorial Societies

While not an alternative arrangement, hundreds of mostly volunteer-run, nonprofit membership groups called memorial societies have been organized around the proposition of simple dignified funerals. Societies in both Canada and the United States negotiate with local funeral directors to provide services for members at a set price. Services may be immediate burials, direct cremations, or traditional funerals. Societies can also aid in arranging body donations.

The Milwaukee Memorial Society, for example, has negotiated a price of $1,000 for a traditional funeral there. This is a considerable savings when compared to the average funeral price of more than $3,300.

Joining a memorial society costs very little, usually a one-time $15 to $20 fee. See Chapter 6 for a list of local societies and the national headquarters, the Continental Association of Funeral and Memorial Societies.

Be aware, however, that some profit-making organizations also use the terms *memorial* or *society* in their names. These groups are not the same as the memorial societies described here.

Planning a Funeral

Funeral planning can take place at the time of death or in advance. In the latter case, it's called preplanning. But whether it's done in advance or at the time of death, the process is similar.

Preplanning a funeral and cemetery arrangement provides survivors and the deceased with distinct advantages. For the survivors, decisions are made in a more settled environment than that surrounding a death. The person whose service is being planned can select the arrangements and type of service. Be aware, however, that state laws may grant the next of kin the final say. As with organ and body donations, plans should be discussed in advance with family members.

Preplanning decisions are usually formalized with a contract for future delivery, or simply reduced to a list of goods and services. A copy can remain with the funeral director and another be retained in one's files with a Letter of Instruction for survivors (see Chapter 4).

Selecting a Funeral Home or Cemetery

There are 22,000 funeral homes and more than 10,000 cemeteries in the United States. Traditionally, selecting a funeral home or cemetery is based on family practice, religion, location, or reputation. There's nothing wrong with limiting a choice to any of these factors. However, if only one funeral home or cemetery is contacted, and no price comparisons are made, the bottom line may be higher than necessary.

Take the case of Mary Bejarano[1] of Phoenix, Arizona, who told her story to the FTC. When she developed cancer, she began to think of final arrangements, and when a door-to-door salesman came to the house selling funerals in advance (pre-need plans), Mary and her husband decided to prepay.

The couple agreed to buy two traditional funerals for $4,000 each. When interest for time payments was added in, the total came to $10,000. But before their cancellation period had expired, the Bejaranos read a newspaper article about funeral price differences. To their surprise, they found that the same traditional funeral they'd bought cost only $1,500 just across town. The Bejaranos canceled the $10,000 contract.

The same funeral may not vary as much in price in Chicago, New York, or Seattle. However, prices vary from funeral home to funeral home. An increasing number of consumers have begun to include price comparisons in their considerations.

The FTC's Funeral Rule requires that funeral homes, but not other elements of the death-services industry, disclose their prices. This information must be made available over the telephone or at the mortuary. Many funeral directors, although not required to do so, will mail a copy of their price lists.

A hospital or nursing home may recommend a funeral home, although some self-interest could be involved in such a referral and these referrals are illegal in some states. It's probably best to start by asking for recommendations from relatives, neighbors, or religious leaders. Ask about the establishment's reputation. It's also a good idea to visit and tour the facility. The telephone directory also lists a community's funeral homes and cemeteries.

It can be helpful to contact the local Better Business Bureau and the state licensing board that regulates funeral directors (see Consumer Protections later in this chapter) to ask about the funeral home you're considering. Ask if any complaints have been filed against either the business or any individuals working there. Ask about the findings of any investigations as well.

Funeral Price Lists

Price information from funeral homes is available in three separate price lists, although they're sometimes combined: one for caskets, another for outer burial containers (concrete or metal containers placed around the casket in graves), and a third for services (the general price list). The Funeral Rule prescribes what must be itemized, but the forms aren't standardized. The terms used and the organization of the lists vary considerably; however, New York state has standardized its forms to some extent.

To compare prices effectively, consumers must determine the total cost for the goods and services selected at each home. For a traditional funeral, the bottom line is determined by summing up the elements listed in Figure 3.2.

Major Components of Funeral Price Lists

Item	Cost
Casket	_____
Outer Burial Container	_____
Transportation of the Body	_____
Care of the Body	_____
Use of Facilities	_____
Services of the Funeral Director	_____
Optional Items (music, flowers, etc.)	_____
Cash Advances (death certificates, permits)	_____

Figure 3.2   Major Components of Funeral Price Lists

CASKETS

While caskets vary widely in both price and style, this item alone accounts for one-third to one-half the retail cost of most traditional funerals. Literally hundreds of different models are produced by more than 300 casket manufacturers. Figure 3.3 gives a small sampling with generic descriptions.

The rule of thumb for wholesale-to-retail markup is 200 to 300 percent. The large markup occurs because funeral directors have traditionally included part of their overhead in the casket price. Some funeral directors charge much more than this, others less.

Caskets

Type	Average Price Range
Minimum Casket	$400–$450
(Cloth-covered wood product with twill or flat crepe interior)	
Minimum Steel	$600
(Normally, 20-gauge steel with twill or flat crepe interior)	
Basic Steel	$950–$1,150
(Normally, gasketed 20-gauge steel with adjustable mattress to facilitate viewing, and twill or flat crepe interior)	
Standard Steel	$1,200–$1,800
(Normally, gasketed 18- or 19-gauge steel with better quality interior and adjustable mattress)	
Premium Steel	$1,500–$2,000
(Normally, gasketed 16-gauge steel with quality interior and adjustable mattress)	
Stainless Steel	$1,700–$2,500
(Stainless steel with quality interior and adjustable mattress)	
Premium Metal	$2,600–$4,000
(Bronze or copper with velvet interior and adjustable mattress)	
Polished Hardwood	$1,400–$1,600
(Normally, pine or poplar with polished finish, crepe interior, and adjustable mattress)	
Oak, Walnut, Cherry, and Mahogany	$1,600–$3,000
(Solid hardwood with polished or semidull finish, crepe interior, and adjustable mattress)	

Figure 3.3   Price Ranges for Casket Types

In some areas of the country, consumers can select a casket at a retail casket store, a cemetery, or from a door-to-door salesperson. In most areas, however, caskets are available only from funeral directors. Be advised that funeral directors often add a service fee for caskets purchased elsewhere. This service fee should be listed on that home's price list, however.

Almost all caskets are made of either metal or wood; fiberglass and plastic models are sometimes available. Most metal caskets are made from rolled steel in different thicknesses (20-, 19-, 18-, and 16-gauge). The thicker the steel, the lower the gauge and the higher the price. Stainless steel, bronze, and copper caskets are significantly more expensive.

Wooden caskets, about 30 percent of the market, come in softwoods (pine), hardwoods (oak, mahogany, cherry, walnut, and poplar), or plywood. Cloth-covered wooden caskets are usually, but not always, the least expensive choice.

Caskets are sold on the basis of visual appeal for social display and protective features. Color, materials, fabric (twills, velours, crepes, or velvet), hardware, and workmanship generally account for the most significant differences. For most consumers, however, the difference between a 20-gauge and an 18-gauge steel casket isn't recognizable except for the price.

In descriptions of metal caskets, the terms *protective, gasketed,* or *sealer* are often used. This means there's a rubber gasket or other special features to retard the entrance of water and rust. Protective features add to the cost of a casket but, according to the FTC, "sealed caskets do not preserve human remains for long periods of time." In a 1988 Gallup Poll survey, 30 percent of funeral planners had been told by funeral directors that protective features would preserve a body indefinitely, even though making this claim is a violation of the Funeral Rule.

Funeral homes exhibit caskets in special rooms or, in some instances, in color catalogues. Critics have long charged that some funeral homes place the most expensive caskets in the best light and setting, and the least expensive ones in unfavorable quarters. Some funeral directors don't display cloth-covered caskets at all so consumers will have to buy the more expensive ones. Sometimes consumers must be persistent to secure the products they want.

Jeanne Karklin[2] of Houston, Texas, testified before the FTC that she'd found a modest casket listed by the mortuary that handled her mother's funeral. She was told it wasn't available and pressured to buy "something better" for her mother. Karklin refused to take no for an answer and prodded the funeral director to find the casket she'd requested. Finally, after much searching, the casket was located on a back shelf of a warehouse. Karklin was satisfied that the casket was both affordable and dignified.

Outer Burial Containers

To prevent ground settlement, most cemeteries require the use of an outer burial container with every in-ground burial; with a crypt in a mausoleum, an outer burial container isn't needed.

An outer burial container is either a grave liner or a vault. A grave liner is made of a rigid material such as concrete. A vault is usually steel-reinforced concrete lined with metal or asphalt; some vaults have bronze, stainless steel, or copper lining. Many vaults are also gasketed and sold with protective claims.

Grave liners average $300 to $400 while a standard vault ranges from $500 to $700. Many cemeteries and all funeral homes sell these items.

TRANSPORTATION COSTS

With any funeral, the remains are transported, usually in a hearse, to the funeral home. From there, the body is borne to the final resting place with a stop at a church or synagogue. The average charge for transporting the body to the funeral home is $75 to $100, and for transferring it to the final place of disposition, $110 to $150.

Sometimes death occurs while a person is away from home. On those occasions, the body is customarily embalmed in the state where death occurred, then transported by air to the location of the funeral or burial. Survivors must pay for air shipment, local transportation to the mortuary (probably in both cities), and a service fee to each funeral director. (In some instances, only one service fee is charged.)

A casket or a special "air pack" or similar container may be purchased to ship the body in. Make sure both funeral directors don't charge for the same item, such as embalming. Ask questions and check prices very carefully when arranging a long-distance shipment.

CARE OF THE BODY

Embalming isn't usually required for immediate burials, direct cremations, or, in some instances, funerals with a closed casket. If the body isn't embalmed, it may require refrigeration to prevent decomposition. Embalming is required by funeral directors, not by state law, to delay decomposition when there is a viewing of the body. Embalming may be legally required when the body is transported across state lines, the funeral is conducted two or three days after death, or when death occurred from a communicable or contagious disease.

The average cost of embalming a body ranges between $225 and $300. Other items may be added to this fee, such as cosmetology, restoration, and special care of an autopsied body. Sometimes an additional charge is tacked on for casketing or dressing, that is, placing a body in a casket or clothing it.

USE OF FACILITIES

Most visitations or wakes are conducted in funeral homes, although more churches are opening their doors for these services. Often the funeral itself is conducted at the mortuary instead of a church or synagogue. The average price for a three-hour viewing at a funeral home is $150 to $250, and for a one-hour service it's an additional $150 to $250. Sometimes, an general use fee or facilities overhead fee is encountered. This additional overhead charge must be included in the bottom line price.

SERVICES OF THE FUNERAL DIRECTOR

With most items on a price list, the consumer chooses what he or she wants. This isn't true with the services of a funeral director. This fee covers much of a funeral home's overhead, including the salary of the funeral director, clerical help, utilities, and other items. Generally, the cost is between $500 and $700. However, some funeral directors charge a lower service fee but more for their caskets, or vice versa.

OPTIONAL AND CASH ADVANCE ITEMS

For many people, a funeral without music or flowers wouldn't be meaningful. These items are optional, and the funeral director can order them for a charge.

With cash advance items, the funeral director pays a third party such as the local newspaper for an obituary, or the public health office for copies of the death certificate, and charges survivors for them. Prices for these items vary too widely to calculate an average cost. Be aware, however, that these items must be paid for.

THE BOTTOM LINE

After selecting the various elements of the funeral, you can sum up the total for all of the goods and services, using a worksheet such as the one in Figure 3.4. To compare prices between funeral homes, be sure to compare the same goods and services. Some funeral homes offer package prices to make the job easier.

Funeral Costs

Item	Cost
Casket	_____
Outer Burial Container	_____
Transportation	_____
Care of Body	_____
Facilities	_____
Services of Director	_____
Optional Items	_____
Cash Advances	_____
Total	$ _____

Figure 3.4   Worksheet for Calculating Funeral Costs

Planning Burial Arrangements

Consumer choice is changing, but most Americans still prefer an in-ground burial. The number of combination funeral home–cemetery operations is increasing, but it's still a common practice to select a graveplot in a cemetery at a separate location. Cemeteries are not required by federal law to provide price information over the phone or in person. Most probably do.

Burial arrangements can include one or more of the following items.

A cemetery lot or burial plot

A crypt or space in a mausoleum or tomb housing many crypts; a mausoleum may be an above- or below-ground (lawn crypt) building

A niche or space in a columbarium

Opening and closing the grave or entombment in a crypt or columbarium

A marker or plaque to memorialize the deceased; these are also sold independently by monument dealers

A charge for installing the marker

An outer burial container for an in-ground burial, if not purchased from a funeral director

Fees, such as a registration fee

Cemetery lots, crypts, and niches vary in cost from as little as $200 to more than $2,000. A large cemetery can have thousands of lots spread over acres of land. Those considered ideal are very costly. Those considered less desirable sell for hundreds less. You're probably safe in budgeting between $200 and $1,000 for a cemetery lot and $2,000 to $4,000 for a crypt. Visit the site, however, to determine if the price and location are right.

Almost always, the plot must be purchased before the burial. Cemetery plots are like real estate, and you will receive a right-of-burial document, which is similar to a deed and can be sold. There may be restrictions on the resale of unused burial plots, however.

A veteran or his or her spouse is eligible for burial at one of the country's national cemeteries (see Chapter 4). There's no charge for veterans to be buried here.

Because of labor costs, many cemeteries are moving to garden-type plots. Here all markers are flat on the ground, permitting easier maintenance. Separate sections are frequently reserved for burials with upright monuments and above-ground headstones. The price for these lots is usually higher. Cemeteries limited to garden-type plots are called memorial parks.

Because both above- and below-ground mausoleums involve masonry construction, crypts almost always cost more than grave lots. Further, crypts at heart or eye level cost more than those at the bottom or top of the building. However, because there are fewer additional charges such as for an outer burial container, the bottom-line cost for a crypt may be no more than for an in-ground burial.

Maintaining grave sites for hundreds of years is an expensive proposition. Cemeteries may or may not assess a separate charge for what is called perpetual care, endowment care, or simply long-term maintenance. Here funds are set aside in trust and the earnings on the principal used to maintain the cemetery over time. Most states require perpetual care funds. Even if it's not mentioned, be sure to ask about perpetual care.

Of the more than 10,000 cemeteries in the nation, over half are owned by the Catholic church. Many are owned by other religious faiths and municipalities. These are nonprofit cemeteries. The remainder are operated by for-profit institutions. Prices at not-for-profit facilities tend to be lower, but not always.

Whether a grave site or crypt is prepaid or purchased at the time of death, there is a charge for opening and closing the grave or entombment. This varies from as little as $250 to more than $1,000. Additional charges may be made if the burial is held on a weekend or after certain hours of the day. There may also be charges for storing a body over the winter for a springtime burial. With crypts, there's no opening or closing fee, but there can be an entombment or inurnment fee, for placing the casket in a crypt or a cremation urn in its niche.

Markers or monuments are frequently selected as a memorial to the deceased. They can range in price from almost $500 for a simple bronze plaque to thousands of dollars for granite or marble markers. Markers and monuments are sold by cemeteries, independent monument builders, and, in some instances, funeral directors. Cemeteries almost always levy a separate charge for installing a marker, though this charge may not be listed separately and may be included in the retail cost. It's been alleged that some cemeteries levy a surcharge for memorials purchased elsewhere. If so, this could offset any savings made by purchasing a monument from a third party. Be sure to check this before you buy.

Purchasing an outer burial container from a cemetery is no different from purchasing one from a funeral director. The products are the same, although prices may vary.

Cemeteries, funeral homes, and some crematories market urns for containing the cremated remains, ranging in price from $50 to more than $1,000.

THE BOTTOM LINE

To assess burial costs, sum up the total for all the needed items. A worksheet such as that in Figure 3.5 may help. To compare prices between cemeteries, use a similar selection of goods and services.

Burial Costs

Item   Cost

Grave, Crypt, or Niche   _____

Outer Burial Container   _____
   (if not purchased from funeral director)

Opening and Closing Grave or Entombment _____
   (usually paid at time of burial)

Marker (bronze or stone) and Installation   _____

Urn (for cremated remains)   _____

Additional Fees (e.g., recording fee)   _____

Total $ _____

Figure 3.5   Worksheet for Calculating Burial Costs

Consumer Protections

Funeral Rule

In 1984, the FTC's Funeral Rule went into effect. This rule was the culmination of a political struggle that began in the 1970s.

The Funeral Rule, which has the effect of law in all states, sets out requirements for funeral directors. Cemeteries, crematories, monument builders, and third-party sellers of caskets and some pre-need plans are not subject to the Funeral Rule. Funeral directors must:

Provide funeral price information over the telephone and itemized price lists at the mortuary for inspection

Secure the approval of the family before embalming a body

Not require the sale of a casket for a cremation

Not sell goods and services as a package without allowing consumer choices

Not make false claims about the preservative value of caskets and outer burial containers

According to the FTC, industry compliance with all requirements of the Funeral Rule is less than 35 percent.[3] Violations include the timing of disclosures, claims about the preservative value of caskets and outer burial containers, and failure to obtain permission to embalm.

While there was significant opposition from the funeral industry when the rule was first issued, funeral directors have learned to live with the regulations. An opinion poll conducted by the American Association of Retired Persons (AARP) found that funeral directors believe the rule is an important consumer protection and should be expanded to cover cemeteries and other elements of the death-services industry.[4]

State Funeral Laws

Many states have adopted statutes or regulations that require similar disclosures. If a funeral director refuses to provide price information, contact a regional FTC office; look in the federal government listings in your telephone book. Second, contact the state attorney general or the state board that licenses funeral directors (see Appendix B).

In most states, the attorney general is the principal consumer advocate. This office investigates consumer complaints and can take legal action. Funeral boards, active in all states except Colorado, license funeral directors. They also conduct investigations and discipline members of the profession. You can contact this board in the state capital.

Mediation and Arbitration

The Funeral Service Consumer Assistance Program was established by the National Funeral Directors Association (NFDA) to mediate and arbitrate funeral, but not cemetery, complaints. It is administered by the National Research and Information Center. Consumers can call a toll-free number (see Chapter 6) with complaints, whether or not the funeral director is a member of the NFDA. This program tries to mediate dispute and, when that doesn't work, it arbitrates. Arbitration is a quasi-legal proceeding in which an arbitrator or panel of arbitrators decides an issue outside the court system. Monetary awards may be made.

There are several drawbacks to this program, however. First, it covers only services. That is, if the consumer has a complaint about caskets or burial vaults, the program cannot help. Second, this is one of the few dispute-resolution programs in which the consumer must agree to binding arbitration, meaning both parties must agree to abide by the decision of the arbitrator rather than appealing to the courts.

Cemetery Regulation

Forty-nine states regulate funeral directors through a state licensing board, but only 37 states oversee cemeteries. In most instances there's a separate board, but, in other cases, cemeteries are regulated by the banking commission or the real estate board. Some locations have county or municipal regulation of cemeteries. In general, protections are limited (see Appendix B for a state-by-state listing) and only state consumer-protection laws apply.

If you have a complaint about a cemetery, file it with a state cemetery board (where it exists), the attorney general, or a consumer-protection office. In some states, such as Ohio, cemeterians have created ethics committees to resolve complaints. There's also a mediation service sponsored by the American Cemetery Association (ACA). The ACA, the largest organization of people in the cemetery business, with 2,000 members, has a code of ethics, including sales practices, to which member cemeteries must subscribe.

ACA sponsors a grave-exchange program, and other such programs also exist. ACA's grave-exchange program includes burial plots and memorials and only applies to some ACA cemeteries. Under this program, a consumer who moves to a new location can secure a credit equal to his or her original purchase price within certain limits. This credit can be applied toward the purchase of a cemetery plot, crypt, and/or marker in a participating cemetery in the new location. When buying, ask the cemeterian if that facility is part of the ACA Credit Exchange or another grave exchange program. Because the ACA exchange doesn't account for price increases over time, a consumer might do better by selling the plot or giving it away.

Together with the Cremation Association of North America and the Pre-Arrangement Association of America, ACA offers a consumer complaint–mediation program called the Cemetery Consumer Service Council. A consumer can write this council with a complaint; see Chapter 6 for the address. The council investigates and then tries to mediate the dispute. Binding arbitration is not included nor are all cemeteries likely to participate.

Conclusion

Planning a funeral reminds people of their own mortality. Death isn't a pleasant prospect, but purchasing a funeral could involve more problems if it's left to survivors in their time of grief.

Those planning a funeral need to remember that it is a consumer purchase. There are choices to be made in goods and services, and there's a large price range. Shopping around can significantly lower costs.

With the Funeral Rule in effect, it's easier than ever to plan ahead and shop wisely. Decide on the goods and services you want and then compare prices among several funeral homes and cemeteries. Make sure you're comparing the same bottom line.

THINGS TO REMEMBER

Plan your funeral before it's needed.

Funeral prices vary widely. Shopping around can save you money.

To compare prices effectively, only look at the bottom line. Cemetery prices vary widely also.

The FTC's Funeral Rule requires that price information be made available by phone and in person.

Notes

1. U.S. Federal Trade Commission, Funeral Industry Practices Mandatory Review, Mary Bejarano, Funeral Consumer, Tr. Vol. III, pp. 1588–1597, Dec. 1988.
2. U.S. Federal Trade Commission, Funeral Industry Practices Mandatory Review, Jeanne Karklin, Funeral Consumer, Tr. Vol. I, pp. 544–546, Oct. 1988.
3. U.S. Federal Trade Commission, Funeral Industry Practices Mandatory Review, "Final Staff Report to the Federal Trade Commission and Proposed Amended Rule," pp. 35–52, June 1990.
4. U.S. Federal Trade Commission, Funeral Industry Practices Mandatory Review, Ayers, Hearing Exhibit–108, Question 10, Dec. 1988.

Chapter 4

Paying or Prepaying for a Funeral

Like many older adults, Leslie Hewitt set aside funds for his funeral. Instead of a savings account for this purpose, the 76-year-old retired janitor bought life insurance.

For six years he paid $415 a year in premiums. But after he'd doled out $2,500, Hewitt found out that his policy would only pay $1,144 in benefits. In other words, he'd lost almost $1,400. There's nothing illegal about this kind of arrangement. Hewitt's policy is like many others sold to older Americans. The details are in the fine print.

After writing the company, Hewitt learned that if he paid $800 more in premiums, his policy would become a "reduced paid-up plan" with benefits of $1,940. So, for a total outlay of $3,300, only $1,940 would be available for his funeral expenses.

Hewitt was irate and contacted his state's attorney general. "I know insurance companies are entitled to a fair profit," he wrote. "But the profits this company made from me seem to be more than enough. . . . I need some help in dealing with this firm."[1]

KEY FACTS

- The cost of a traditional funeral and an in-ground burial is between $5,000 and $6,000.

- Historically, funeral prices have increased by 4–6 percent a year.

- Social Security provides a $255 death allowance to eligible survivors.

- The Veterans Administration (VA) provides a burial plot and a marker in a national cemetery at no charge to eligible veterans.

- The number of deaths per year in the United States is close to 2.1 million. That number is expected to increase slowly until it reaches 2.7 million by the year 2010.

- Since 1985, the death-services industry has aggressively marketed funerals and burials to be bought in advance of death, called pre-need plans.

- In 1990, 1 million pre-need funeral contracts were sold, primarily to older consumers.

- Pre-need sales are regulated on a state-by-state basis and the oversight is inconsistent. In one case alone, fraudulent activities have dissipated millions of dollars spent by consumers.

It's common these days for older people to receive solicitations trumpeting the high costs of a funeral. Some prey on emotions with questions like, Do you want your funeral to be a burden for your children? By paying in advance, you can have peace of mind, urges the script in a typical direct-mail piece.

Most people who prepay for their funerals are 60 years old or older, according to industry statistics. Pre-need, or paying in advance, is a megatrend in the death-services industry. All the tools of advertising are used (television, radio, newspapers, direct mail, and even billboards) to send the message: Buy now!

And this hoopla seems to work. In 1960 only 22,000 consumers paid for funerals in advance. Thirty years later, 1 million people purchased a pre-need funeral plan, and the number of buyers increases by about 100,000 every year.[2] William Hocker, the former president of the National Funeral Directors Association (NFDA), the nation's largest membership organization of funeral directors, estimated that "funeral directors will soon be selling more pre-need than at-need [at the time of death] funerals."

The $5,000 to $6,000 price tag for a traditional funeral with cemetery expenses establishes it as one of the largest payments a consumer makes in a lifetime. Consumers are wise to plan their funerals and determine how these goods and services will be paid for. These financial arrangements can be made by earmarking funds or by paying in advance.

Prepaying makes sense for some people. For example, Anne Anderson of Columbus, Ohio, paid only $1,271 in life insurance premiums but received a $3,100 funeral from the proceeds.[3] But whether to prepay or not is a question involving more than peace of mind.

This chapter continues the discussion of funeral planning introduced in Chapter 3. Chapter 3 covered the elements of a funeral and burial and their costs. This chapter addresses two questions: how to pay for a funeral or burial at the time of death or in advance, and whether or not a consumer should prepay. The first part of the chapter reviews financial planning for a funeral, including various available death benefits and eligibility requirements for them. The latter part examines the variety of pre-need options available and looks at costs, earnings, portability (whether the plan can move with the owner), and security. This chapter concludes with a discussion of consumer-protection issues surrounding pre-need funeral plans.

Resources To Pay for Funeral and Burial Expenses

When planning a funeral or burial, consumers select the goods and services they want, mindful of what their pocketbooks permit. Knowing the bottom line, or total cost, is crucial to any decision. However, making financial arrangements for a funeral in the future (preplanning) must also include the impact of inflationary increases over time. The life expectancy for a 65-year-old is 17 years and funeral prices will increase during that time.[4] Financial planning for a funeral means assuring that adequate funds are on hand now as well as 10 or more years from now.

It's always hard to predict prices. One measure of future costs is a review of past rates of increase. Historically, over the last 25 years, funeral prices have increased at only a modest 4–6 percent a year, even in years when the government's Consumer Price Index of inflation was much higher.[5] From 1987 through 1990, funeral prices rose an average of $100 to $200 a year. If prices continue to escalate at an average rate of 5 percent a year, today's $5,500 traditional funeral with in-ground burial will cost about $9,000 10 years from now and almost $15,000 20 years from now.

If a $5,500 price tag appears formidable, consider the various options. First, determine if any savings can be accomplished by reducing the bottom line. For example, could a 20-gauge metal casket serve instead of an 18-gauge one, thereby reducing costs? Could the answer be another type of disposition (as described in Chapter 3)? Does another funeral home offer lower prices?

Next, after all cost reductions have been made, determine the survivors' eligibility for death benefits from Social Security, the VA, and other sources. As with any other major consumer purchase, review existing assets and liabilities to determine whether funeral and burial expenses can be paid from benefits and available funds. Finally, if the bottom line can't be reduced, and existing benefits and assets are insufficient, borrowing money may be the only option.

There are several public and private benefits that can be investigated. Consumers should try to determine their eligibility for these death benefits.

Social Security

Surviving spouses and dependent children are eligible for a $255 payment from Social Security for the funeral expenses of a deceased recipient. If there is no eligible survivor, no payment is made.

Veterans' Burial Benefits

All veterans of the armed services who were discharged under other than dishonorable conditions are eligible for certain benefits. Burial in a national cemetery is available at no charge, for example. A veteran's spouse and dependent children are also eligible for this burial benefit. Some states also have veterans' cemeteries.

Veterans, whether or not they're buried in a national cemetery, are also eligible for a bronze marker; 300,000 veterans benefited from this service in 1990. The cost of installing the marker in a private cemetery is borne by survivors. In a national cemetery, the VA installs the marker. An American flag to drape over the casket is also available to all veterans.

If the deceased was receiving VA disability compensation, was collecting a VA pension, or died in a VA medical facility, he or she may be eligible for a $300 burial allowance and a $150 burial plot allowance.

All of these benefits are granted in addition to what Social Security may pay. Contact the nearest VA office for more information.

Other Death Benefits

Death benefits may also be available from current or former employers, labor unions, or civil service pension systems. Check with former employers of the deceased. See Chapter 5 for more details.

Public Benefit Programs

For older persons receiving Supplemental Security Income (SSI), a federally funded cash assistance program, and/or Medicaid, the state-federal, low-income health-care program, there is no death benefit. Figure 4.1 outlines the way that recipients may be able to set aside money for burial. Some states provide special-needs assistance for a funeral or burial for eligible low-income applicants. Most do not, however, provide these benefits.

In some jurisdictions, a county or city public assistance program known as general assistance provides a minimum amount for a funeral or burial. Check with the local office of social services or an Area Agency on Aging.

Existing Assets

Many older people already have savings and investments earning interest. Can a portion of these savings, together with any death benefits, be earmarked for that person's funeral expenses? If so, can price increases over time be fully funded with earnings on the deposit or investment?

Setting Aside Funds for a Funeral under SSI and Medicaid

Eligibility for both SSI and Medicaid is based upon the assets and income of the applicant. Frequently, nursing home expenses force older adults to "spend down" (reduce) their assets to become eligible for Medicaid. While there are no death benefits under either SSI or Medicaid, in most instances, recipients can set aside funds to pay for funeral and burial expenses without jeopardizing their eligibility.

SSI permits an individual to irrevocably (permanently) set aside funds for a funeral. These can be placed in a cash value life insurance policy, a trust (property or money set aside on behalf of another), or a bank account. However, the irrevocable funds must be used exclusively for a funeral or burial. At this time, there's no limit on the amount that can be irrevocably set aside.

An SSI recipient can also set aside $1,500 as a burial fund in a separate but revocable account. But a recipient can't have both irrevocable and revocable funds.

While SSI is federally operated, Medicaid, on the other hand, is administered by the various states. Many states follow the same standards as SSI in determining eligibility, including the amount of money that can be set aside as a burial fund. However, other states follow their own standards. The best advice is to check with your local social services agency or Area Agency on Aging for current information.

Figure 4.1   Setting Aside Funds for a Funeral or Burial under Public Benefit Programs Such as Medicaid and SSI

For example, the market rate for a certificate of deposit (CD) is over 7 percent at the writing of this book. Depositing $5,000 to accumulate at 7 percent interest compounded will earn more than $4,800 after 10 years for a total of $9,800. Even with the tax liabilities on the earnings, this should be more than enough to cover funeral and burial cost increases over time.

However, many savings and investment accounts contain a hidden defect that prevents their use at the time of death. Unless the ownership records include the name of someone other than the deceased, the account will almost surely be frozen until after the estate has gone through probate. To avoid this delay on using the funds, more than one name should be listed and the person should have a right of survivorship (see Chapter 5 for more information).

While some funeral directors are willing to wait for payment, most want to be paid at the time of the funeral. One study shows that probate proceedings in some areas averaged a year and a half in length.[6]

Two solutions are to add the name of a spouse or close relative to a savings account with rights of survivorship (see Chapter 5) or to create a payable-on-death (P.O.D.) account (see below). Be sure to ask about payment in a conference with your funeral director, either at the time of the death or while prearranging.

The asset review should also include existing life or burial insurance policies. How many policies are owned? What is the total amount in insurance benefits available? Does the death benefit increase over time? Are there any outstanding debts that will reduce the death benefit? Are the benefits earmarked for another purpose such as reducing outstanding debts or income protection? Who's the named beneficiary? Can the benefits be assigned to a funeral director? Discuss the latter topic with the funeral director, particularly if you're making arrangements at the time of a death.

Finally, is a burial plot already part of the assets? For many older people, this is the first and often the only prearrangement they've made. One opinion survey found that about 60 percent of the 65-plus population already owned a burial plot.[7] If a plot has been purchased, the total amount earmarked for a funeral and burial can be reduced.

Pre-Need Arrangements

A consumer can prearrange a funeral or burial. To pay in advance of the need for a funeral is called pre-need. It's not a new concept. Pre-need statutes have been on the books in some states since the 1950s. If burial or industrial insurance (small policies paid on a weekly or monthly basis) is considered pre-need, it's been around a lot longer than that. What's new is the marketing of pre-need plans. Today, the concept is advertised everywhere.

Pre-need arrangements permit the funeral director and cemeterian to expand their businesses in a time of increasing life expectancy. The national death rate is relatively constant at around 2 million deaths a year and isn't expected to rise significantly until after the year 2010. Pre-need can increase sales at a time of a relatively constant death rate. Selling the plans is also a matter of survival. If a funeral director doesn't sell pre-need plans, competitors can lock up the lion's share of future business.

The benefits aren't all one-sided, however. Advertising for pre-need focuses public attention on the need to preplan. Planning in advance eases decision making for a family because it can be done in a less emotionally charged atmosphere. With many pre-need plans, consumers can also lock in a price and, if the plan is carefully selected, provide survivors with funds left after the funeral is paid for.

Pre-need arrangements can provide what the industry calls peace of mind because the consumer knows these arrangements have been made and survivors won't have to struggle at an emotional time. Remember, however, $3,000 or $4,000 invested over time is more than peace of mind.

What Is a Pre-Need Plan?

Most pre-need plans contain two elements: a prearrangement agreement listing the goods and services selected, and a funding mechanism to pay for these items. Most plans are binding agreements stipulating that the funeral director or cemeterian must provide these items at a specified price.

Currently there are three types of pre-need plans to prepay funeral or burial expenses. These are: personal or individual trusts, state-regulated trusts, and insurance-funded plans.

PERSONAL TRUSTS

Charles Andrews met with his local funeral director, who also owns a cemetery, and selected a traditional funeral with an in-ground burial worth $4,500. Once he selected the goods and services, Andrews completed a prearrangement agreement listing each item.

Then he created a Totten Trust (personal trust) at the First National Bank. Andrews deposited $4,500 into the trust account. During his lifetime, he is the trustee and controls the account. At his death, the $4,500, together with any earnings, will be paid to the funeral director as the beneficiary of the trust. Any funds in excess of actual costs will go to Andrews' estate. If there is a shortfall, his survivors would need to make up the difference. To create the trust, he paid an attorney $200.

This is one way to prepay for a funeral. Instead of a trust, Andrews could have created a special payable on death (P.O.D.) savings account payable to the funeral director on Andrews's death. Normally there is no charge for setting up such an account, but it may be a good idea to discuss it with an attorney, banker, and funeral director.

Finally, although it would not be a pre-need plan, Andrews could have simply created a separate savings account earmarked for funeral expenses with or without the knowledge of the funeral director. But at least one other person, with rights of survivorship, must have access to the account.

Instead of making a lump sum payment of $4,500, Andrews could pay into the savings account over time. However, if death occurs before the funeral is fully funded, Andrews's estate or survivors would be liable for any shortfall.

A personal trust provides Andrews with maximum control of the funding mechanism. He can cancel without penalty and can earn the market rate of interest. On the other hand, there may be fees involved in creating a formal trust, and of course Andrews is liable for income taxes on the earnings. Since he's living on a fixed retirement income, taxes are minimal.

For the funeral director, the advantage is that future business is locked in with this arrangement. Cost increases are also funded.

STATE-REGULATED TRUSTS

Andrea Percy decided she simply wanted to pay a funeral director in advance rather than create her own trust. Percy selected a $2,500 traditional funeral, contracted for the delivery of it upon her death, and paid for it. The funeral director guaranteed that she would deliver the services for a payment of $2,500 plus any interest earned by the trust.

State law where Percy lives specifies that 100 percent of the $2,500 must be deposited by the funeral director in a financial institution until the time of need. The funeral director doesn't have access to these funds until Percy's death since they are held in trust. Any interest is paid directly into the trust. Every year the state funeral board audits the funeral director's books to ensure that the trust accounts are maintained properly.

Percy bought a burial vault and marker from a cemetery for an additional $1,500; she already owns a burial plot. Again, she signed a contract for future delivery. But here, only $1,000 was deposited in a trust account and the other $500 remains with the cemetery. Trust requirements are different for cemeteries and for funeral homes in Percy's state. The cemeterian is under contract to deliver these goods but can have use of the $500 until the time of need.

Every state except Alabama, Vermont, and the District of Columbia regulates the prepayment of funerals. These laws require that a set percentage of the funds and earnings be placed in trust. The percentage varies from 50 percent in Mississippi to 100 percent in 26 states; see Appendix B for a state-by-state listing of pre-need laws. Any funds not held in trust are available for use by the funeral director.

Trust laws for cemeteries not only vary from state to state, but are usually distinct from funeral-related pre-need laws. In California and other states, for example, 100 percent trusting is required for the fee for cemetery merchandise and services. However, the consumer can also take "constructive delivery." Here, the seller holds the vault, memorial, or other items in a warehouse until needed and issues a certificate of ownership to the purchaser. In California, this is considered the same as an actual delivery and trust requirements don't apply. Other states have no trust requirements for cemetery pre-need sales.

Regulated trust funds can be commingled (combined) for investment, or segregated, kept in separate trust accounts. This varies, depending upon state law and the contract. Most trust funds earn interest until the death, although some are sold like Christmas Club funds and earn no interest. Most accounts are insured by a federal agency such as the Federal Deposit Insurance Corporation (FDIC). With many state-regulated trusts, the seller guarantees that the cost of the funeral, as spelled out in the pre-arrangement agreement, will never exceed the amount paid. Any earnings in excess of funeral cost may go to survivors or to the seller, depending upon the contract and state law.

According to the Internal Revenue Service (IRS), in most instances the consumer is liable for any taxes on the earnings of such a funeral trust. This is true even if they never personally benefit from the earnings since they are held in trust. For most older adults, the amount involved is insignificant. However, the funeral director or the bank must send a 1099 or K-1 form to both the consumer and the IRS.

Payments to the trust can be made in installments but are usually lump-sum deposits. If the trust isn't fully funded, survivors or the estate are liable for unfunded costs at the time of death. In some instances, consumers can borrow money to create a trust. The borrower repays the debt over time. As in any other credit transaction, federal truth-in-lending consumer protections apply.

Regulated trusts provide users with some protections, such as trust requirements and audits in some states. They also may provide guaranteed costs and the potential for higher earnings than in insurance-funded plans. The risks are that a funeral director or cemeterian can make a bad investment, go out of business, or go bankrupt, losing the consumer's funds. See Security below.

For the funeral director, the advantage is locking in future business with the potential of gaining all or part of the interest earned on the deposited funds. The disadvantage is the paperwork required for the IRS and state regulators. And with 100 percent trusting, none of the funeral director's expenses in selling pre-need plans are recovered until the time of death. This could be years away.

INSURANCE-FUNDED PLANS

Louis Ramicone decided he wanted to pay his funeral director in advance. Ramicone selected a $5,000 traditional funeral and signed a contract for future delivery. To pay for this, he purchased a life insurance policy from the funeral director with a face amount of $5,000. The funeral director guaranteed the price and was named the beneficiary of the policy.

The premiums paid by Ramicone go to the insurance company for investment until the time of need. The funeral director received a commission from the insurance company for the sale. The larger the funeral policy, the higher the fee.

Ramicone also selected a burial vault and marker from a cemetery for an additional $1,500; he already owns a burial plot. He signed a contract for future delivery and the cemeterian sold him a life insurance policy for the face amount of $1,500. Like the funeral director, the cemeterian became the beneficiary of the policy.

Should Ramicone change his mind or move to another state, he can appoint a different beneficiary. This can be his next of kin or a funeral director or cemeterian in the new city.

Insurance-funded pre-need arrangements are the newest and fastest growing pre-need product on the market. A life insurance policy or annuity (a tax-deferred investment similar to life insurance) is used to finance the funeral. Usually, the funeral director or cemeterian guarantees that the life insurance policy will cover charges listed in the prearrangement agreement. Funds in excess of these costs are paid to survivors or the funeral director, depending upon the contract.

Some of the largest insurance companies selling insurance-funded products are Forethought Life Insurance, Franklin Life Insurance (sold by funeral directors who are members of the Order of the Golden Rule), Torchmark Life Insurance, American Funeral Security Life Insurance, Monumental Life Insurance (sold by members of the National Selected Morticians), and PFS Life Insurance. Insurance-funded pre-need plans are sold in most states but not all products are available in every state. Insurance-funded pre-need plans are prohibited in Georgia, Maryland, New York, South Carolina, and Wyoming.

The life insurance policy is purchased with multiple (usually five or ten) payments or a single lump-sum premium. Some are written as guaranteed issue policies, meaning no health questions are asked. Others have limited underwriting, and health conditions determine eligibility. If someone is ineligible for a life insurance policy, an annuity is sold. Purchasing a guaranteed issue policy may mean the death benefit is limited to the premiums paid for several years. Check the contract.

For the consumer, the benefits of an insurance-funded product are that immediate, complete coverage of the funeral cost is provided even if he or she doesn't live long enough to pay the total price, except in a guaranteed issue policy. There's also a price guarantee with most plans, some state regulation of insurance sales, and no income tax liability for earnings. The principal disadvantage is the lower earnings with these products.

With insurance-funded plans, the seller both secures future business and receives a commission for the sale. However, some states prohibit a funeral director from becoming the beneficiary of a life insurance policy and some states prohibit funeral directors from receiving commissions.

FINAL EXPENSE LIFE INSURANCE

While it's not a pre-need product tying funeral goods to an insurance policy, an ever-increasing number of final expense life insurance policies are being sold to older people. These are small policies of $10,000 or less, typically marketed in television ads, through the mail, and by funeral directors. The death benefit can be used to pay for a funeral or any other expense.

The cost of this insurance can be very high, and in a number of instances, consumers pay more in premiums than they will receive in death benefits unless they die during the first few years. Take Leslie Hewitt, who was mentioned at the beginning of this chapter. He paid more than $2,500 in premiums but was eligible for only $1,144 in benefits from his life insurance policy. His complaint was instrumental in the development of new insurance regulations in Washington state.

The state insurance commissioner there issued a rule banning the sale of small, multiple-payment life insurance policies in which the death benefit is less than the premiums paid, plus 5 percent interest, for the first 10 years. This means the death benefit must be greater than what consumers pay during the first 10 years. Similarly, the Virginia legislature passed a law in 1991 requiring any life insurance policy funding a funeral to earn at least 5 percent interest compounded. Whether or not a consumer lives in Washington state or Virginia, 5 percent should be a minimum standard for any life insurance policy.

Factors To Consider

Costs and Earnings of Pre-Need Plans

Most pre-need plans are sold at or near the price of the funeral or burial as listed in the prearrangement agreement. That is, a consumer selecting a $2,500 or $3,000 funeral should expect to pay this amount of money whether the pre-need plan is a trust or an insurance policy. The premiums for some insurance-funded policies are somewhat less than the face amount of the policy. But the major difference is the earnings of the different plans.

Some state-regulated trust plans have earned as much as 10 percent interest compounded. Some insurance-funded plans pay less than 5 percent interest. The earnings differences between these two types of plans can be dramatic over time. With higher earnings, survivors will likely receive funds in excess of the funeral cost. Check the contract to determine earnings over time and who receives any funds remaining after the funeral is paid for. Also, be sure to consider any tax liabilities on earnings.

Some funeral directors and cemeterians argue that a pre-need plan isn't an investment. In part, they're right. It's a payment for the future delivery of goods and services. However, buyers must also consider a factor called the time value of money. In 1990, a sum of $3,000 deposited in a certificate of deposit can earn 7 percent interest or more. Over 10 years, $3,000 will almost double to $5,800; the average life of a pre-need contract is 10 to 12 years. But this projection doesn't consider the tax implications. These factors indicate that pre-need planning should be compared to a long-term deposit.

Pre-Need Portability

Most older people retire in the communities where they've always lived. However, a significant number move to be near children or grandchildren or simply want to live in the Sunbelt. Buyers need to ask whether the pre-need plan can move if they move.

The consumer controls an individual trust. It's easy to move the funds around with little or no penalty from the financial institution. However, funeral costs vary from area to area, and consumers must select a funeral home in the new community and review prices there. As always, use caution and compare prices.

A state-regulated trust plan can be transferred within and outside the state in some instances. Usually, however, a consumer who moves must cancel the trust and deposits the funds with a new funeral director. There may be penalties involved (see Appendix B for more details).

Insurance-funded plans offer more options than state-regulated trusts. An insurance policy, though probably not the prearrangement agreement tied to it, is portable and valid no matter where the consumer lives. In some instances, the insurance company will aid policy owners in finding another funeral home to honor the prearrangement agreement. However, the $3,000 funeral bargained for in Boston may cost more or less than that in Ft. Lauderdale. Additional insurance may be needed to cover costs and a new prearrangement required.

Revocation and Cancellation

Because people change their minds, and because many pre-need plans aren't portable, a consumer should review a contract before signing to determine if the plan is revocable or cancelable, that is, whether the buyer can cancel the contract. Some plans are sold as irrevocable agreements with a particular funeral home. Unless SSI or Medicaid eligibility is an issue, it's almost always best to have a revocable plan.

With personal trusts, the only penalty for cancelation, if any, is for the early withdrawal of funds.

Laws for regulated trusts differ from state to state. A consumer may or may not receive his or her full deposit and/or earnings when canceling a state-regulated trust. With many state plans, no penalty is involved (see Appendix B). However, with some plans, in California, for example, an administrative fee of 10 percent may be deducted from the earned interest.

In life insurance sales, every state has a "look-see" regulation. After purchasing a policy, a consumer can look it over and within a certain number of days (usually 10 to 30) cancel without penalty. However, after the look-see period, policyholders are severely penalized for canceling life insurance. The cash surrender value (money paid when canceling) won't come close to the premiums paid for many years. It's best to hang on to any recently purchased life insurance policy even if the prearrangement agreement is canceled.

Security

If funeral funds have disappeared when death occurs, the consumer's peace of mind is only an illusion. The risks with pre-need plans are real.

Poor investment decisions made by funeral directors in Ohio and Pennsylvania have placed thousands of pre-need consumers at risk. Instead of banking trust funds in secure accounts, funeral directors deposited them with an investment firm that purchased rare coins and a 32-carat diamond—hardly safe and secure investments. In addition, the chief executive officer of this firm squandered $500,000 in consumer pre-need funds on improvements and furnishings to his house, spent $300,000 on jewelry, and traveled to Las Vegas.

His firm filed for bankruptcy. Ohio funeral directors will receive about 25 cents for every pre-need dollar invested, but their colleagues in Pennsylvania may receive no more than a nickel.

The Ohio and Pennsylvania funeral directors involved remain contractually bound to provide the funerals consumers paid for. The consumers' risk is that some directors have lost hundreds of thousands of dollars and may be forced into bankruptcy themselves before they can provide those funerals.

This example may be an exception. Many states prohibit the commingling of pre-need funds and require regular audits. But allegations of fraud involving pre-need contracts are increasing in states including Missouri, California, Iowa, Texas, and Wisconsin. The fraud has occurred primarily with state-regulated trusts.

Personal trusts are probably the safest of the three plans because the individual controls them. As long as the funds are deposited in a federally insured account, they should be safe.

In Florida, Indiana, Iowa, Missouri, Oregon, and West Virginia, state-regulated trust funds are protected by guarantee funds. This is a state fund to insure that consumers receive the funeral they paid for in the event of fraud or bankruptcy by a funeral home. Even with such a fund, however, consumers need to ask where their trust funds are invested. Are they insured? How regularly are these accounts audited and by whom?

Life insurance has been more tightly regulated and, as a result, these plans have not been subject to the same kinds of fraud problems. Abuses here have been in other areas. For example, consumers have filed complaints alleging they were never informed they were buying life insurance. In some states, trust funds were converted to life insurance products without the consent of the consumers. Other policies are sold without an explanation of the earnings or penalties involved.

Every state, but not the District of Columbia, has established a life insurance guarantee fund to insure that, should an insurance company go bankrupt, individual policyholders will be protected. However, with large insurance companies in trouble, news reports have questioned the size of these funds. To date there have been delays, but benefits are paid.

Consumer Protections in Pre-Need Plans

There are no federal regulations for pre-need plans although the FTC's Funeral Rule covers most funeral sellers. But every state except Alabama, Vermont, and the District of Columbia regulates the sale of pre-need trusts. All states regulate the sale of life insurance. However, the laws vary widely as to trusting requirements, where and how the funds are deposited, auditing, investigations, and regulatory authority. See Appendix B for the names of the agencies that regulate pre-need arrangements in each state.

The better state trust laws require that most of the funds be trusted, create a guarantee fund for consumer losses from fraud or bankruptcy, and require unannounced audits of pre-need accounts. In addition, the regulating agency should have clear authority to investigate and inspect pre-need sales.

With insurance-funded plans there's usually dual jurisdiction. Insurance departments regulate life insurance sales, but the pre-arrangement agreement is regulated by a different state agency such as a funeral board, banking commission, or the attorney general's office. Although the prearrangement agreement and the insurance policy are tied together, it's not clear in most states who regulates the entire package, if anyone. In Iowa, Colorado, Florida, Nebraska, and Nevada, the insurance commissioner regulates all pre-need sales.

In addition, pre-need sales, like any other consumer purchase, fall under the state's unfair and deceptive practices acts. These laws vary, but in all states they prohibit fraudulent and deceptive sales practices. The attorney general and, in some instances, district or state attorneys have authority under these statutes. Pre-need sellers can sometimes be prosecuted under these laws. Statewide consumer-protection agencies may also have authority to investigate and take legal action.

Is there adequate consumer protection for buyers of pre-need plans? At this point, the answer must be no. Regulations, investigations, and auditing are minimal in most states. In at least one instance, some of the worst abuses surfaced as a result of private legal actions rather than state enforcement activities.

The consumer's guide in other consumer purchases should be followed in buying pre-need funeral arrangements: Caveat emptor, or buyer beware!

Conclusion

Whether or not consumers prepay, consumer groups, funeral directors, and cemeterians all agree that it's best to preplan a funeral. Along with selecting the goods and services, financial arrangements should be made.

Funerals and burial expenses can be paid for from existing assets, life insurance policies, and death benefits. The costs can also be paid over time in advance or by borrowing money. Pre-need arrangements or paying in advance may be a good idea, but each consumer should weigh the cost, earnings, portability, revocation and cancelation, and security of a plan before buying.

THINGS TO REMEMBER

Consider all personal benefits and assets in funeral financial planning.

If a consumer decides to prepay, the seller should be thoroughly investigated. Will he or she provide the goods and services at the time of need? If not, who will?

What happens if the seller goes out of business or bankrupt?

In any pre-need plan, consider cost, earnings, portability, revocability, and security.

Remember, a $3,000, $4,000, or $5,000 payment earns money over time. It's an investment that involves more than just peace of mind.

Notes

1. Letter from Leslie Hewitt to Office of Washington Attorney General dated April 18, 1988. Letter filed with *Omega v. Marquardt.*

2. Fred W. Rockwood, "Changing Consumer Needs Altering Some Policies," *American Funeral Director,* Vol. 114, No. 4, April 1991, pp. 20–21.

3. Example supplied by Forethought Life Insurance, Batesville, Indiana.

4. American Council of Life Insurance, *1990 Life Insurance Fact Book* (Washington, DC: American Council of Life Insurance, 1991), p. 147.

5. George W. Lemke, "FTC Findings Contradicted; Funeral Costs Drop over 20 Year Period," *American Funeral Director,* Vol. 112, No. 8, August 1989, pp. 22–24.

6. Michael J. Klug, *Probate* (Washington, DC: AARP, 1989), p. 30.

7. U.S. Federal Trade Commission, Funeral Industry Practices Mandatory Review, "Excel Survey," Hearing Exhibit–8, Oct. 1988.

Chapter 5

Sorting Out the Final Details

Last July, Jim Edwards received word that his stepmother had died. It came as a total surprise. Only a month before, she'd visited him in Washington.

Jim is an only child who was raised by his father's second wife. In fact, his stepmother is the only mother he knows. His father passed away some time ago.

At the family home in Boston, everything was chaos. His mother had left no instructions, nor had she made any funeral plans. Worse, there was no will.

Jim's stepmother wasn't wealthy, although her house was worth $175,000. Besides the house, her estate consisted of an insurance policy, some savings, and family heirlooms.

It's December now and Jim has paid $3,000 in mortgage payments, heating bills, and insurance on his mother's house. He still doesn't know when the house will be sold or if he'll inherit anything.

Since his stepmother died intestate, or without a will, her estate will be distributed according to Massachusetts law. As a stepson who was never legally adopted, Jim isn't considered her next of kin. He may inherit nothing.

The case has been in court for months, as the heating bills for a Boston winter continue to mount.

KEY FACTS

- Three out of four Americans die without a will.

- Nine out of ten probate cases involve the estate of a person over the age of 60. Probate is the legal process of gathering and distributing the assets of the deceased.

- Even with real estate appreciation, most estates are moderate in size, worth less than $200,000.

- The largest single asset most older Americans own is their home.

- More than two-thirds of people over 65 own their homes and 80 percent of these own them outright.

- In one study, the length of time required to probate a will was almost a year and a half.

- Probate fees for attorneys and personal representatives, also called executors or administrators, consume as much as $2 billion annually.

- Surviving spouses at age 65 receive an average of $522 a month in Social Security benefits.

After the funeral, the children returned to their homes and families. Sophia Damato is now alone in her Tampa, Florida, home. Retirement was good for Sophia and her recently deceased husband, Tom. But now, like 50 percent of all women over 65, she's a widow.

The Damatos had been as close as two people can be except for one item: Family finances were Tom's domain. Like many men of his generation, Tom Damato didn't want to burden his wife with either the paperwork or the decision making of family finances. He always provided for the family. Even in retirement there was a pension, Social Security, and savings. Sophia didn't ask questions or get involved.

Now that he's gone, Sophia must establish her own legal and financial identity. The titles to the house and the car must be transferred and life insurance benefits applied for. Automobile and homeowner's insurance must be maintained and banking accounts changed. The debts, including the cost of the funeral, must be paid and Tom's stamp and coin collections passed on to a grandson.

The surgeon Christiaan Barnard said, "The burden is borne by those that mourn." So it is with Sophia. As she mourns, the burden of the final details is hers. Sophia must write the insurance companies and Tom's former employers. She must talk to bankers, attorneys, Social Security bureaucrats and government officials, and attend to a whole host of details.

The actuarial tables say she's got another 15 to 20 years to live. To protect herself during that time, Sophia needs to make all the right decisions. Otherwise, she'll face poverty and dependence in her last years. Now she's taking a crash course to learn her financial ABCs.

This chapter addresses the legal and financial issues of settling the final details of a life. Its goal is to help survivors work through the required steps and develop the right questions and strategies. By necessity, it's a brief review providing general information rather than an in-depth, state-by-state analysis. Many decisions about final details depend on state laws; if specific information about a state is required, Part Two of this book lists several resources to review.

Figure 5.1 contains a checklist of final details to attend to. Each item on the list is discussed in this chapter, including the steps to take when action is required. For example, the chapter outlines how to change the title to a house or a bank account. The same checklist can also be used as a planning tool.

Chapter 5 also summarizes the making of wills or will substitutes and the probate process, including tax implications, and it highlights elements of estate planning. It's written with the viewpoint that survivors can handle many of the details themselves. Professional help from accountants and attorneys is needed with some estates and makes life easier with others. Ultimately the reader must decide when it's necessary to bring in a professional.

Letter of Instruction

For survivors struggling to put their lives back together, the questions are endless. Is there a will? When is the mortgage due? What about homeowner's insurance? Where's the safe deposit box and what's in it? What about checking and savings accounts? Investments? Real estate titles? And so on.

Many of these items should be attended to in the first few weeks after a death. Without any groundwork, the job can be difficult. A smart detective with enough time, clues (canceled checks and incoming mail, for example), and a clear mind could sort out most of the details. But a clearly written Letter of Instruction makes life easier for survivors.

A Letter of Instruction is not a legal document but a list of everything the deceased person owns and owes. Items listed should include: bank accounts, life insurance policies, real estate, investments, personal property, mortgages, and credit cards. It's

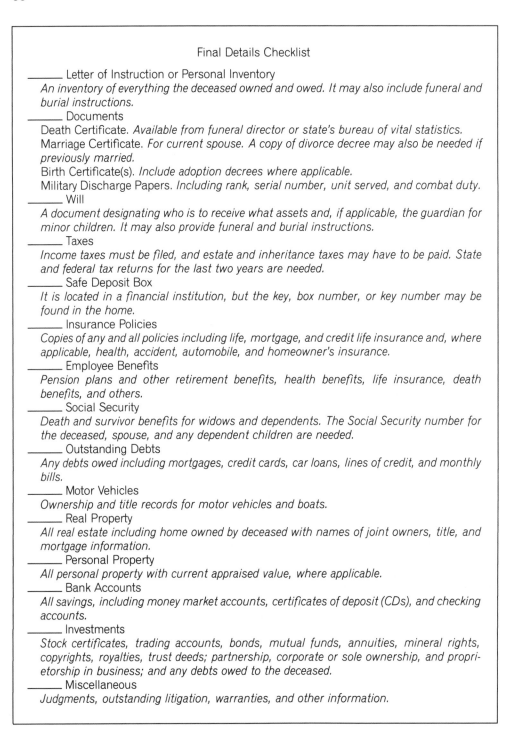

Final Details Checklist

_____ Letter of Instruction or Personal Inventory
An inventory of everything the deceased owned and owed. It may also include funeral and burial instructions.
_____ Documents
Death Certificate. *Available from funeral director or state's bureau of vital statistics.*
Marriage Certificate. *For current spouse. A copy of divorce decree may also be needed if previously married.*
Birth Certificate(s). *Include adoption decrees where applicable.*
Military Discharge Papers. *Including rank, serial number, unit served, and combat duty.*
_____ Will
A document designating who is to receive what assets and, if applicable, the guardian for minor children. It may also provide funeral and burial instructions.
_____ Taxes
Income taxes must be filed, and estate and inheritance taxes may have to be paid. State and federal tax returns for the last two years are needed.
_____ Safe Deposit Box
It is located in a financial institution, but the key, box number, or key number may be found in the home.
_____ Insurance Policies
Copies of any and all policies including life, mortgage, and credit life insurance and, where applicable, health, accident, automobile, and homeowner's insurance.
_____ Employee Benefits
Pension plans and other retirement benefits, health benefits, life insurance, death benefits, and others.
_____ Social Security
Death and survivor benefits for widows and dependents. The Social Security number for the deceased, spouse, and any dependent children are needed.
_____ Outstanding Debts
Any debts owed including mortgages, credit cards, car loans, lines of credit, and monthly bills.
_____ Motor Vehicles
Ownership and title records for motor vehicles and boats.
_____ Real Property
All real estate including home owned by deceased with names of joint owners, title, and mortgage information.
_____ Personal Property
All personal property with current appraised value, where applicable.
_____ Bank Accounts
All savings, including money market accounts, certificates of deposit (CDs), and checking accounts.
_____ Investments
Stock certificates, trading accounts, bonds, mutual funds, annuities, mineral rights, copyrights, royalties, trust deeds; partnership, corporate or sole ownership, and proprietorship in business; and any debts owed to the deceased.
_____ Miscellaneous
Judgments, outstanding litigation, warranties, and other information.

Figure 5.1   Final Details Checklist

also a registry of the whereabouts of legal papers such as a will, safe deposit boxes, and post office boxes, and a place to communicate special wishes such as funeral plans or how personal property is to be distributed.

Preprinted letters of instruction are often available at stationary stores under titles such as "What My Family Should Know." They're available in book form from several publishers (see Chapter 7), and Citibank published a sample letter in its consumer newsletter several years ago. This three-page document is reprinted in Appendix A.

The format of the Letter of Instruction isn't all that important. A looseleaf notebook or simple notations on index cards would serve just as well as a preprinted form. The most critical question about the inventory is, Is it complete?

The value of such an inventory is lost when it's inaccessible. Storing it in a safe deposit box is counterproductive because these boxes are frequently sealed at the time of death. Store it in a secure place at home after notifying survivors of its existence and location.

Sophia Damato found no letter or inventory of assets and debts from her husband. As a result, she was forced to assemble her own. It was important for three reasons.

> First, it measured the size of the estate, including debts, and estimated how much would be passed on.

> Second, by separating probate and nonprobate assets (see below), her inventory became the basis for determining if probate was required and, if so, the complexity of the proceedings.

> Third, the inventory assisted her in preparing tax returns and maintaining important items such as health insurance.

Collecting Documents

To apply for Social Security, change the name on a motor vehicle registration, or apply for life insurance benefits, one or more of the documents listed below is required. A Letter of Instruction can guide survivors to their location. If there are no instructions, it's necessary to collect the documents. Inspect the safe deposit box, shoe boxes, strongboxes, or filing cabinets. If the documents aren't found, copies can be secured at public health or other government offices.

The required documents include:

Death Certificate. Copies are needed to file for insurance benefits and apply to Social Security and other agencies. As many as 15 copies may be needed. They're available at county or state public health departments or from the funeral director. There is a charge for certified copies.

Certificate of Honorable (or other than dishonorable) Discharge. If the deceased was a veteran, this document is important in applying for veteran's or Social Security benefits. If a copy can't be found, write the National Personnel Record Center, Department of Defense, 9700 Page Boulevard, St. Louis, MO 63132.

Marriage Certificate. If the spouse of the deceased is applying for survivor benefits, this document is important. Copies are available from the county clerk's office in the county where the marriage was performed. A prenuptial agreement may also be relevant.

Birth Certificate, Guardianship, or Adoption Decree. These are required when there are dependent children and for proof of age when applying for survivor benefits. Copies are available from state or county public health offices or the clerk of the court.

Wills and Probate

Wills

Although three out of four people die without one, a will can be fundamental in determining how the personal and real property in an estate is divided. A will isn't the only way to pass on property such as real estate, savings accounts, investments, and personal property. Will substitutes and trusts can also be used (see below). However, when minor children or grandchildren are involved, or there are significant assets to be transferred, a will should be written.

Property laws relating to marriage in each state affect how assets can be disposed of in a will. If there is no will, the estate of a married person will be distributed according to state laws (see Figure 5.2 for further information).

A will doesn't mean the estate can bypass probate, the legal process of distributing the deceased's assets in a probate court. (For ways to do that, see the discussion under "Probate" later in this chapter.) In fact, the will typically governs how the estate is settled.

If a person doesn't have a will, it's called dying intestate, and a probate judge determines how the estate will be settled. The judge decides on distribution based on a legal formula specified in state law. Generally speaking, the basis for these laws is that "blood is thicker than water." A son or daughter may

---

Separate and Community Property Laws

How an estate is distributed can depend upon who owns the property in a marriage. Forty-one states and the District of Columbia have separate property laws, under which property is owned separately by each spouse unless there's a joint ownership agreement. Separately owned property can be passed on to anyone of the owner's choice without the consent of the spouse. Under these same laws, a spouse may not be liable for the debts of his or her partner, unless both signed for them.

Eight states (Arizona, California, Idaho, Louisiana, New Mexico, Nevada, Texas, and Washington) have community property systems. In these systems, marriage is considered an economic partnership and all property acquired during the union is jointly owned. When one spouse dies he or she can only will one-half of any property acquired during a marriage. The other half is owned by the surviving spouse. Similarly, a spouse is responsible for at least 50 percent of any of his or her partner's debt.

Wisconsin's property system is a hybrid of both types.

Figure 5.2   Separate and Community Property Laws

have the strongest claim on assets. Dying intestate usually means that the surviving spouse receives one-third to one-half of the estate and may not receive legal title to the home he or she lives in.

The location of the will should be specified in the Letter of Instruction or other communication. If not, it may be necessary to play detective to track it down, even if survivors aren't sure whether a will exists. A common location is a safe deposit box. If the box has been sealed, a court order can be issued to open it. Other locations may include the registry service of the probate court, the trust department of a bank, an attorney's office, or personal files including shoe boxes and strongboxes. If all else fails, a classified ad in a legal newspaper may attract the attention of the attorney who drafted the will.

WHAT DOES A WILL DO?

A will accomplishes four purposes.

1. A will can name a guardian to care for minor children until they are adults. If significant financial assets are transferred to minor children, a conservator may be named to oversee investments and disbursements.

2. A will determines how to distribute the estate to beneficiaries or heirs. It can specify that 75 percent of the assets go to a surviving wife and 25 percent to their children or vice versa.[1] It can set up contingencies if the named beneficiary has died, and it can forgive a debt. Further, a will can designate gifts of property or cash to a favored charity and can specify how personal property, like Tom Damato's stamp and coin collections, will be disbursed.

3. A will designates a personal representative, also called an executor or executrix. This person administers an estate in probate. Usually a trusted relative serves in that capacity but an attorney or bank could also serve. Personal representatives are entitled to compensation for their efforts, although friends and relatives often waive their fees.

4. A will can limit the role of the probate court by expanding the powers of the personal representative. For example, the personal representative can be given authority to sell real property without court approval. This can save time and money.

To execute or write a self-proving will (a witnessed will meeting all state legal requirements), a person can consult any number of do-it-yourself legal manuals or computer programs (see Chapter 7). The risk of writing one's own will is that an imperfectly expressed will could become the basis for court challenges and delays.

Most people hire an attorney to prepare their will. A lawyer isn't legally required, but should be familiar with state requirements. Attorneys' fees for executing a will are generally minimal, ranging from $100 to $300 in one study.

If the estate isn't very large or complicated, writing a will without an attorney shouldn't pose major difficulties. But, as with any legal document, all requirements of state law must be met, including the sworn or notarized signatures of two or three unrelated witnesses (most states require two but a few require three). As a safeguard, an attorney could review a self-written will.

Other forms of wills are recognized in some states. Holographic wills, that is, unwitnessed wills written in longhand by the deceased, are recognized in half the states, primarily in the South and the Southwest. Oral wills are acknowledged in 20 states. In the other states, having only a holographic or oral will is the same as dying intestate. But even if oral or holographic wills are accepted, to avert disputes it's best to execute a self-proving will.

A will can be revised, revoked, or rewritten at any time. Small amendments, called codicils, make simple changes such as naming a different guardian or adding a beneficiary. The signing of a codicil, however, must be witnessed just as a will must be.

Probate

More than a century ago Charles Dickens scathingly cautioned readers about probate court: "Suffer any wrong that can be done you rather than come here." A modern American critic, Norman

Dacey, calls probate a "form of private taxation levied by the legal profession upon the rest of the population."

Modern probate is certainly not the onerous process Dickens described in his novel *Bleak House*. Nonetheless, probate in this country takes 17 times longer and costs 100 times more than in modern Great Britain, according to one legal scholar. Probate normally takes more than a year to complete, even with a will, and even in routine and uncomplicated cases. Although most estates are small to moderate in size, with the house the only significant asset, probate still takes more than a year.

Probate can be expensive; attorneys' fees in some cases consume as much as 20 percent of the estate. Fees for both attorneys and personal representatives are based on a percentage system or a negotiated rate basis, depending on state law and the attorneys involved. As a rule of thumb, attorney fees average 3 percent of the estate's value unless an hourly rate is negotiated. Hourly rates are usually lower.

The first question to ask is, Is probate necessary? Second, if it's necessary, What level of court involvement is required? To answer these questions, the first task is to separate probate from nonprobate assets. If an inventory has been completed, this task should be relatively easy. Ways to bypass probate are described in Figure 5.3.

All property jointly owned with a right of survivorship (the ability to pass property on to the co-owner automatically) is nonprobate property. In some states this arrangement is called tenancy in common or tenancy in the entirety. Transfer of ownership is conducted outside probate with a minimum of paperwork. Sophia Damato's house, for example, became hers outside probate. In addition, life insurance benefits are nonprobate property.

All property owned individually or jointly with no right of survivorship is subject to probate, no matter what size. The bank accounts, investments, and other property that were in Tom Damato's name alone went through probate.

The professional services of an attorney, accountant, or bank trust department may be required to handle probate property. However, survivors can also secure guidance by consulting the clerk of probate court and by studying some of the publications listed in Chapter 7.

Bypassing Probate

By planning ahead using will substitutes, people can bypass probate or minimize its effect. Joint ownership or tenancy with rights of survivorship is called a poor man's will because it bypasses probate. It's easy to establish and can cover almost any asset.

Another option is to distribute the assets before death. An annual gift of $10,000 or $20,000, if the spouse consents, can be made to a person without triggering federal gift taxes.

The disadvantage of these will substitutes is their permanency. Once property is in joint ownership, it's difficult to convert to sole ownership should there be a dispute. Similarly, when a gift is granted, it's irretrievable.

A third option is a living trust. Here probate property is placed in a trust (property held on behalf of another) and administered by a trustee. Since these assets are no longer legally owned by the individual, they're not subject to probate upon his or her death. However, the individual can still control them as the trustee. Upon death, the assets are disbursed according to the terms of the trust agreement, outside of probate.

The problem with this arrangement is the cost of creating and administering a trust. Creating such a trust could cost between $500 and $1,000 in legal fees.

Figure 5.3   Bypassing Probate

When probate is required, it may be handled at various levels of court involvement. The simplest and easiest form of probate is often called small estate administration. The court is barely involved in this process and because of its simplicity, an attorney is normally not required. Any survivor can handle the legal details and transfer assets, although in some states the court appoints a personal representative.

But only the smallest estates qualify for this type of handling. The definition of a small estate varies from state to state. In some states it's an estate worth $2,000. In others it could be $50,000 or $100,000. If a house is involved, the estate is probably too large to qualify as a small estate.

For estates that exceed the definition of small estate, but are routine in nature, the next level is called unsupervised administration or informal probate. Court involvement is minimal, but all the steps of probate must be followed. An attorney may not be needed.

The highest level of probate administration is called supervised administration or formal probate. Here the court must give its consent to all sales and distribution of assets. Formal probate is required with the largest estates and when there's a dispute over distribution of assets. An attorney is usually necessary.

STEPS IN THE PROBATE PROCESS

The process begins with the survivors' filing the deceased person's will with the clerk of the probate or orphan's court, also called the register of wills. Next, an interested party such as an heir, the personal representative, or a creditor files a written request or petition for probate.

The court names a personal representative, usually the executor named in the will, or appoints an administrator when there's no will. Legal notices are published to inform potential heirs and creditors of the death and distribution of the deceased's assets. As a result, claims may be filed against the estate. A formal inventory and appraisal of the estate's assets is conducted.

All debts, including taxes, are paid, as well as legal and personal representative fees. After these payments, a final accounting is made and the remaining assets are distributed to the beneficiaries according to the terms of the will or according to state law if the deceased died intestate. A case is closed when the personal representative submits a sworn statement and a financial report to the court and other interested parties. In some cases, this may require a hearing.

Taxes

The old saying is, No one escapes death or taxes. The truth is that even after death there are taxes. While technically separate from probate, tax matters are interwoven with the probate process and other estate settlement activities.

Tax liability for income and death taxes, which include estate and inheritance taxes, is based on the entire or gross estate before any fees are paid or assets are distributed. The gross estate includes both probate and nonprobate property, including the proceeds from life insurance policies and the sale of personal homes. Funeral expenses, outstanding debts, and mortgages are subtracted from the total, however. The tax returns for death and income taxes are completed and any amount owing is paid personal representative during the probate process or by a survivor when probate is bypassed.

Four different taxes may arise as a result of a death.

Personal income taxes for the year in which the deceased died. This may include capital gains tax when property is sold.

Estate income taxes for any income earned by the estate.

Federal and state estate taxes. The latter is an excise tax levied on the transfer of property.

Inheritance taxes owed by the heir receiving the bequest.

A more detailed discussion of each of these taxes follows.

Personal Income Taxes

Federal income tax returns and state returns, where required, are filed for any income earned by the deceased in the year in which he or she died. Federal returns are filed on a form 1040. Joint returns with a surviving spouse are permitted.

Copies of past returns should be obtained and reviewed. These are important for two reasons. First, they show prior deductions and credits; deductions are permitted until the date of death. Second, past returns may be used when applying for survivor benefits from Social Security. The Letter of Instruction should specify where past tax returns are stored. If not, the IRS and state revenue departments can provide copies of past returns.

Federal tax returns, together with any taxes owed, are filed on the April deadline in the year after the death. Filing requirements for state returns vary.

For more information, the Internal Revenue Service (IRS) publishes a helpful booklet titled "Tax Information for Survivors,

Executors, and Administrators." It's IRS Publication number 559 and is available at any regional office.

Estate Income Taxes

If the estate earns any income in excess of the tax minimum ($600) during the probate process, estate income taxes may be owed to the federal government. Income could come from interest, dividends, rents, or other sources. File a federal return on form 1041 or the U.S. Fiduciary Income Tax Return. It's best to contact the IRS for advice and to secure a federal estate-tax identification number. For state requirements, contact the state revenue department.

Federal and State Estate Taxes

Most estates never need pay federal estate taxes because most estates are far below the $600,000 federal threshold for gross estates. But for an estate of $600,000 or larger, a federal return must be filed within nine months of the death.

However, no matter what the size of the gross estate, any amount of personal or real property can be transferred to a surviving spouse without triggering federal estate taxes. The next generation of heirs, usually the children, will pay federal estate taxes.

States, on the other hand, may levy an estate or inheritance tax no matter what the size of an estate. Some states levy a tax as high as 20 percent of the gross estate. Check with the state revenue department or the clerk of the probate court for more information. The personal representative is responsible for paying this tax before the final accounting in the probate process.

Inheritance Taxes

While estate taxes are levied on the property before disbursement, inheritance taxes are levied on the inheritance received by an heir. The amount of this tax varies from 2 to 20 percent depending upon state law and the blood relationship between the deceased and the heir. Spouses and children, for example, pay less tax than nieces and nephews or unrelated persons. In some states, the personal representative must compute and pay inheritance taxes before the final probate accounting. Again, check with the state revenue department or clerk of the court for details.

Safe Deposit Boxes

In settling the affairs of the deceased, a safe deposit box can be important. It often contains assets such as collectibles, jewelry, savings passbooks, stock certificates, and so on. In addition, the box may contain the will, life insurance policies, a Letter of Instruction, military service records, or other documents.

Only a co-renter of the box or the personal representative in the probate proceeding has access to it. Frequently the bank seals the box after the renter's death for tax purposes. A state revenue department representative can conduct an inventory of its contents. If sealed, the box can only be opened in the presence of a representative of the state revenue department or by court order.

Sometimes the ownership of a safe deposit box is assumed but the box can't be located. To determine if there is one, first inquire at the financial institutions where the deceased held accounts. Second, review canceled checks to determine if they indicate payments made to a bank. If all else fails, write or call the American Safe Deposit Association, 330 West Main Street, Greenwood, IN 46142; telephone (317) 888-1118.

This association, with a membership of 4,000 financial institutions, will query members. For a $75 fee and an additional $5 for each alias, the association publishes the deceased's name in its quarterly newspaper. If a match is found, the financial institution contacts the survivor directly.

Insurance Policies

According to the American Council of Life Insurance, an industry trade group, 63 percent of people over 65 own some form of life insurance. Annually, the insurance industry pays out $23 billion in death benefits.

For Sophia Damato, who received almost $200,000 from her husband's policies, life insurance benefits were a godsend. She used them to pay funeral costs and living expenses while the estate was probated.

Similarly, the benefits of a mortgage insurance policy, another form of life insurance, could pay off the outstanding debt on a home or be invested for long-term gain. Credit life insurance can also zero out a credit card balance or pay off a car loan. Finally, most credit unions maintain either credit life or a life insurance policy on borrowers. Benefits may be available to reduce or erase outstanding debts.

No insurance policy, however, pays benefits automatically. The company or lender must be notified of the policyholder's death. A request should be made for the payment of benefits, including any unpaid dividends or unearned premiums. A written request is usually required although a telephone call may work in some instances. Be sure to give the policy number. A certified copy of the death certificate may be required. The insurance agent who sold the policy could be helpful in filing for benefits.

If no policies are located, yet survivors believe they exist, ask the insurance agent who handles family insurance needs to review his or her records. Review canceled checks for a record of premium payments or loan agreements that would indicate mortgage or credit life insurance. Inquire also with lenders.

If none of these methods is successful, write the American Council of Life Insurance, 1001 Pennsylvania Avenue, NW, Washington, DC 20004-2599. Ask for a copy of the "Information for Missing Policy Inquiry" and enclose a stamped, self-addressed envelope. After completing this form, mail it back to the same address. The country's largest life insurance companies are members of this council. Using this form, the association circulates the deceased's name among its members. If a policy is found, the insurance company contacts the survivor directly.

Death benefits under a life insurance policy aren't subject to income taxes or probate unless the beneficiary is the deceased's estate. However, benefits are part of the gross estate and may be subject to death taxes. Benefits may be paid in a lump sum or in annual, quarterly, or monthly disbursements. Check the policy or ask the company about options.

In addition to life insurance, review other insurance coverage carried by the deceased. This includes health insurance (major medical and Medicare supplements), automobile, homeowner's or renter's, and disability policies. Maintain coverage as needed. Ask that policies be amended or rewritten in the name of the new owner. Where coverage is no longer needed, cancel the policy and ask for a refund. Contact the insurance company or an agent for more information about individual policies.

Employee Benefits

Whether the deceased was working at the time of death or had been retired for many years, contact the most recent employers. When applicable, also contact any labor union of which the deceased was a member. Employers and unions frequently pay pensions and retirement benefits that can be helpful with both short-term cash needs such as funeral and burial expenses and long-term income security. For example, 45 percent of people over 65 receive a private or public (civil service, military, etc.) pension. Similarly, nearly all large companies and some labor unions provide retiree health benefits.

If the deceased was employed at the time of death, there may be vacation and sick leave benefits; this usually isn't considered probate income. If the death occurred on the job, survivors may be eligible for accidental death benefits or workmen's compensation. Free or reduced-cost health coverage may be available.

Even if an employer doesn't provide health insurance for a deceased employee's family as a benefit, survivors who were covered by the deceased's policy may be able to continue their coverage. Under a federal law called COBRA, (Title X of the Consolidated Omnibus Budget Reconciliation Act of 1985) surviving spouses and dependent children may be entitled to continue under their spouse's work-related medical insurance plan for up to 36 months. Survivors must pay the premiums, however.

As with insurance benefits, call or write the employer or labor union as soon as possible and ask about the following, where applicable.

Unpaid vacation or sick time

Death or burial benefits

Life insurance policies

Health benefits

Accidental death insurance

Workmen's compensation

Pension plans with survivor benefits

Deferred compensation, independent retirement funds, annuities, and profit-sharing plans

Any other benefits

Pension plans, deferred compensation, and independent retirement accounts provide different payout options, similar to life insurance benefits. Survivors must decide whether a lump-sum or multiple-payment plan best meets their financial needs.

Social Security Benefits

More than 90 percent of Americans over 65 receive either retirement or survivor benefits under Social Security. It represents the largest single source of income for older people in this country. The average benefit in 1990 for an aged widow or widower was $522 a month.

Benefit levels are determined by years of coverage and past earnings. Almost all jobs are now covered by Social Security, but this wasn't always the case. Until 1950, agricultural workers, for example, were excluded. Federal, state, and local government employees were enrolled in independent civil service retirement systems. Railroad workers continue to be covered by the independent Railroad Retirement System and by Social Security.

Survivors' benefits are based on the deceased's earnings and years of coverage. A wife who has been married to the deceased for at least nine months before his death may qualify for benefits as a surviving widow. She may also qualify for retirement benefits based on her own work history, but not for both. The larger of the two benefits is paid. At age 65, a widow is eligible for full survivor benefits (100 percent of her deceased spouse's benefits). If she applies before age 65 but after age 60, benefits are reduced. If the deceased was already receiving Social Security, his widow may be eligible for a death benefit of $255 (see Chapter 3).

Some other eligibility categories include:

Divorced surviving ex-spouses

Widows with dependent children and grandchildren under age 16

Dependent children and grandchildren (in some instances) under the age of 19 and attending elementary or high school full-time

Disabled widows over age 50

To determine eligibility and benefit levels, file an application with the Social Security Administration as soon as possible. An application can be made by visiting the nearest office or by calling the toll-free number, (800) 772-1213.[2] The application must be accompanied by the following documents.

A copy of the death certificate, which includes the deceased's Social Security number

Social Security numbers for eligible beneficiaries

Proof of age (birth certificate) for the applicant

Birth certificates, with adoption decrees or guardianship documents when applicable, for dependent children

A copy of the marriage license

Military discharge papers for the deceased (additional work credit may be given for active duty)

Income tax returns for the two prior years to bring the earnings record up to date

While an eligibility determination is usually made at the Social Security office, the first check may not arrive for six months or more. This check is retroactive, however, covering benefits accrued since the death.

If the deceased person was receiving Social Security retirement benefits, he or she isn't entitled to a Social Security check for the month in which the death occurred. That is, if the deceased died in January, the check arriving in early February as a January payment must be returned. If the check is written to both the husband and wife, consult Social Security before cashing.

Civil service pensions and the Railroad Retirement System also issue survivors' benefits. The Veterans Administration (VA) provides survivor benefits for widows and dependent children of veterans receiving disability benefits. To determine eligibility and benefits, consult these agencies.

If a surviving spouse receives little or no income, he or she may be eligible for Supplemental Security Income (SSI). SSI is a program administered by the Social Security Administration for low-income older adults, the blind, and people with disabilities. It isn't based on work history or earnings and the income can be combined with Social Security benefits up to the SSI federal base benefit of $407 per month for an individual and $610 for a couple (in 1991).

Some states supplement federal payments with state funds. Contact a local social service agency or an Area Agency on Aging. In addition, SSI recipients are usually eligible for Food Stamps and Medicaid, the federal-state health program.

Debts

As a group, older Americans have far fewer delinquent payments and bankruptcies than any other segment of the population. Paying bills is a mark of personal integrity and one's good name. For many people who lived through the Great Depression, personal debt is anathema.

Because of this, there may be no debts to settle after the death of an older person. Family records or a Letter of Instruction should indicate any debts. Further, it should provide a list of both short-term and long-term debts. Even so, it's also important to monitor incoming mail for indications of other indebtedness. If no inventory exists, survivors must construct one. In addition, the legal notices required in probate may attract creditors.

With an inventory in hand, sort the debts into at least three categories, listing the person responsible for each obligation. First, some debts are solely the responsibility of the deceased person and therefore the estate is obligated for payment. Medical bills not covered by Medicare or insurance, for example, are normally the obligation of the estate, not a surviving spouse, unless the spouse cosigned. Another debt frequently paid by the estate is funeral expenses.

Second, some debts are the responsibility of the deceased and the spouse (joint) or other survivor. In these cases, payments should be made to preserve a good credit rating. Although laws vary, in community-property states the spouse is responsible for half the debts incurred during a marriage, whether or not the debts are in his or her name.

With joint credit accounts, contact the creditor and ask that the name on the account be changed or the card be canceled. The terms of the agreement may also be renegotiated at this time; also see Equal Credit below.

Third, some debts are secured (guaranteed) with real estate, an automobile, or other property. Here, no matter who's responsible for the debt, if payments aren't made, the lender may act to foreclose on a mortgage or repossess a motor vehicle or other property. Survivors or the personal representative should either make payments or negotiate with the creditor. If not, an important asset may be lost.

To maintain the value of a home, heating bills should be paid when a house is up for sale during winter. Without heat, the water pipes may burst, decreasing the value of the house. With utilities, it's usually best to notify the creditor of the death and request that the account name be changed. If the applicant doesn't have a separate credit history, a security deposit may be required. In some areas, state laws require families to pay utility bills even if the accounts were in the name of the deceased.

With some estates, the assets are inadequate to pay all debts. In this instance, the probate code in some states allows the court to ignore the debt or requires only a partial payment. In other states, creditors are ranked in order of priority for payment. Those with the lowest priority may receive nothing.

Creditors may make a claim for payment against survivors even if the estate alone is responsible. If this happens, it may be wise to consult an attorney. When there's no legal obligation to pay, there's no reason to pay. If a survivor feels morally obligated to pay, an agreement should be negotiated that recognizes the survivor's true financial condition.

Equal Credit

For many older women like Sophia Damato, all family credit is listed in the husband's name. Instead of a joint account with a department store, Visa, or MasterCard, she carried courtesy or user cards as Mrs. Tom Damato. Many widows continue using and paying on their husbands' accounts long after his death for fear of losing credit.

Even if a wife has never held credit in her own name, it's important that she build her own financial identity. It's easiest to do this while a husband is alive, but after his death it's absolutely necessary. Sophia Damato notified the creditors with which she had courtesy cards of her husband's death and asked that the accounts be transferred into her name.

Under the federal Equal Credit Opportunity Act, a widow's courtesy card or other credit can't be cut off simply because her husband has died. Nor can she be denied credit based simply on her age, sex, or race. A creditor may, however, ask the widow to reapply in her own name. If her income is insufficient or there's no credit history, the account may be canceled or the line of credit reduced. This decision can be appealed.

Motor Vehicles

For many couples like the Damatos, the family car is registered in the husband's name alone. Besides a passenger car, there might also be a pickup truck, motor home, or recreational vehicle. If the estimated value of a motor vehicle is less than $10,000, the title can usually be transferred directly outside probate. If the value is more than this amount, it may have to go through probate. Of course, if the title is in both names with a right of survivorship, it can be readily transferred.

For details, contact the state motor vehicle agency. A local office can explain transfer procedures and the dollar threshold. A copy of the current registration or title and a certified copy of the death certificate are usually required.

If a widow or next of kin doesn't want the automobile, it may still be in her best interest to assume ownership and then sell it. Otherwise, the car becomes part of probate.

Real Property

Real property consists of a personal home, rent-producing property, and unimproved land. It is the largest single asset in most estates. Years of escalating property values make real estate an important asset. Further, more than two-thirds of people over 65 own their homes and 80 percent of these own them outright.

If ownership of property is joint with a right of survivorship, title readily passes to the survivor outside probate. To complete the transfer, a survivor files a certified copy of the death certificate with the register of deeds in the county where the property is located. This establishes the new owner's right to occupy, rent, sell, or borrow against the property.

If, on the other hand, title was solely in the name of the deceased, real estate becomes part of probate. The personal representative, under court supervision, appraises and disposes of it according to the will. When a sale is contemplated, to ensure that full value is received, real property must be maintained and protected. This means the mortgage, utility bills, and homeowner's insurance must be maintained. These expenses are reimbursable in probate.

Personal Property

Generally speaking, personal property, such as home furnishings, a stamp collection, jewelry, antiques, and so on, is considered joint property and passes to a surviving spouse. In some instances it goes to the new owner of a house. Personal property can be willed when there's a sole owner or when the spouse agrees. Unless the value is substantial or there's a dispute, most personal property (like Tom Damato's stamp and coin collections or family heirlooms) passes outside probate.

If there's no surviving spouse and the disposition of personal property isn't specified in the will, it is sold through an estate auction and the proceeds divided among designated heirs.

Bank Accounts and Investments

If accounts at banks, savings and loan associations, and credit unions were jointly held, the survivor need only complete a new signature card, identifying the new owner. Some financial institutions require a certified copy of the death certificate to make this change.

With individually owned retirement accounts, Individual Retirement Accounts (IRAs), and Keogh plans, the funds pass to the named beneficiary outside probate. When there's no beneficiary, these accounts are treated as probate assets.

If an account was individually owned or there's no beneficiary, it becomes part of the probate process. In this instance, the personal representative closes individual accounts and makes them part of the estate.

Investments

These are handled in a way very similar to bank accounts. Instead of a banker, survivors may work with a stockbroker or a company agent. Stocks and bonds, including trading accounts, mutual funds, and futures, pass directly to the surviving holder if held in joint ownership. Here again, one or more certified copies of the death certificate may be required. In some instances, the corporate transfer agent has to reissue a stock or bond in the name of the new owner. With other accounts, the stockbroker may be able to make the necessary changes. Check with a broker or investment firm.

Other investments, such as business partnerships, royalties, mineral rights, and so on, also pass directly to the survivor with joint ownership.

When stocks, bonds, or other investments are solely owned, they're considered probate property and must go through that process. Because these investments fluctuate in value, it may be important for the personal representative or survivor to proceed quickly with the management or disposition of these assets.

With some investments, where payments could be made far into the future—royalties or mineral rights, for example—the personal representative in probate may assign an account or asset to a beneficiary. This is done to avoid keeping the estate open indefinitely. If there's more than one beneficiary, a bank could be designated as a collection agent. In turn, the bank distributes these funds to the heirs.

Miscellaneous

In completing the details of closing an estate, whether or not it has passed through probate, there are likely to be items that don't fit into any of these categories. For example, warranties or maintenance agreements on motor vehicles, furnaces, water heaters, and personal property have monetary value but aren't necessarily considered assets in probate. A Letter of Instruction should specify when and where major items were purchased and what warranties and maintenance agreements exist. With this information, an asset might increase in value or the cost of repairs could be covered without any additional outlays.

If the information isn't recorded, a bill of sale or canceled check may indicate when and where the item was purchased. A survivor may need to query the vendor to determine what, if any, warranty coverage exists.

Other items to look for include any lawsuits filed against the deceased. There may be an outstanding judgment seeking monetary damages or other actions. A pending lawsuit could also affect an estate. It's possible that probate may not proceed until such a case has been resolved.

Other unfinished business may include a legal right of action for wrongful death, membership fees, and subscriptions. Some of these may be continued; others can be canceled and a refund sought.

Planning for the Future

Even before the estate is closed, the benefits paid, or the final details worked out, it's time for the survivor to begin planning for the future.

Women outlive men in our society and will do so for the foreseeable future. The present generation of older men often manages family finances. Taken together, these facts guarantee that many older women suddenly become responsible for managing financial details late in life.

It's important that any survivor put finances on a firm footing. It's not within the scope of this book to delineate what's involved in short- or long-term financial planning. Other publications, courses, and professionals can assist people in need of these services. But it's important that this process begin almost immediately. A budget should be created, bills paid, insurance maintained, and wise investment decisions made regarding any asset, even during the grieving process.

In addition, a survivor must think about the future of his or her own estate and how to pass on the assets. Will it be through joint ownership? A trust? By updating or executing a will? What about a Durable Power of Attorney, written to maintain property if the grantor becomes incapacitated? A Living Will or Durable Power of Attorney for Health Care (see Chapter 1)? Finally, a new Letter of Instruction should be drafted.

Conclusion

Settling the affairs of a loved one doesn't end with the funeral. There are countless legal and financial details to work through. Property must be passed on through a will and the probate process, through joint ownership, or through a trust. Taxes must be paid and insurance benefits applied for. There may be debts to pay and benefits from an employer or Social Security to collect. Titles to property and cars all must be changed.

All of these and many more items must be settled. In addition, for many older women, settling the estate also means building a new financial and legal identity.

Planning for the inevitability of death takes time and may cost money. However, it helps survivors in their time of grief more easily find and handle the documents needed to start and complete the process.

Consumer writer Jane Bryant Quinn said it best when she urged older people to plan ahead: "You own stuff, you're gonna die. Someone's going to get your stuff."

THINGS TO REMEMBER

Professional help from lawyers, accountants, and financial planners is important, but many of the final details can be handled by survivors.

Look for a Letter of Instruction. If there is none, create an inventory of everything owned and owed.

Locate all life insurance policies and file for benefits.

Apply for survivor and funeral benefits from Social Security.

Contact past employers and labor unions for possible benefits.

Plan ahead for and document your wishes with a will or will substitute.

Notes

1. A number of states have laws providing a minimum percentage for the spouse, no matter what the will specifies.
2. During the late 1980s, the Social Security Administration stopped listing phone numbers for local offices. This was to encourage the use of the toll-free number. Social Security reversed this policy in 1990, and local telephone numbers are reappearing in telephone directories.

PART
TWO

Resources

Chapter 6

Directory of Organizations

This section offers a listing of organizations and associations that may provide useful information, referrals, or assistance.

National Organizations

Funeral Service, Death, and Dying

American Association for International Aging
Dr. Helen K. Kerschner, President
1511 K Street, NW, Suite 443
Washington, DC 20005
(202) 638-6815

> Members of this association include advocates, organizations, corporations, foundations, and individuals concerned about the interests and needs of the aged in the United States and world-wide, particularly in the Third World. This organization seeks to improve the socioeconomic conditions of older, low-income persons in developing countries through self-help, mutual support, and economic development activities.

American Association of Retired Persons (AARP)
Horace B. Deets, Executive Director
601 E Street, NW
Washington, DC 20049
(202) 872-4880

> AARP is a nonprofit, nonpartisan organization dedicated to helping older Americans achieve dignity, independence, and purpose.

It was founded in 1958, and membership is open to anyone over age 50 whether working or retired. Membership dues are $8 per year. The organization offers a wide range of legislative representation at federal and state levels, and educational and community services using a national network of volunteers and local chapters. The AARP Program Division provides information on funerals, pre-need plans, and probate; an extensive network of support groups for the recently widowed (see Widowed Persons Service below); and information on bioethical issues such as Living Wills. Members receive *Modern Maturity*, a bimonthly magazine, and a monthly newsletter, *AARP News Bulletin*. The National Retired Teachers Association (NRTA) is a division of AARP.

American Board of Funeral Service Education (ABFSE)
Dr. Gordon S. Bigelow, Executive Director
14 Crestwood Road
Cumberland Center, ME 04021
(207) 829-5715

The purpose of the ABFSE is to formulate and enforce rules and regulations setting up standards for institutions teaching mortuary science, and to accredit schools and colleges of mortuary science. It sponsors the National Scholarship for Funeral Service program to provide financial assistance to capable young men and women.

American Cemetery Association (ACA)
Stephen L. Morgan, Executive Vice President
Three Skyline Place
5201 Leesburg Pike
Falls Church, VA 22041
(703) 379-5838

The American Cemetery Association is the largest trade association of cemeteries. Members include owners and managers of cemeteries and funeral homes, related suppliers, and professional service firms. The association also sponsors educational seminars.

Associated Funeral Directors Service International
Richard A. Santore, Executive Director

P.O. Box 23023
St. Petersburg, FL 33742
(813) 579-1113

> This group serves other funeral directors in the handling of human remains for shipping. It provides members with business and professional aids, including public relations and advertising programs, booklets, and cooperative buying of products. It also conducts an annual seminar.

Casket Manufacturers Association of America
George W. Lemke, Executive Director
708 Church Street
Evanston, IL 60201
(708) 866-8383

> Members of this association include manufacturers and distributors of caskets and other funeral supplies. It holds an annual series of regional management and educational seminars.

Cemetery Consumer Service Council
Robert M. Fells, Assistant Secretary
P.O. Box 3574
Washington, DC 20007
(703) 379-6426

> The council acts as a central clearinghouse for consumer inquiries and complaints concerning the cemetery industry, including cremations. It establishes uniform guidelines for handling inquiries and complaints on national, state, and local levels.

Center for Death Education and Research
Dr. Robert L. Fulton, Director
University of Minnesota
267 19th Avenue South, 1167 Social Science
Minneapolis, MN 55455
(612) 624-1895

> This agency conducts original research into grief and bereavement as well as studies of attitudes and responses to death and dying. It conducts college and university classes, television and newspaper educational programs, and symposia and workshops

for caregiving professionals. The center provides research opportunities for graduate and undergraduate students and speakers for regional and national conclaves.

Center for Public Representation
Michael Pritchard, Executive Director
121 South Pinckney Street
Madison, WI 53703
(608) 251-4008

> This nonprofit, public-interest law firm represents citizen groups including consumers, children, and the elderly in Wisconsin's administrative agencies, legislature, and courts. It seeks to clarify, through litigation, laws and issues concerning groups represented by the center. The center conducts research and trains students and other citizens to become involved in government decision making. Publications include pamphlets and books that address issues of guardianship, Living Wills, and other Advance Medical Directives.

Commission on Legal Problems of the Elderly (CLPE)
American Bar Association
Nancy Coleman, Director
1800 M Street, NW
Washington, DC 20036
(202) 331-2297

> The American Bar Association established this 15-member interdisciplinary commission in 1978 to analyze and respond to the legal needs of older persons. The commission's work focuses on Social Security, housing, long-term care, age discrimination, consumer and legal rights including the right to die, and improved availability of legal services to the elderly. The commission issues a number of publications including *Bifocal*, its quarterly newsletter.

Conference of Funeral Service Examining Boards
Charles Lindquist, Director
520 East Van Trees
P.O. Box 497
Ashington, IN 47501
(812) 254-7887

The conference studies and recommends educational standards for funeral directors and embalmers and examines candidates for licensure. It also cooperates in obtaining uniformity of rules and regulations governing state licensing boards. Its standard examination to use in testing applicants is available to all member state boards and licensing agencies.

Continental Association of Funeral and Memorial Societies
John Blake, Executive Director
6900 Lost Lake Road
Egg Harbor, WI 54209
(800) 765-0107

This membership organization is dedicated to promoting the "dignity, simplicity, and spiritual values of funeral rites and memorial services." Members believe in reducing the unjustifiable costs of burials and other funeral services and promoting the opportunity for every person to predetermine the type of funeral or memorial service desired. The association makes available information on how members "by body or organ donation, may render assistance for medical, educational, and research purposes." A complete listing of memorial society chapters is provided beginning on page 138.

Cremation Association of North America
Jack Springer, Executive Director
401 North Michigan Avenue
Chicago, IL 60611
(312) 644-6610

The association maintains a speakers' bureau and biographical archives, conducts research, and compiles statistics. It sponsors technical and procedural seminars.

Federal Trade Commission (FTC)
Janet Steiger, Chairperson
6th Street and Pennsylvania Avenue, NW
Washington, DC 20580
(202) 326-2000

The FTC is a federal regulatory agency. It has the power to conduct investigations, issue rules and regulations that have the force of law, and conduct enforcement proceedings. The FTC is the principal federal consumer protection agency. Through the Funeral Rule, it has jurisdiction over funeral sales throughout the country.

Foundation for Hospice and Homecare (FHHC)
William Halamandaris, Chief Executive Officer
519 C Street, NE
Stanton Park
Washington, DC 20002
(202) 547-6586

> The foundation has two divisions. The National HomeCaring Council accredits homemaker–home health aide services, conducts research, provides technical assistance, and is establishing a certification program for homemaker–home health aides. The council promotes understanding of the value of homemaker–home health aide services, conducts a consumer-education and consumer-protection program, provides a central source of information, promotes development of standards, and administers an agency accreditation and approval program. The other division, the Caring Institute, is devoted to research and maintains a lending library of materials and visual aids of interest to communities and agencies seeking to initiate and improve homemaker and home health aide service programs. FHHC publishes books, pamphlets, and audiovisual aids.

Foundation of Thanatology
Dr. Austin H. Kutscher, President
630 West 168th Street
New York, NY 10032
(212) 928-2066

> Members of the foundation include health, theology, psychology, and social science professionals devoted to scientific and humanistic inquires into death, loss, grief, and bereavement. The foundation promotes improved psychosocial and medical care for critically ill and dying patients and assistance for their families.

Funeral Service Consumer Assistance Program (FSCAP)
c/o National Research and Information Center
David L. Reiners, Executive Director

2250 East Devon Avenue
Suite 250
Des Plaines, IL 60016
(800) 662-7666

> The Funeral Service Consumer Assistance Program provides informal, third-party dispute resolution for complaints regarding the purchase of funeral service merchandise. The program focuses on positive resolution of consumer complaints. When informal mediation is unable to resolve a dispute, the case may be resolved by a third-party, binding arbitration panel.

Gerontological Society of America
John Cornman, Executive Director
1275 K Street, NW
Suite 350
Washington, DC 20005
(202) 842-1275

> The society includes physicians, other medical professionals, and business professionals interested in improving the well-being of older people by promoting scientific study of the aging process, publishing information about aging, and bringing together groups interested in older people. Advance Medical Directives, Living Wills, and health care decision making are among the areas being researched. The society encourages education on the aging process.

Hebrew Free Burial Association
Allan Manheim, Secretary
1170 Broadway
New York, NY 10001
(212) 686-2433

> This association provides burial services for indigent Jewish citizens in the New York City area. It operates a 24-hour phone line. Services are provided at the time of need according to the Orthodox Jewish tradition, and no prearrangements are available. The association promotes projects and information campaigns in support of Israel.

Hemlock Society
Derek Humphrey, Founder

P.O. Box 66218
Los Angeles, CA 90066
(213) 391-1871

> This organization provides support and information about voluntary euthanasia for people who are terminally ill.

International Order of the Golden Rule (OGR)
Dale Rollings, Executive Director
1000 Churchill Road
P.O. Box 3586
Springfield, IL 62718
(217) 793-3322

> This service organization is comprised of funeral directors united for public relations, advertising, and educational purposes. The OGR operates a follow-up program for families served by its members. It also provides informal mediation for consumer disputes. Its motto is, "Service measured not by gold but by the Golden Rule."

Jewish Funeral Directors of America
Judith L. Weiss, Executive Director
250 West 57th Street, Suite 2329
New York, NY 10107
(212) 582-9744

> This is a professional society of Jewish funeral directors. Its publications include "How To Explain Death to Children" and "If You Will Lift the Load."

Legal Counsel for the Elderly
Wayne Moore, Director
601 E Street, NW
Washington, DC 20049
(202) 662-4933

> This agency provides direct, free legal services to Washington, D.C., residents 60 years of age and older, and backup assistance and training to extend legal services and nursing home advocacy to the elderly nationally. It conducts training for attorney and nonattorney advocates in issues affecting older adults. Programs and activities of this group include individual advocacy and guardianship, legislative activities, community activities, and education.

The Living Bank
Bruce Conway, Director
P.O. Box 6725
Houston, TX 77265
(800) 528-2971

> The Living Bank is an organ and tissue donor registry with almost 300,000 members. The goals of this national organization are to educate the public on the importance of organ and tissue donation; to maintain a registry of informed, registered donors wishing to donate; and to make placements.

Living/Dying Project
Dale Borglum, Director
P.O. Box 357
Fairfax, CA 94930
(415) 456-3357

> The purpose of this project is to "consciously and compassionately explore life through the mirror of the dying process." It provides outreach services to terminally ill patients as well as national telephone and mail counseling services.

Monument Builders of North America
John E. Dianis, Executive Vice President
1612 Central Street
Evanston, IL 60201
(708) 869-2031

> This group provides sales, advertising, and management materials to members and conducts sales institutes and a national management school. It also develops modern and religious memorial designs. It encourages growth and expansion of traditional cemeteries through a cemetery assistance program. This group opposes restrictive business practices and unfair competition.

National Anatomical Service
John Scalia, President
28 Eltingville Boulevard
Staten Island, NY 10312
(800) 727-0700

> This organization provides information to individuals about schools and organizations in their areas that accept donations of human cadavers.

National Association of Attorneys General
Christine T. Milliken, Executive Director
444 North Capitol Street
Washington, DC 20001
(202) 628-0435

> This association sponsors legal-education seminars on consumer protection, environmental protection, antitrust, charitable trusts and solicitations, commerce, bankruptcy, tax, utility rate regulation, and construction claims. In addition, it serves as a clearinghouse for information about state statutes and regulations.

National Association of Consumer Agency Administrators
Anna Flores, Executive Director
1010 Vermont Avenue, NW
Suite 514
Washington, DC 20005
(202) 347-7395

> The membership of this group consists of executive directors of state, county, and local governmental consumer-protection agencies; and staff members of federal agencies, universities, and foreign consumer agencies. The association seeks to enhance consumer services available to the public. It also sponsors seminars and public policy forums, and acts as a clearinghouse for consumer-oriented education and legislation information.

National Association of Insurance Commissioners
Sandra Gilfillan, Executive Director
120 West 12th Street, Suite 1100
Kansas City, MO 64105
(816) 842-3600

> The membership consists of state officials who supervise insurance. The association promotes uniformity of legislation and regulations affecting insurance to protect the interests of policyholders. In addition, it has developed model regulations for insurance-funded pre-need and life insurance products marketed to older persons.

National Catholic Cemetery Conference
Leo A. Droste, Executive Director

710 North River Road
Des Plaines, IL 60016
(708) 824-8131

> Membership consists of archdiocesan and diocesan directors of Catholic cemeteries. Associate members are administrators of Catholic cemeteries. The conference maintains a library on cemetery monuments and shrines.

National Consumers League
Linda F. Golodner, Executive Director
815 15th Street, NW
Suite 516
Washington, DC 20005
(202) 639-8140

> The league encourages citizen participation in governmental and industry decision making. It conducts research, education, and advocacy programs on consumer and worker issues. In addition, the league researches and publishes pamphlets on issues related to the elderly, such as Medicare, hospices, and health care.

National Foundation of Funeral Service
David L. Reiners, Director
1614 Central Street
Evanston, IL 60201
(708) 328-6545

> The foundation offers educational programs, including extension courses, on funeral service management. It maintains a library devoted exclusively to services provided by the funeral industry and conducts public education on these services. The foundation also researches programs on funeral service for consumers and for the industry.

National Funeral Directors Association (NFDA)
Robert E. Harden, Executive Director
11121 West Oklahoma Avenue
Milwaukee, WI 53227
(414) 541-2500

> NFDA is a federation of state associations of funeral directors. It maintains a speakers' bureau and a library of 400 volumes and

films on subjects relating to dying, death, and bereavement. It also conducts professional education programs. NFDA provides information on a variety of subjects dealing with providing funerals such as: grief, support groups, suicide, Sudden Infant Death Syndrome, and the technical aspects of funeral service. NFDA provides outreach through its membership and has published a "Code of Ethics and Professional Practices."

National Hospice Organization
John J. Mahoney
1901 North Moore Street, Suite 901
Arlington, VA 22209
(703) 243-5900

Hospice is a concept of caring for the terminally ill and their families which enables the patient to live as fully as possible, makes the entire family the unit of care, and centers the caring process in the home whenever appropriate. Inpatient facilities are available for those unable to be cared for at home. The organization promotes standards of care in program planning and implementation, and monitors health care legislation and regulation relevant to the hospice movement. It encourages recognized medical and other health-related teaching institutions to provide instruction in hospice care of terminally ill patients and their families.

National Interfaith Coalition on Aging
Rev. John F. Evans, President
298 South Hull Street
P.O. Box 1924
Athens, GA 30603
(404) 353-1331

The coalition identifies, supports, and sponsors programs and services for the aging which are best carried out through the resources of the religious sector. This group encourages the elderly to remain active in community life. It also provides information to vitalize and develop the role of churches and synagogues in improving the quality of life and spiritual well-being of the aging. This group stimulates cooperation between the religious sector and national, secular, private, and public organizations that support programs on aging, and it advocates for the inclusion of gerontology in religious education.

National Kidney Foundation
John Davis, Director
30 East 33rd Street
New York, NY 10016
(800) 622-9010

> This is a national voluntary health agency primarily seeking answers to diseases of the kidney and urinary tract, including prevention, treatment, and cure. The National Kidney Foundation is also an organ and tissue donor registry committed to the goal of ensuring that anyone who needs a transplant gets one. It conducts public relations campaigns on the importance of organ donation.

National Selected Morticians (NSM)
Fred L. Bates, Executive Director
1616 Central Street
Evanston, IL 60201
(708) 475-3414

> This service organization is comprised of funeral directors united for public relations, advertising, and educational purposes. NSM conducts a follow-up program for families served by its members. It also operates an informal mediation program for consumer disputes.

Pre-Arrangement Association of America (PAA)
Dan Brady, Executive Director
401 North Michigan Avenue
Chicago, IL 60611
(312) 644-6610

> The Pre-Arrangement Association of America (PAA) is a national organization dedicated to promoting understanding and awareness of the importance of prearrangement. PAA is dedicated exclusively to issues related to prearrangement. Membership in PAA is open to any person or entity "that is engaged in or interested in promoting prearrangement." PAA membership is composed of both funeral directors and cemetarians. In addition, consumers, representatives of consumer organizations and regulators are also welcome in the organization. PAA promotes ethical competition throughout the death care industry, as it believes that it is through such competition that the interests of the consumer are best served.

St. Francis Center
Helen Quick, Deputy Executive Director
5417 Sherier Place, NW
Washington, DC 20016
(202) 363-8500

> This is a nondenominational organization that provides information, counseling, and personal support to individuals and families affected by life-threatening illnesses, impairments, or other emotional difficulties associated with death. It sponsors thanatology programs in elementary and secondary schools in order to provide young people with a realistic and compassionate understanding of death and dying. It maintains the CARING Program, in which professionally trained volunteers provide emotional and practical support to individuals in homes and institutions who are coping with life-threatening illnesses or problems related to grief, separation, and loss.

Seasons: Suicide Bereavement
Joan Clark, Contact
1358 Sunset Drive
Salt Lake City, UT 84116
(801) 596-2341

> This is a support group of families and individuals united to bring together survivors of a person who has committed suicide so they may help each other develop a healthy understanding of their loss and grief, and work toward recovery. The group provides a place to discuss difficult issues and an opportunity to benefit from others' experience in coping with a suicide. The organization also offers information and referrals.

Society for the Right to Die (SRD)
Fenella Rouse, Executive Director
250 West 57th Street
New York, NY 10107
(212) 246-6973

> The SRD and its sister group Concern for Dying have championed Living Wills, fought for legal recognition of the right to refuse treatment, and educated both the public and health care professionals on the importance of the individual's voice in

decisions about life-sustaining medical care. These organizations distribute Advance Medical Directives, including the Durable Power of Attorney. A membership organization, it can provide the appropriate documents for each state at no charge.

Thanatos
Jan Scheff, Editor
520 East Jefferson Street
P.O. Box 6009
Tallahassee, FL 32313
(904) 224-1969

> This quarterly publication reflects the humanistic approach to death, dying, and bereavement. It includes nonsectarian articles submitted by individuals and grief-counseling professionals. It also provides information on support groups. The subscription rate is $16.00 annually.

Theos Foundation
Barbara Moore, Board President
1301 Clark Building
717 Liberty Avenue
Pittsburgh, PA 15222
(412) 341-0820

> The Theos Foundation was established to assist in the planning and development of spiritual enrichment and educational programs for people who have been widowed. Its church-affiliated chapters are found nationwide.

Third Age Center (TAC)
Msgr. Charles Fahey, Director
Fordham University
113 West 60th Street
New York, NY 10023
(212) 814-5347

> The Third Age Center concentrates on the intellectual, emotional, economic, spiritual, and cultural opportunities that confront older people. Its programs include studies of the interface of informal and formal support systems, long-term care and service, delivery, alternative forms of housing, and older persons in families.

Widowed Persons Service
American Association of Retired Persons (AARP)
601 E Street, NW
Washington, DC 20049
(202) 872-4700

> This service assists in developing local support groups for widowed persons across the country. It provides a directory of services for the widowed and is part of the American Association of Retired Persons.

Older Adults and the Terminally Ill

Administration on Aging (AoA)
Joyce Berry, Commissioner
330 Independence Avenue, SW
Room 4146
Washington, DC 20201
(202) 245-0724

> AoA is the principal federal agency responsible for programs authorized under the federal Older Americans Act of 1965. It is the focal point for the aging network, which includes AoA, the Federal Council on Aging, 50 State Units on Aging (SUAs), and Area Agencies on Aging (AAAs). This agency advises federal departments and agencies on the characteristics and needs of older people and develops programs designed to promote their welfare. It also advocates for the needs of this population and provides advice, funding, and assistance to promote the development of state-administered systems of social services for older people.

Aging in America
Ralph Hall, President
1500 Pelham Parkway, South
Bronx, NY 10461
(212) 824-4004

> Aging in America is a research and service organization for professionals in gerontology. The objectives of this organization are to produce, implement, and share effective, affordable, programs

and services that improve the quality of life for the elderly community; and to better prepare professionals and students interested in, or involved with, the aging and the aged. The agency conducts research projects, educational and training seminars, and in-service curricula for long-term and acute-care facilities.

American Senior Citizens Association (ASCA)
Ben Sutton, President
P.O. Box 34
Fayetteville, NC 28302

The goal of ASCA is to promote the physical, mental, emotional, and economic well-being of senior citizens. Members believe that senior citizens have a right to live with competence, security, and dignity. ASCA promotes activities that help senior citizens be active participants in their communities.

American Society on Aging (ASA)
Gloria H. Cavanaugh, Executive Director
833 Market Street, Suite 516
San Francisco, CA 94103
(415) 543-2617

This organization works to enhance the well-being of older individuals and to foster unity among those working with and for the elderly. It maintains the Training Center on Aging, which offers continuing education in aging-related fields. This organization also sponsors the Community Education in Aging Program, which brings professional education to both urban and rural areas and works with local agencies to offer programs meeting community needs.

Beverly Foundation
Dr. Carroll Wendland, President
70 South Lake Avenue, Suite 750
Pasadena, CA 91101
(818) 792-2292

The foundation seeks to encourage "creative aging," which it defines as fostering a fresh perspective on problems and opportunities concerning the elderly and promoting a positive attitude toward and among the elderly. The Beverly Foundation works to create imaginative, flexible programs and opportunities for older adults and their communities and programs designed to improve long-term care service systems and methods through education, research, and demonstrations.

Center for Social Gerontology
Penelope A. Hommel, Executive Director
117 North First Street, Suite 204
Ann Arbor, MI 48104
(313) 665-1126

> The purpose of the center is to advance the well-being of older people through research, education, technical assistance, and training. The focus is primarily on legal rights, employment, guardianship and alternative protective services, and housing for the elderly. The center produces educational films and materials, and provides consultation services.

Center for the Study of Aging
Sara Harris, Executive Director
706 Madison Avenue
Albany, NY 12208
(518) 465-6927

> The Center for the Study of Aging promotes education, research, and training in the field of aging. The services include programs for volunteers and professionals in aging, gerontology, geriatrics, wellness, fitness, and health. The center also provides consultant services on areas including adult day care, nutrition, physical and mental fitness, nursing homes, housing, retirement, and a speakers' bureau. The center offers expert assistance in research, institutional and community program development, planning, and organization.

Children of Aging Parents (CAPS)
Mirca Liberti, Co-Executive Director
2761 Trenton Road
Levittown, PA 19056
(215) 945-6900

> This self-help group is devoted to the education, support, guidance, and development of coping skills for caregivers of the elderly. It holds an Instant Aging Workshop for community groups and in-house training for social workers and for nurses in

hospitals, nursing homes, and rehabilitation centers. It also conducts outreach programs for hospitals and for gerontology classes in nearby colleges.

Gray Panthers (GP)
Cheryl Clearwater, Director
311 South Juniper Street, Suite 601
Philadelphia, PA 19107
(215) 545-6555

> The Gray Panthers is a membership organization of people of all ages founded in 1970 by Maggie Kuhn. The organization carries out programs of consciousness-raising and education, petition drives, lawsuits, congressional testimony, and media monitoring on a variety of aging issues.

Jewish Association for Services for the Aged
Bernard Warach, Executive Director
40 West 68th Street
New York, NY 10023
(212) 724-3200

> The objective of this social welfare organization is to provide the services necessary to enable the older adult to remain in the community. It maintains 23 community service offices and 24 local senior citizens centers in New York City and Nassau and Suffolk counties, New York. Services include case management, information and referrals, personal counseling, financial assistance, health and medical service counsel, counsel on housing and long-term care, information and guidance for social action on legislative issues affecting the elderly, legal services, and protective services.

Legal Services for the Elderly
Jonathan A. Weiss, Executive Director
132 West 43rd Street, 3rd Floor
New York, NY 10036
(212) 391-0120

> This agency includes lawyers who advise and litigate concerning problems of the elderly. It is funded through the Legal Services Corporation in New York City, attorneys' fees, and grants. It conducts research, litigation, and educational programs.

National Alliance of Senior Citizens (NASC)
Curt Clinkscales, Executive Director
2525 Wilson Boulevard
Arlington, VA 22201
(703) 528-4380

> This group consists of persons advocating the advancement of senior Americans through sound fiscal policy and belief in individuality and personal freedom. Its purpose is to inform the membership and the American public of the needs of senior citizens and of the programs being carried out by the government and other specified groups. It represents the views of senior Americans before Congress and state legislatures.

National Association for the Advancement of the Black Aged
Jim Bush, Chairperson
150 Michigan Avenue, 4th Floor
Detroit, MI 48226
(313) 224-4966

> The association seeks to advocate for the rights of all needy people, not only blacks or senior citizens. It organizes letter-writing and telephone campaigns on legislative issues pertaining to the welfare of senior citizens.

National Association of Area Agencies on Aging (N4A)
Jonathan Linkous, Executive Director
600 Maryland Avenue, SW
West Wing 208
Washington, DC 20024
(202) 484-7520

> The association seeks to promote and achieve a reasonable and realistic national policy on aging. It also aims to assist the process of partnership and regular communication within the national network on aging, which is composed of the U.S. Administration on Aging, State Units on Aging, and Area Agencies on Aging. The association acts as an advocate for the needs of older persons at the national level.

National Association of State Units on Aging (NASUA)
Dr. Daniel A. Quirk, Executive Director

2033 K Street, NW
Suite 304
Washington, DC 20006
(202) 785-0707

> This public-interest organization provides information, technical assistance, and professional development support to State Units on Aging. (A state unit is an agency of state government designated by the governor and legislature to be the focal point for all matters relating to older persons within the state and to administer the Older Americans Act.) This association works to promote social policy regarding the needs of older Americans at the federal and state levels.

National Council of Senior Citizens (NCSC)
Lawrence Smedley, Executive Director
925 15th Street, NW
Washington, DC 20005
(202) 347-8800

> This educational and action group supports Medicare; increased Social Security benefits; improved recreational, educational, and health programs; increased voluntary services programs; reduced costs of drugs; better housing; and other programs to aid senior citizens. In addition, it sponsors mass rallies, educational workshops, and leadership-training institutes; provides speakers on Medicare and other issues concerning senior citizens; and helps organize and develop programs for local and state groups.

National Council on Aging (NCOA)
Dr. Daniel Thursz, Executive Director
600 Maryland Avenue, SW
West Wing 100
Washington, DC 20024
(202) 479-1200

> The council cooperates with other organizations to promote concern for older people and to develop methods and resources for meeting their needs. It provides a national information and consultation center, and holds conferences and workshops.

National Hispanic Council on Aging
Dr. Marta Sotomayor, President

2713 Ontario Road, NW
Washington, DC 20009
(202) 265-1288

> The membership of this organization consists of individuals who work in administrative, planning, direct services, research, or educational areas for the benefit of the aging. It fosters the well-being of the Hispanic elderly, and provides a network for organizations and community groups interested in this population.

National Indian Council on Aging
Curtis D. Cook, Executive Director
P.O. Box 2088
Albuquerque, NM 87103
(505) 242-9505

> The council seeks to bring about improved, comprehensive services to the Indian and Alaskan native elderly. The objectives of the council are to act as a focal point for the articulation of the needs of the Indian elderly, to provide information on Indian aging programs, and to provide technical assistance and training opportunities to tribal organizations in the development of their programs.

National Senior Citizens Law Center
Burton Fretz, Executive Director
2025 M Street, NW
Suite 400
Washington, DC 20036
(202) 887-5280

> The center specializes in the legal problems of the elderly. It acts as an advocate on behalf of elderly, poor clients in litigation and administrative affairs. It sponsors conferences and workshops on areas of the law affecting the elderly.

Select Committee on Aging
Representative Edward Roybal (D-CA), Chair
U.S. Congress, House of Representatives
Room 712, House Office Building, Annex 1
300 New Jersey Avenue, SE
Washington, DC 20515
(202) 226-3375

The Select Committee on Aging, established in 1974, is primarily a fact-finding body and has no legislative responsibility. It has four subcommittees: Retirement Income and Employment, Health and Long-Term Care, Housing and Consumer Interests, and Human Services. The committee informs the House of Representatives of problems of older Americans, advises House committees that have legislative jurisdiction over issues that affect the elderly, and oversees the executive branch to ensure that laws applicable to the elderly are properly executed.

Special Committee on Aging
Senator David Pryor (D-AR), Chair
U.S. Congress, Senate
G-41 Dirksen Building
Washington, DC 20510-6400
(202) 224-5364

The Special Committee on Aging, established in 1961, is charged with responsibility for studying all issues affecting older people. It conducts studies and investigations into issues such as Medicare, Social Security, health, retirement income, employment, housing, energy assistance, and crime. The committee's housing team focuses on both federal and private housing options. Its findings and recommendations are submitted to other Senate committees for legislative action. The committee also conducts oversight of federal agencies and programs designed to assist older people.

State and Local Organizations

Directory of Memorial Societies

These nonprofit societies were organized by church and consumer groups to work with local funeral directors and encourage members to plan before the time of need. Membership is open to anyone for a small fee, and the membership may be transferred if the member moves to another area. Members are encouraged to express their own religious and philosophical values. For more information contact your local society or:

Continental Association of Funeral and Memorial Societies, Inc.
33 University Square, Suite 333
Madison, WI 53715
(800) 458-5563
(414) 868-2729

Alaska
Anchorage
Cook Inlet Memorial Society, Inc.
P.O. Box 102414
Anchorage, AK 99510
(907) 563-7507

Arizona
Phoenix
Valley Memorial Society, Inc.
P.O. Box 3074
Scottsdale, AZ 85271-3074
(602) 990-3055

Prescott
Memorial Society of Prescott
335 East Aubrey Street
Prescott, AZ 86303
(602) 778-3000

Tucson
Tucson Memorial Society, Inc.
P.O. Box 12661
Tucson, AZ 85732-2661
(602) 721-0230

Yuma
Memorial Society of Yuma
P.O. Box 4314
Yuma, AZ 85366
(602) 726-8014

Arkansas
Fayetteville
Northwest Arkansas Memorial
 Society
P.O. Box 3055
Fayetteville, AR 72702
(501) 443-1404

Little Rock
Memorial Society of Central Arkansas
12213 Rivercrest Drive
Little Rock, AR 72212
(501) 225-7276

California
Bakersfield
Kern Memorial Society
P.O. Box 1202
Bakersfield, CA 93302-1202
(805) 831-6176
(805) 366-7266

Berkeley
Bay Area Funeral Society
P.O. Box 264
Berkeley, CA 94701
(415) 841-6653

Fresno
Valley Memorial Society
P.O. Box 101
Fresno, CA 93707
(209) 268-2181

Los Angeles
Los Angeles Funeral Society
P.O. Box 92313
Pasadena, CA 91109-2313
(818) 791-4829

McKinleyville
Humboldt Funeral Society
P.O. Box 2716
McKinleyville, CA 95521-2716
(707) 822-2445

Modesto
Stanislaus Memorial Society
P.O. Box 4252
Modesto, CA 95352
(209) 523-0316

Palo Alto
Peninsula Funeral and Memorial
 Society
P.O. Box 60448
Palo Alto, CA 94306-0448
(415) 321-2109

Sacramento
Sacramento Valley Memorial
 Society
P.O. Box 161688
Sacramento, CA 95816
(916) 451-4641

San Diego
San Diego Memorial Society
P.O. Box 16336
San Diego, CA 92176-6336
(619) 293-0926

San Luis Obispo
Central Coast Memorial Society
P.O. Box 679
San Luis Obispo, CA 93406
(805) 543-6133

Santa Barbara
Channel Cities Memorial Society
P.O. Box 424
Santa Barbara, CA 93102
(805) 569-1794

Santa Cruz
Funeral and Memorial Society of
 Monterey Bay
P.O. Box 2900
Santa Cruz, CA 95063-2900
(408) 462-1333
(408) 462-6832

Stockton
San Joaquin Memorial Society
P.O. Box 4832
Stockton, CA 95204
(209) 466-7743

Colorado
Denver
Rocky Mountain Memorial
 Society
4101 East Hampden Avenue
Denver, CO 80222
(303) 759-2800

Delaware
(See Maryland)

District of Columbia
Washington
Memorial Society of Metropolitan
 Washington
1500 Harvard Street, NW
Washington, DC 20009
(202) 234-7777

Florida
Cocoa
Funeral and Memorial Society of
 Brevard County
P.O. Box 276
Cocoa, FL 32923-0276
(407) 453-4109
(407) 636-4002

De Land
Funeral Society of Mid Florida
125 S. High Street
De Land, FL 32720
(904) 734-9280

Ft. Myers
Funeral and Memorial Society of
 Southwest Florida
P.O. Box 7756
Ft. Myers, FL 33911-7756
(813) 939-3368

Ft. Walton Beach
Memorial Society of Northwest
 Florida, Inc.
P.O. Box 4122
Ft. Walton Beach, FL 32549-4122
(904) 862-6706

Gainesville
Memorial Society of Alachua County,
 Inc.
P.O. Box 14662
Gainesville, FL 32604
(904) 372-2873
(904) 335-6635

Miami
Miami Memorial Society, Inc.
1115 Country Club Prado
Coral Gables, FL 33134
(305) 266-1403

Orlando
Memorial and Funeral Society of
  Greater Orlando
1815 East Robinson Street
c/o Church
Orlando, Fl 32803
(407) 898-3621
(407) 647-0631

Pensacola
Funeral and Memorial Society of
  Pensacola and West Florida
7804 Northpointe Boulevard
Pensacola, FL 32514
(904) 932-9566
(904) 477-8431

Sarasota
Memorial Society of Sarasota, Inc.
P.O. Box 15833
Sarasota, FL 34277
(813) 953-3740

St. Petersburg
Suncoast–Tampa Bay Memorial
  Society
719 Arlington Avenue North
St. Petersburg, FL 33701
(813) 898-3294

Tallahassee
Funeral and Memorial Society of
  Leon County
1006 Buena Vista Drive
Tallahassee, FL 32304
(904) 224-2082

Tampa
Tampa Memorial Society, Inc.
3915 North "A" Street
Tampa, FL 33609
(813) 877-4604

West Palm Beach
Palm Beach Funeral Society
P.O. Box 2065
West Palm Beach, FL 33402-2065
(407) 833-8936

Georgia
Atlanta
Memorial Society of Georgia
1911 Cliff Valley Way, NE
Atlanta, GA 30329
(404) 634-2896

Hawaii
Honolulu
Memorial Society of Hawaii
2510 Bingham Street, Room A
Honolulu, HI 96826
(808) 946-6822

Idaho
Boise
Idaho Memorial Association, Inc.
P.O. Box 1919
Boise, ID 83701
(208) 343-4581

Illinois
Chicago
Chicago Memorial Association
P.O. Box 2923
Chicago, IL 60690-2923
(312) 939-0678

Urbana
Champaign County Memorial
  Society
309 West Green Street
Urbana, IL 61801
(217) 384-8862

Indiana
Bloomington
Bloomington Memorial Society
2120 North Fee Lane
Bloomington, IN 47408
(812) 332-3695

Fort Wayne
Northeast Indiana Memorial
  Society
2923 Woodstock Court
Fort Wayne, IN 46815
(219) 484-4385

Indianapolis
Indianapolis Memorial Society
5805 East 56th Street
Indianapolis, IN 46226
(317) 545-6005
(317) 844-1371

Valparaiso
Memorial Society of Northwest Indiana
356 McIntyre Court
Valparaiso, IN 46383
(219) 462-5701

West Lafayette
Memorial Society of Mid-North
  Indiana, Inc.
P.O. Box 2155
West Lafayette, IN 47906
(317) 744-9871

Iowa
Ames
Central Iowa Memorial Society
1015 Hyland Avenue
Ames, IA 50010

Davenport
Iowa Memorial Funeral Society
3011 West 70th Street
Davenport, IA 52806
(319) 391-1886

Iowa City
Memorial Society of Iowa River Valley
20 North Dubuque Street
Iowa City, IA 52245
(319) 338-2637

Kentucky
Lexington
Memorial Society of Central Kentucky
1704 Betta Drive
Lexington, KY 40515
(606) 223-1448

Louisville
Memorial Society of Greater Louisville
891 Minoma Avenue
Louisville, KY 40217
(502) 637-5911

Louisiana
Baton Rouge
Memorial Society of Greater Baton
  Rouge
8470 Goodwood Avenue
Baton Rouge, LA 70806
(504) 926-2291

Maine
Auburn
Memorial Society of Maine
P.O. Box 3122
Auburn, ME 04212-3122
(207) 786-4323

Maryland
Bethesda
Memorial Society of Maryland
9601 Cedar Lane
Bethesda, MD 20814
(301) 564-0006

Massachusetts
Brewster
Memorial Society of Cape Cod
45 Foster Road
Brewster, MA 02631
(617) 896-3370

Brockton
Memorial Society of Greater Brockton
325 West Elm Street
Brockton, MA 02401
(508) 238-6373

Brookline
Memorial Society of New England, Inc.
25 Monmouth Street
Brookline, MA 02146
(617) 731-2073

New Bedford
Memorial Society of Southeast
  Massachusetts, Inc.
71 Eighth Street
New Bedford, MA 02704
(508) 994-9686
(508) 679-6835

Springfield
Springfield Memorial Society, Inc.
P.O. Box 2821
Springfield, MA 01101
(413) 783-7987

Michigan
Ann Arbor
Memorial Advisory and Planning
  Service
2030 Chaucer Drive
Ann Arbor, MI 48103
(313) 665-9516

Detroit
Greater Detroit Memorial Society
P.O. Box 1321
Royal Oak, MI 48068
(313) 547-1330

East Lansing
Lansing Area Memorial Planning
  Society
P.O. Box 925
East Lansing, MI 48823
(517) 351-3980

Flint
Memorial Society of Flint
P.O. Box 4315
Flint, MI 48504
(313) 239-2596

Grand Rapids
Memorial Society of Greater Grand
  Valley
2121 Michigan Street, NE
Grand Rapids, MI 49503-2114
No telephone

Minnesota
St. Cloud
Minnesota Funeral and Memorial
  Society
717 Riverside Drive, SE
St. Cloud, MN 56304
(612) 252-7540

Missouri
Kansas City
Greater Kansas City Memorial Society
4500 Warwick Boulevard
Kansas City, MO 64111
(816) 531-2131

St. Louis
Memorial and Planned Funeral
  Society
5007 Waterman Boulevard
St. Louis, MO 63108
(314) 361-0595

Montana
Billings
Memorial Society of Montana
1024 Princeton Avenue
Billings, MT 59102
(406) 252-5065

Missoula
Five Valleys Burial Memorial
  Association
405 University Avenue
Missoula, MT 59801
(406) 543-6952/

Nevada
Reno
Memorial Society of Western Nevada
P.O. Box 8413
University Station, NV 89507-8413
(702) 852-4600

New Hampshire
Concord
Memorial Society of New Hampshire
P.O. Box 702
Concord, NH 03302-0702
(603) 224-8913

New Jersey
Cherry Hill
Memorial Society of South Jersey, Inc.
401 North Kings Highway
Cherry Hill, NJ 08034
(609) 667-3618

East Brunswick
Raritan Valley Memorial Society
176 Tices Lane
East Brunswick, NJ 08816
(201) 246-9620
(201) 572-1470

Lincroft
Memorial Association of Monmouth
County
1475 West Front Street
Lincroft, NJ 07738
(201) 747-0707

Madison
Morris Memorial Society, Inc.
P.O. Box 507
Madison, NJ 07940
(201) 540-1177

Montclair
Memorial Society of Essex
P.O. Box 888
Upper Montclair, NJ 07043
(201) 783-1145

Paramus
Central Memorial Society
156 Forest Avenue
Paramus, NJ 07652
(201) 836-7267

Plainfield
Memorial Society of Plainfield
858 Princeton Court
Branchburg, NJ 08853
(908) 369-7260

Princeton
Princeton Memorial Association
48 Roper Road
P.O. Box 1154
Princeton, NJ 08540
(609) 924-5525

New Mexico
Las Cruces
Memorial and Funeral Society of
Southern New Mexico
P.O. Box 6531
Las Cruces, NM 88006
(505) 522-3335

New York
Albany
Memorial Society of Hudson Mohawk
Region
405 Washington Avenue
Albany, NY 12206-2604
(518) 465-9664

Binghamton
Southern Tier Memorial Society, Inc.
183 Riverside Drive
Binghamton, NY 13905
(607) 729-1641

Buffalo
Greater Buffalo Memorial Society
695 Elmwood Avenue
Buffalo, NY 14222
(716) 885-2136

Corning
Memorial Society of Greater Corning
Area
P.O. Box 23
Painted Post, NY 14870
(607) 936-6563
(607) 962-7132

Hornell
Upper Genesee Memorial Society
33 South Main Street
Alfred, NY 14802
(607) 587-8429

Ithaca
Ithaca Memorial Society, Inc.
P.O. Box 134
Ithaca, NY 14851
(607) 273-8316

New Hartford
Mohawk Valley Memorial Society
P.O. Box 322
New Hartford, NY 13413
(315) 797-2396
(315) 735-6268

New York
Community Church of New York
    Funeral Society
40 East 35th Street
New York, NY 10016
(212) 683-4988

New York
Memorial Society of Riverside
    Church
490 Riverside Drive
New York, NY 10027
(212) 222-5900

Pomona
Rockland County Memorial Society
P.O. Box 461
Pomona, NY 10970
(914) 354-1789

Port Washington
Memorial Society of Long Island,
    Inc.
P.O. Box 303
Port Washington, NY 11050
(516) 627-6590
(516) 944-9035

Poughkeepsie
Mid-Hudson Memorial Society
249 Hooker Avenue
Poughkeepsie, NY 12603
(914) 454-4164
(914) 462-2768

Rochester
Rochester Memorial Society, Inc.
220 Winton Road South
Rochester, NY 14610
(716) 461-1620

Syracuse
Syracuse Memorial Society
P.O. Box 67
Dewitt, NY 13214-0067
(315) 446-1199
(315) 478-2258

Watertown
Memorial Society of Northern New
    York, Inc.
1138 Harrison Street
Watertown, NY 13601
(315) 782-4999

White Plains
Westchester Funeral Planning
    Association
Rosedale Avenue and Sycamore Lane
White Plains, NY 10605
(914) 946-1660

North Carolina
Asheville
Blue Ridge Memorial Society
P.O. Box 2601
Asheville, NC 28802
(704) 669-2587

Chapel Hill
Triangle Memorial and Funeral Society
P.O. Box 1223
Chapel Hill, NC 27514
(919) 942-4994

Greensboro
Piedmont Memorial and Funeral
    Society
P.O. Box 16192
Greensboro, NC 27406
(919) 674-5501

Laurinburg
Scotland County Funeral and
    Memorial Society
P.O. Box 192
Laurinburg, NC 28352
(919) 276-6536

Wilmington
Memorial Society of the Lower Cape Fear
P.O. Box 4262
Wilmington, NC 28406
(919) 762-5252

Ohio
Akron
Memorial Society of Akron-Canton Area
3300 Morewood Road
Akron, OH 44333
(216) 836-2206

Cincinnati
Memorial Society of Greater
    Cincinnati, Inc.
536 Linton Street
Cincinnati, OH 45219
(513) 281-1564

Cleveland
Cleveland Memorial Society
21600 Shaker Boulevard
Shaker Heights, OH 44120
(216) 751-5515

Columbus
Memorial Society of the Columbus Area
P.O. Box 14835
Columbus, OH 43214-0835
(614) 267-4946

Dayton
Dayton Memorial Society
665 Salem Avenue
Dayton, OH 45406
(513) 274-5890

Toledo
Memorial Society of Northwest Ohio
610 Stickney Avenue, Suite 2809
Toledo, OH 43604
(419) 729-4437

Waverly
Waverly Branch of Memorial Society
    of Columbus
111 Wendy Lane
Waverly, OH 45690
(614) 947-2118

Yellow Springs
Memorial Society of the Columbus
    Area
317 Dayton Street
Yellow Springs, OH 45387
(513) 767-1659

Youngstown
Memorial Society of Greater
    Youngstown
75 Jackson Drive
Campbell, OH 44405
(216) 755-8696

Oregon
Eugene
Emerald Memorial Association
P.O. Box 11347
Eugene, OR 97440-3547
(503) 345-0639

Portland
Oregon Memorial Association
811 East Burnside, Suite 122
Portland, OR 97214
(503) 239-0150

Pennsylvania
Bethlehem
Lehigh Valley Memorial Society
701 Lechauweki Avenue
Bethlehem, PA 18115
(215) 866-7652

Erie
Thanatopsis Society of Erie
P.O. Box 3495
Erie, PA 16508
(814) 864-9300

Harrisburg
Memorial Society of Greater
    Harrisburg, Inc.
1280 Clover Lane
Harrisburg, PA 17113
(717) 564-4761

Philadelphia
Memorial Society of Greater Philadelphia
2125 Chestnut Street
Philadelphia, PA 19103
(215) 567-1065

Pittsburgh
Pittsburgh Memorial Society
605 Morewood Avenue
Pittsburgh, PA 15213
(412) 621-4740

State College
Memorial Society of Central
 Pennsylvania
780 Waupelani Drive
State College, PA 16801-2820
(814) 237-7605

Wilkes-Barre
Memorial Society of Northeast
 Pennsylvania
P.O. Box 2216
Wilkes-Barre, PA 18703-2216

Rhode Island
East Greenwich
Memorial Society of Rhode Island, Inc.
119 Kenyon Avenue
East Greenwich, RI 02818
(401) 884-5933

Tennessee
Chattanooga
Memorial Society of Chattanooga
3224 Navajo Drive
Chattanooga, TN 37411
(615) 899-9315

Knoxville
East Tennessee Memorial Society
P.O. Box 10507
Knoxville, TN 37919
(615) 523-4176

Nashville
Middle Tennessee Memorial Society
1808 Woodmont Boulevard
Nashville, TN 37215
(615) 383-5760

Pleasant Hill
East Tennessee Memorial Society
Cumberland Branch
P.O. Box 246
Pleasant Hill, TN 38578
(615) 277-3795

Texas
Austin
Austin Memorial and Burial
 Information Society
P.O. Box 4382
Austin, TX 78765
(512) 477-5238

Dallas
Dallas Area Memorial Society
4015 Normandy
Dallas, TX 75205
(214) 528-6006

El Paso
Memorial Society of El Paso
P.O. Box 4951
El Paso, TX 79914
(505) 824-4565
(915) 541-0812

Houston
Houston Area Memorial Society
5200 Fannin Street
Houston, TX 77004
(713) 526-4267

San Antonio
San Antonio Memorial Society
807 Beryl Drive
San Antonio, TX 78213
(512) 341-2213

Utah
Salt Lake City
Utah Memorial Association
3306 East Oakcliff
Salt Lake City, UT 84117
(801) 272-7764
(801) 581-6608

Vermont
Burlington
Vermont Memorial Society
P.O. Box 67
Burlington, VT 05401
(802) 862-7474

Virginia
Arlington
Memorial Society of Northern
  Virginia
4444 Arlington Boulevard
Arlington, VA 22204
(703) 271-9240

Charlottesville
Memorial Planning Society of the
  Piedmont
717 Rugby Road
Charlottesville, VA 22903
(804) 293-8179

Fort Lee
Virginia State Memorial Society
P.O. Box 5176
Fort Lee, VA 23801
(804) 541-1043

Richmond
Memorial Society of Greater Richmond
  Area
P.O. Box 29315
Richmond, VA 23229
(804) 285-9157

Salem
Roanoke Valley Memorial Society
2152 Bainbridge Drive
Salem, VA 24153

Virginia Beach
Memorial Society of Tidewater, Inc.
P.O. Box 4621
Virginia Beach, VA 23454
(804) 481-2991

Washington
Seattle
People's Memorial Association, Inc.
2366 Eastlake Avenue, E-409 Areis
Seattle, WA 98102
(206) 325-0489

Spokane
Spokane Memorial Association
P.O. Box 13613
Spokane, WA 99213
(509) 924-8400

Yakima
Funeral Association of Central
  Washington
P.O. Box 379
Yakima, WA 98907
(509) 452-1712

Wisconsin
Egg Harbor
Memorial Society of Door County
6900 Lost Lake Road
Egg Harbor, WI 54209
(414) 868-3136

Madison
Memorial Society of Madison
5235 Harbor Court
Madison, WI 53705
(608) 238-4422

Milwaukee
Funeral and Memorial Society of
  Greater Milwaukee
13001 West North Avenue
Brookfield, WI 53005
(414) 782-3535

Racine
Memorial Society of Southeastern
  Wisconsin
625 College Avenue
Racine, WI 53403
(414) 868-3136

Chapter 7

Reference Materials

The reference materials listed in this chapter include books, articles, pamphlets, brochures, audiovisual materials, and computer-based information. These materials are organized according to the chapter headings in Part One.

The Right To Die

Books and Articles

Dicks, Helen Marks. *Power of Attorney for Health Care*. Madison, WI: Center for Public Representation, 1991. 132p. $49.95. ISBN 0-932622-38-0.

> This manual is a guide to Wisconsin's Power of Attorney for Health Care law. It was written to answer the questions of attorneys, physicians, social workers, and other professionals about using this law and the Living Will. The manual has practical advice for professionals who assist clients and includes sample forms and suggested language for use in creating Advance Medical Directives.

Lynn, Joanne, M.D., ed. *By No Extraordinary Means: The Choice To Forgo Life-Sustaining Food and Water*. Bloomington, IN: Indiana University Press, 1989. 323p. $16.95 (paper). ISBN 0-253-20517-4.

> A collection of essays written by scholars in ethics, law, religion, public policy, and health care concerning the issue of whether

eliminating food and water should be regarded as killing a person or allowing the person to die. The editor, who also authored a number of the papers, served as the assistant director of the President's Commission for the Study of Ethical Problems in Medicine.

Pamphlets and Brochures

American Association of Retired Persons. *A Matter of Choice: Planning Ahead for Health Care Decisions.* Washington, DC: American Association of Retired Persons, 1989. 87p. No charge. Stock no. D12776.

> Prepared as a report to the U.S. Senate Special Committee on Aging, this small book views health care choices as a fundamental right and a question of dignity. Living Wills, Durable Powers of Attorney for Health Care, and anatomical gifts are all reviewed. In addition, there's a checklist for health care advisors, a list of resources for more information, and extensive appendices.

American Association of Retired Persons. *Tomorrow's Choices: Preparing Now for Future Legal, Financial, and Health Care Decisions.* Washington, DC: American Association of Retired Persons, 1988. 65p. No charge. Stock no. D13479.

> This is a guide to planning for difficult decisions in the future. It reviews choices in living arrangements, managing financial assets, and health care decisions such as Living Wills and Durable Powers of Attorney for Health Care.

Sabatino, Charles P., J.D. *Health Care Powers of Attorney.* Washington, DC: Commission on Legal Problems of the Elderly of the American Bar Association, 1990. 11p. No charge. Distributed by the American Association of Retired Persons. Stock no. D13895.

> A short description of what a Durable Power of Attorney does and how to establish one. It also contains a sample power-of-attorney form, which may not fit the requirements of every state.

Coping with Death

Books and Articles

Brooks, Anne. *The Grieving Time.* Garden City, NY: Dial Press, 1985. 64p. $12.95. ISBN 0-385-19801-9.

> This book is based on a monthly journal kept by the author for a year following her husband's death. It helps readers understand that the depth of their personal grief is real and honest and that they're not alone.

Brothers, Joyce. *Widowhood.* New York: Simon and Schuster, 1990. 256p. $19.95. ISBN 0-671-55266-X.

> The famous psychologist discusses how she dealt with the death of her husband. She writes about the despair and loneliness she experienced, and how she was able to put her life back together. This book helps chart the course of the pain called grief.

Caine, Lynn. *Being a Widow.* New York: Arbor House, 1988. 261p. $18.95 ISBN 0-87795-966-8.

> This self-help book is full of practical advice and words of wisdom written by women who have lived through widowhood. The book covers the early shock of the death through the first steps toward a new life. It discusses the impact of death, depression, legal and financial problems, re-emerging sexuality, dreams, rebuilding self-confidence, stress, and grieving children.

Carroll, David. *Living with Dying: A Loving Guide for Family and Close Friends.* New York: McGraw-Hill, 1985. 381p. $17.95. ISBN 1-07-010098-5.

> Information and advice are provided from doctors, psychiatric nurses, gerontologists, thanatologists, and the dying. This book answers the most common practical and emotional concerns.

Colgrove, Belba, Harold Bloomfield, and Peter McWilliams. *How To Survive the Loss of a Love: 58 Things To Do When There Is Nothing To Be Done.* New York: Bantam Books, 1976. 119p. $3.95. ISBN 0-553-20624-9.

This book helps define the loss of a loved one and offers guide-lines to encourage survival, healing, and growth.

Foehner, Charlotte, and Carol Cozurt. *The Widow's Handbook: A Guide for Living*. Golden, CO: Fulcrum, 1988. 301p. $18.95. ISBN 1-55591-014-9.

This book is designed to help a woman confront the first two years of widowhood and look ahead to starting a new life. A practical and sensitive guide, it includes checklists, sample forms and letters, guidelines, and lists of support groups, all in an easy-to-use format. It features the personal experiences of widows from ages 29 to 88.

Gates, Philomen. *Suddenly Alone: A Woman's Guide to Widowhood*. New York: Harper and Row, 1990. 248p. $18.95. ISBN 0-06-016352-6.

For the newly bereaved or the experienced widow, this book offers the companionship of shared experience and clear, down-to-earth advice on how to cope with a new life-style and handle the practical problems that accompany widowhood.

Grollman, Earl. *Concerning Death*. Boston: Beacon Press, 1974. 365p. $9.95. ISBN 0-8-70-2764-2.

A source of practical help for coping with all facets of a death in the family.

————. *Explaining Death to Children*. Boston: Beacon Press, 1967. 296p. $4.95. ISBN 0-8070-2385-X.

An anthology to help children deal with their first experience with the death of a loved one. The book blends information and perspectives from the fields of religion, psychology, psychiatry, sociology, anthropology, biology, and children's literature. It attempts to provide a healthy basis for useful communication between children and their parents, teachers, and other adult counselors.

————. *Living When a Loved One Has Died*. Boston: Beacon Press, 1977. 115p. $7.95. ISBN 0-8070-2740-5.

This book argues that an individual can be harmed by not griev-ing to the extent of his or her need. It helps guide survivors through emotional turmoil into a new life. It also seeks to comfort the grieving so that they can go on living.

———. *Talking about Death*. Boston: Beacon Press, 1990. 118p. $9.95. ISBN 0-8070-2364-7.

A dialogue to be shared between parent and child concerning death. The text brings emotions and fears into the open where they can be honestly confronted.

———. *What Helped Me When My Loved One Died*. Boston: Beacon, Press, 1981. 158p. $9.95. ISBN 0-8070-3228-X.

This is a collection of personal stories of many people who have mourned the death of a loved one. Contributors talk about their experiences with bereavement. Each chapter deals with the sense of overwhelming sadness experienced in grief, and each contributor offers insights about death and grieving.

Humphrey, Derek. *Final Exit*. Eugene, OR: National Hemlock Society, 1991. 190p. $16.95. ISBN 0-9606030-3-4.

This book explains how terminally ill people can commit suicide painlessly with prescription sleeping pills. Other suicide options such as starvation are also discussed. A table of lethal drug dosages is featured along with instructions on their usage.

Hyde, Margaret Oldroyd. *Meeting Death*. New York: Walker Publishing, 1989. 129p. $15.95. ISBN 0-8027-68773-3.

This book seeks to teach the reader that death is a part of life.

James, John W., and Frank Cherry. *The Grief Recovery Handbook: A Step-by-Step Program for Moving beyond Loss*. New York: Harper and Row, 1988. 175p. $15.95. ISBN 0-06-015939-1.

A step-by-step recovery program for survivors. Part One prepares the reader for a new understanding of how to grieve. Part Two introduces the tools for recovery: honesty, willingness, and commitment. Part Three defines the five stages necessary for recovery from grief.

Kübler-Ross, Elisabeth. *Death: The Final Stage of Growth*. Englewood Cliffs, NJ: Prentice-Hall, 1975. 175p. $2.95 (paper). ISBN 0-13-197012-7.

This volume offers a spectrum of viewpoints on death and dying from ministers, rabbis, doctors, nurses, sociologists, persons near death, and their survivors. The author shows how, by accepting the finiteness of living, readers can grow. Death provides a key to the meaning of human existence.

————. *Living with Death and Dying*. New York: Macmillan, 1981. 181p. $10.95. ISBN 0-02-567140-3.

Kübler-Ross and several of her colleagues provide answers to critical questions regarding children and death.

————. *On Children and Death*. New York: Macmillan, 1983. 279p. $5.95 ISBN 0-02-567110-3.

Kübler-Ross here confronts the difficulties faced by parents of dying children and offers loving and practical help. This book contains ideas, methods, and examples that demonstrate how children and parents can live with love and understanding during a difficult time.

————. *On Death and Dying*. New York: Macmillan, 1969. 289p. $11.95. ISBN 0-02-089130-X.

Written by a former therapist, this book is regarded as a classic text in the study of dying. It describes the five stages of dying: denial, anger, bargaining, depression, and acceptance. It offers insights about death and the terminally ill. The book provides case histories to illustrate the various stages and contains interviews with terminally ill patients.

————. *Questions and Answers on Death and Dying*. New York: Macmillan, 1974. 177p. $4.95. ISBN 0-02-567120-0.

This sequel to *On Death and Dying* contains answers to the most commonly asked questions about death and dying.

————. *To Live Until We Say Good-Bye*. Englewood Cliffs, NJ: Prentice-Hall, 1978. 160p. $12.95. ISBN 0-13-922955-8.

An intimate view of Kübler-Ross's counseling work with terminally ill patients as she helps them reach an acceptance of their own deaths.

————. *Working It Through*. New York: Macmillan, 1982. 144p. $15.95. ISBN 0-02-567160-X.

The story of Kübler-Ross's workshops for people whose lives are touched by death. The book is geared to those who are terminally ill, those who have lost a loved one, and professionals such as doctors, nurses, social workers, clergy members, and others.

Kushner, Harold S. *When Bad Things Happen to Good People.* New York: Schocken Books, 1981. 149p. $10.95. ISBN 0-8052-3773-9.

This book seeks to bring faith, comfort, and inspiration to survivors of deaths and other crises. It argues that survivors are not alone in their pain and sorrow.

Loewinsohn, Ruth Jean. *Survival Handbook for Widows (and for Relatives and Friends Who Want To Understand).* 2d ed. Glenview, IL: AARP Books and Scott, Foresman, 1984. 129p. $5.95. ISBN 0-673-24820-8.

This book discusses the phases of the widowhood experience. It describes grieving and offers ideas and suggestions for coping with the grieving process. Special problems such as suicide and institutionalized spouses are also addressed.

Osterweis, Marian, Fredric Solomon, and Morris Green, eds. *Bereavement: Reactions, Consequences and Care.* Washington, DC: National Academy Press, 1984. 312p. $29.95 ISBN 0-309-03438-8.

Bereavement is a fact of life, especially for older people. This book was commissioned by the National Institute of Mental Health to review the consequences of bereavement and its impact on general and mental health. It reviews risk factors, adults' and children's reactions to grief, and the impact of certain kinds of losses such as those of a spouse or a child. It also discusses ways of assisting the bereaved.

Rando, Therese A. *Grieving: How To Go On Living When Someone You Love Is Dying.* Lexington, MA: Lexington Books, 1988. 330p. $17.95. ISBN 0-699-17021-6.

The author guides the reader through the bereavement process. The book dispels myths about mourning and provides information and support to help the reader cope with a loss. It offers solace, comfort, and guidance to those mourning a loved one.

Raphael, Beverly. *The Anatomy of Bereavement.* New York: Basic Books, 1983. 440p. $27.50. ISBN 0-465-00289-7.

The author shares her broad experience with the bereaved by revealing how people cope with, understand, and eventually adapt to the many different bereavements encountered in a lifetime.

Robertson, John, and Betty Utterback. *Suddenly Single: Learning To Start Over through the Experience of Others.* New York: Simon and Schuster, 1986. 223p. $15.95. ISBN 0-671-54442-X.

A collection of authentic stories by people who have lived through a sudden death. The book follows them through their dark period, taking into account all the personal and social pressure that must be confronted, the hard choices that must be considered, and the repercussions of such decisions on family and friends.

Rose, Xenia. *Widow's Journey.* New York: Holt, Rinehart and Winston, 1990. 205p. $19.95. ISBN 0-8050-1193-5.

This book helps guide the widow through her bereavement.

Sarnoff-Schiff, Harriet. *Living through Mourning: Finding Comfort and Hope When a Loved One Has Died.* New York: Viking Press, 1986. 300p. $15.95. ISBN 0-670-80028-7.

The text discusses the process of grieving, from the acknowledgment of conflicting and painful feelings, through stages of denial, anger, helplessness, despair, and powerlessness, to the point of acceptance. It offers understanding, support, and practical advice for those in mourning.

Shuchter, Stephen R. *Dimensions of Grief: Adjusting to the Death of a Spouse.* San Francisco: Jossey-Bass, 1986. 376p. $39.95 ISBN 1-55542-003-6.

Written by a clinical psychiatrist, this book tries to answer questions about grief. For example, what is normal grief and when is it harmful? How long does it last? How effective are the support groups designed to assist the bereaved? This work contains a series of case histories describing people's experiences and emotions associated with the death of a spouse.

Simpson, Michael A. *The Facts of Death: A Complete Guide for Being Prepared.* Englewood Cliffs, NJ: Prentice-Hall, 1979. 276p. $9.95. ISBN 0-13-299636-7.

A guide to coping with the emotional and practical aspects of death. Tips include: helping an individual face his or her own death; talking with the dying; comforting the bereaved; and practical advice on items such as writing a will, planning a funeral, and reducing inheritance taxes.

Viorst, Judith. *Necessary Losses: The Loves, Illusions, Dependencies and Impossible Expectations That All of Us Have To Give Up in Order To Grow.* New York: Simon and Schuster, 1988. 447p. $17.95. ISBN 0-671-45655-5.

This book discusses a subject central to all of life: loss. The losses of childhood, youth, and the people we love are explored. The author thoughtfully and compassionately argues that, in order to grow, every individual must give up what is known. Practical advice on dealing with losses is provided.

Pamphlets and Brochures

American Association of Retired Persons. *Grief Support Training for Clergy and Congregations.* Washington, DC: American Association of Retired Persons, 1989. 57p. No charge. Stock no. D13643.

This training manual provides helpful information about grief, mourning, and aiding someone who is grieving. It includes exercises to help students identify and evaluate their own attitudes about areas connected with assisting those faced with death and dying issues. The manual contains comprehensive training information about long-term grief support. It is published as a project of the Interreligious Liaison Office and the Widowed Persons Service Program of the AARP.

American Association of Retired Persons. *On Being Alone.* Washington, DC: American Association of Retired Persons, 1990. 15p. No charge. Stock no. D150.

An overview of how to survive a loss, this publication reviews the various aspects of widowhood. It covers bereavement and the phases of grief, personal adjustment, and taking care of business.

National Funeral Directors Association. *Helping Groups.* Milwaukee: National Funeral Directors Association, undated. 5p. No charge.

Primarily a listing of various support groups across the country, this guide provides the names, addresses, and telephone numbers of these organizations. There are support groups for survivors of suicide, widowed persons, bereaved children, and bereaved parents.

National Funeral Directors Association. *Parent Death*. Milwaukee: National Funeral Directors Association, undated. 6p. No charge.

Written for the adult child of a deceased parent, this guide discusses reactions to losing the parent and coping with grief.

National Funeral Directors Association. *What Can I Do To Help?* Milwaukee: National Funeral Directors Association, undated. 4p. No charge.

Another in a series of pamphlets from the country's largest funeral directors' association. It asks and answers a series of questions about helping the family of the recently deceased.

Audiovisual Materials

Death and Dying: A Conversation with Elisabeth Kübler-Ross, M.D.

Type: Video
Length: 29 min.
Cost: $59.95
Source: PBS Video
1980 Braddock Place
Alexandria, VA 22314
Date: 1974

Dr. Elisabeth Kübler-Ross, author of *On Death and Dying*, discusses her work in caring for dying persons and their families.

Death Notification

Type: Video
Length: 27 min.
Cost: $420
Source: Coronet/MTI Film & Video
108 Wilmot Road
Deerfield, IL 60015
Date: 1988

This video explores the effects of a sudden death on a spouse and other survivors.

The Death of Ivan Ilych
Type: Video
Length: 28 min.
Cost: $49.95
Source: Mass Media Ministries
           2116 North Charles Street
           Baltimore, MD 21218
Date: 1979

> One in a series of productions by United Methodist Communications, this video explores the issues confronting an individual's own death.

Deathing: An Introduction to Conscious Dying
Type: Video
Length: 30 min.
Cost: $49.95 plus $3.00 shipping
Source: Hartley Film Foundation, Inc.
           Car Rock Road
           Cos Cob, CT 06807
Date: 1989

> A video geared to the hospice patient or any individual facing death. It helps prepare patients for what lies ahead.

Invincible Summer: Returning to Life after Someone You Loved Has Died
Type: Video
Length: 16^{1}/$_{2}$ min.
Cost: Purchase $59.95, preview $10
Source: Willowgreen Productions
           P.O. Box 25180
           Ft. Wayne, IN 46825

> A discussion of the grieving process and its stages. It also offers practical suggestions for each stage of grief.

Living—When a Loved One Has Died
Type: Video
Length: 19 min.
Cost: Purchase $79
Source: Batesville Management Services
           P.O. Drawer 90
           Batesville, IN 47006-9989

This video explains the normal reactions individuals experience in dealing with grief. It suggests ways to cope with depression, guilt, and anger.

When Your Loved One Is Dying

Type: Video
Length: 16 min.
Cost: Purchase $79
Source: Batesville Management Services
           P.O. Drawer 90
           Batesville, IN 47006-9989

Designed to assist the living in coping with their emotions when a loved one is dying, this video is based on the book of the same name.

Widows and Widowers—Problems and Adjustments

Type: Video
Length: 20 min.
Cost: Purchase $79
Source: Batesville Management Services
           P.O. Drawer 90
           Batesville, IN 47006-9989

Based on a research project, this video reviews the problems faced by widows and widowers in the first year after a spouse's death. It discusses factors that affect adjustment and focuses on those in a helping relationship.

Arranging or Prearranging a Funeral

Books and Articles

Carlson, Lisa. *Caring for Your Own Dead.* Hinesburg, VT: Upper Access Publishers, 1987. 343p. $17.95. ISBN 0-942679-00-8.

A handbook for people who want to take charge of funeral and body disposition arrangements for their own family members. For financial reasons, the author took care of transporting the body and arranging the cremation and burial of her husband. From this experience she researched the laws in all 50 states regarding legal requirements, where to secure permits, body and organ donation, and issues for legal reform.

Goodman, Rabbi Arnold M. *A Plain Pine Box: A Return to Simple Jewish Funerals and Eternal Traditions*. New York: KTAV Publishing House, 1981. 123p. ISBN 0-87068-895-2.

> This is the story of the Chervra Kevod Hamet (Society To Honor the Dead) of Minneapolis. This Jewish society is organized to care for the dead without the use of the funeral industry, or to return to "traditional Jewish burial and mourning practices."

Mitford, Jessica. *The American Way of Death*. New York: Macmillan, 1982. 144p. $15.95. ISBN 0-02-567160-X.

> First published in 1963, this book stirred up a controversy that culminated in federal regulation of the funeral industry. Mitford describes the technical, financial, and social customs surrounding the American funeral. Chapters describe funerals, cemeteries, costs, memorial societies, and other organizations.

Morgan, Ernest. *Dealing Creatively with Death: A Manual of Death Education and Simple Burial*. 11th ed. Burnsville, NC: Celo Press, 1988. 170p. $9. ISBN 0-914064-26-6.

> This book introduces many death-related issues, including the right to die, how to live with a dying person, and bereavement. It also reviews simple burials and cremations, memorial societies, death ceremonies, and body and organ donations. Eight appendices include hospices in the various states, instructions for simple burials, sample death ceremonies, organizations, anatomical gifts, and an extensive bibliography.

Nelson, Thomas C. *It's Your Choice*. Glenview, IL: AARP Books and Scott, Foresman, 1983. 118p. $4.95. ISBN 0-673-24804-6.

> Although somewhat dated, this is a consumer-friendly publication on funeral planning. The guide is written primarily for older persons, the principal consumers of funeral goods and services. It discusses various options, costs, caskets, cemetery plots, and paying for a funeral. It also has several appendices with checklists and comparison forms for consumer use.

Pamphlets and Brochures

American Association of Retired Persons. *Cemetery Goods and Services.* Washington, DC: American Association of Retired Persons, 1988. 12p. No charge. Stock no. D13162.

> Similar to the AARP's book *It's Your Choice,* this brochure reviews the goods and services needed for an in-ground or above-ground burial together with price information. It also discusses cremation, urns, and disposition of the cremated remains.

American Association of Retired Persons. *Product Report: Funeral Goods and Services.* Washington, DC: American Association of Retired Persons, 1989. 8p. No charge. Stock no. D13496.

> A guide to assist consumers in planning or preplanning a funeral. It reviews the various elements of a traditional funeral and provides a range of retail prices for each item. The guide also discusses alternative arrangements for funerals.

American Cemetery Association. *Cemeteries and Memorial Parks.* Falls Church, VA: American Cemetery Association, 1979. 8p. No charge.

> A series of questions and answers about cemeteries and memorial parks (cemeteries without tombstones). The brochure also describes cemetery goods such as mausoleums and columbariums and how to pay for these items.

Cemetery Consumers Service Council. *Having a Problem with a Cemetery?* Washington, DC: Cemetery Consumers Service Council, 1979. 3p. No charge.

> This brochure describes how to file a complaint with the service council regarding a consumer cemetery problem.

Council of Better Business Bureaus, Inc. *Tips on Planning a Funeral.* Arlington, VA: Council of Better Business Bureaus, 1985. 11p. $1 plus a stamped, self-addressed envelope. No. 24-196-A400385.

> A quick review, in a short brochure, of the major issues in planning a funeral.

The Living Bank. *Questions on Organ Donation.* Houston: The Living Bank, 1990. 5p. No charge.

This handout discusses the issues surrounding organ and tissue donation and how to become a donor. The Living Bank is one of a number of organ and tissue registries.

Monument Builders of North America. *Your Right To Choose.* Evanston, IL: Monument Builders of North America, 1985. 5p. No charge.

A small brochure discussing monument selection, styles, and sellers. It also describes cemetery requirements for monuments.

National Funeral Directors Association. *Death away from Home.* Milwaukee: National Funeral Directors Association. 5p. No charge.

Death is difficult to face, but when someone dies away from home, it's even more difficult. This brochure offers suggestions on how to handle such a situation.

National Funeral Directors Association. *A Way To Remember: Choosing a Funeral Ceremony.* Milwaukee: National Funeral Directors Association. 4p. No charge.

One of a series of consumer brochures about funeral planning from the largest association of funeral directors.

National Funeral Directors Association. *When Death Occurs.* Milwaukee: National Funeral Directors Association. 5p. No charge.

This pamphlet reviews the steps to take and people to contact in the event of a death.

National Kidney Foundation. *The Organ Donor Program.* New York: National Kidney Foundation, 1987. 7p. No charge.

A series of questions and answers about organ and tissue donation and how to become a donor. The brochure also contains a uniform donor card.

National Research and Information Center. *Funeral Service Consumer Assistance Program.* Evanston, IL: National Research and Information Center, 1990. 4p. No charge.

A short guide to filing a complaint against a funeral director regarding goods and services contracted for. The center has a consumer arbitration program that may pay a refund if the panel decides in the buyer's favor.

Audiovisual Materials

Because Life Was Lived
Type: Video
Length: 10 min.
Cost: Purchase $99
Source: Batesville Management Services
           P.O. Drawer 90
           Batesville, IN 47006-9989

A short introduction exploring the question, Why have a funeral? It discusses costs, prearrangements, and what a funeral director does.

It's Your Choice: A Consumer Education Program on Funeral Planning
Type: Slides and tape
Length: 13 min.
Cost: Purchase $17, rental free to nonprofit groups
Source: American Association of Retired Persons
           Program Scheduling Office
           1909 K Street, NW
           Washington, DC 20049
Date: 1983

This is a companion to the book by the same name. It reviews the elements of a funeral, prices, options, and legal requirements. Handouts are included.

Paying or Prepaying for a Funeral

Books and Articles

Babbitt, Wendy. "The Funeral Industry: A Business You'd Rather Ignore—But Shouldn't." Washington, DC: *Public Citizen* 11, no. 4 (July/August 1991): 24–26. ISSN 0738-5927.

A short review of funeral costs, purchasing a funeral, and how the Federal Trade Commission's Funeral Rule is working.

Hughes, Theodore E., and David Klein. *A Family Guide to Estate Planning, Funeral Arrangements and Settling an Estate after Death.*

New York: Charles Scribner's, 1983. 258p. $15.95. ISBN 0-684-17920-2.

> This two-part book, written by an assistant attorney general and a consumer advocate, discusses end-of-life planning and coping with death. Part One reviews wills, Living Wills, avoiding probate, death taxes, and funeral planning. Part Two covers funeral arrangements, sorting out assets, and wills and the probate process. Included are sample copies of a will, a Letter of Instruction for survivors, a Living Will, and a universal donor card. There are also several tables of state-by-state requirements for wills, estate taxes, inheritance taxes, and the various forms of legal ownership of property.

McManus, Kevin. "Keeping Funeral Costs in Line: After All, King Tut Had a Lot More Money Than You Do." *Changing Times* 45, no. 6 (June 1991): 57–60. ISSN 0009 143X.

> A review of funeral pricing including caskets, headstones, cemetery perpetual care, cremation, and pre-need plans.

Streitfeld, David. "Consummate Consumer, Death and the Salesman." *Washington Post,* May 29, 1990.

> A critical review of pre-need funeral plans. This article describes both insurance-funded and trust-funded pre-need plans and compares their earnings over time.

Pamphlets and Brochures

American Association of Retired Persons. *Product Report: Pre-Paying Your Funeral?* Washington, DC: American Association of Retired Persons, 1988. 8p. No charge. Stock no. D13188.

> A consumer guide to prepaying a funeral with a comparison of nine different pre-need plans. The publication also highlights important questions such as portability, guarantees, revocation, availability, and security.

The Forethought Group. *Buyer's Guide to Pre-Need Funeral Planning.* Batesville, IN: Batesville Management Services 1989. 9p. No charge.

Published by the country's largest pre-need insurance company, this is a guide to prepaid funeral arrangements. It discusses how to establish a pre-need agreement and describes the various funding arrangements available. It also answers several other consumer questions.

National Funeral Directors Association. *Easing the Burden—Prearranging Your Funeral.* Milwaukee: National Funeral Directors Association, undated. 6p. No charge.

A guide to prearranging and prefunding a funeral. It contains a series of questions about the kind of funeral desired and special instructions for survivors.

Pre-Arrangement Association Educational Foundation. *13 Basic Questions about Pre-Arrangement and Pre-Payment.* Chicago: Pre-Arrangement Association Educational Foundation, 1991. 10p. No charge.

A small guide in question-and-answer format that argues consumers should both prearrange and prepay their funerals. Questions answered include: What does prearrangement mean? Why should I prearrange? What does prepayment mean? What type of prepayment options exist? How do I know if I am getting a fair price?

U.S. Veterans Administration. *Interments in National Cemeteries.* Washington, DC: Department of Veterans Affairs, 1987. 8p. No charge.

A guide to eligibility requirements for burial in a national cemetery, along with a list of these facilities.

Audiovisual Materials

Planning Ahead
Type: Video
Length: 12 min.
Cost: Purchase $99
Source: Batesville Management Services
           P.O. Drawer 90
           Batesville, IN 47006-9989

A consumer-oriented video outlining the need for estate planning as well as funeral prearrangement. This factual presentation offers many suggestions.

Sorting Out the Final Details

Books and Articles

Appel, Jens C., III, and F. Bruce Gentry. *The Complete Will Kit.* New York: John Wiley, 1990. 146p. $17.95. ISBN 0-471-51295-8.

> This is one of a number of self-help, will-writing guides. It provides detailed steps for writing or amending a will with state-specific information on legal requirements. There are extensive appendices with forms for all states and worksheets for estate taxes.

Brown, Judith N., and Christina Baldwin. *A Widow's Guide to Financial Survival at a Time of Emotional Crisis.* New York: Simon and Schuster, 1986. 223p. $16.95. ISBN 0-671-60349-3.

> This book is a practical guide for newly widowed women facing critical financial decisions. It focuses on the emotional, financial, and legal needs of the widow. There are sample letters, charts, and lists of items to attend to. It is authored by an attorney–investment advisor and a clinical psychotherapist.

Dacey, Norman F. *How To Avoid Probate.* 3d ed. New York: Macmillan, 1990. 715p. $24.95. ISBN 0-02008181-2.

> This is an exhaustive review of lawyers, probate, as well as inter vivos or living trusts and how to create one. The 13 chapters address how to avoid probate for personal real estate, bank accounts, partnerships, personal effects, and so on. There are also worksheets to use in creating a trust document. This is largely a self-help book with order forms to secure additional trust documents.

Daly, Eugene J. *Thy Will Be Done: A Guide to Wills, Taxation, and Estate Planning for Older Persons.* Buffalo, NY: Prometheus Books, 1990. 230p. $14.95 (paper). ISBN 0-87975-586.

Written by an attorney for the older adult, this is a practical guide to how assets are distributed after death. Included are will preparations, probate, tax issues, and miscellaneous items. There are also sample forms and tax tables.

Esperti, Robert A., and Renno L. Peterson. *Loving Trust: The Right Way To Provide for Yourself and Guarantee the Future of Your Loved Ones.* New York: Viking Press, 1988. 293p. $19.95. ISBN 0-670-81881-X.

Written by two financial planners, this book discusses why consumers need a trust as opposed to a will. It provides details on how to establish such a trust and how to find a professional to help create one.

Jurinski, James. *Keys To Preparing a Will.* Hauppauge, NY: Barron's, 1991. 160p. $5.95 (paper). ISBN 0-8120-4594-7.

From the series "Keys to Retirement Planning," this book explains what a legal will is, how to prepare for a meeting with the attorney drafting one, and how to amend the will.

Matthews, Joseph L., and Dorothy Berman. *Social Security, Medicare and Pensions.* 5th ed. Berkeley: Nolo Press, 1990. 231p. $15.95. ISBN 0-87337-128-3.

Authored by an attorney in laymen's language, this book is written for the over-55 population. It discusses in detail the ins and outs of Social Security benefits, Medicare, Supplemental Security Income (SSI), Medicaid, and veterans' benefits. It also reviews railroad retirement benefits, public and private pension systems, and the federal Age Discrimination in Employment Act. The book provides a wealth of information with charts, graphs, and sample letters to file.

Ostberg, Kay, in association with HALT (Halt All Legal Tyranny). *Probate: Settling an Estate: A Step-by-Step Guide.* 3d ed. New York: Random House, 1990. 162p. $8.95. ISBN 0-679-72960-7.

An overview of the probate process, this book assists survivors in administering an estate, deciding whether or not an attorney is needed, and securing additional information. It reviews wills, taxes, claims against the estate, taking inventory of the assets, and closing the estate. The appendices provide state-specific information about probate rules and procedures as well as tax information. There is also a checklist for personal representatives to follow.

Petterle, Elmo A. *Legacy of Love: How To Make Life Easier for the Ones You Leave Behind*. Bolinas, CA: Shelter Publications, 1986. 194p. $12.95 + $1.50 for postage. ISBN 0-89586-478-9.

> A four-part workbook and planning tool. Part One describes how to make and record end-of-life decisions. It includes will preparations, funeral arrangements, investments, insurance, property inventories, family history, and personal notes. Part Two is written from the perspective of a survivor attending to these details. Included in this book are forms and directions for survivors.

Soled, Alex J. *The Essential Guide to Wills, Trusts, and Death Taxes*. Glenview, IL: AARP Books and Scott, Foresman, 1984. 252p. $12.95. ISBN 0-673-24809-7.

> A practical guide to assist consumers in planning an estate. It discusses wills, probate, trusts, and death taxes (gift, inheritance, and estate taxes). Legal terms are clearly defined in a glossary, and state-specific information is provided as to probate requirements and death taxes.

Pamphlets and Brochures

American Association of Retired Persons. *A Consumer's Guide to Probate*. Washington, DC: American Association of Retired Persons, 1989. 10p. No charge. Stock no. D13822.

> A consumer pamphlet offering a generic overview of the probate process. It describes the basic steps such as filing a will, appointing a personal representative, paying debts, and distributing assets. It also tries to answer questions about cost and how long the process will take.

American Association of Retired Persons. *Final Details: A Guide for Survivors When Death Occurs*. Washington, DC: American Association of Retired Persons, 1990. 4p. No charge. Stock no. D14168.

A short guide for survivors on handling the financial arrangements and other decisions required after a death. It lists documents to collect, Social Security and other benefits, wills, probate, taxes, credit, ownership titles, and professional assistance.

American Association of Retired Persons. *What To Do If You're Denied Credit.* Washington, DC: American Association of Retired Persons, 1988. 10p. No charge. Stock no. D13285.

Developed by AARP's Consumer Affairs Section, this booklet explains the rights of older persons under the federal Equal Credit Opportunity Act. It is a self-help guide to assist older women and men who have been denied credit.

Older Women's League. *The Owl Observer, Special Edition: Women and Health Insurance.* Washington, DC: Older Women's League, Winter/Spring 1991. 8p. No charge. Distributed by the American Association of Retired Persons. Stock no. D14284.

A detailed description of how to maintain health insurance coverage under COBRA (Title X of the Consolidated Omnibus Budget Reconciliation Act of 1985). This special newsletter discusses how to secure COBRA rights and how this federal law applies to widows, divorced or separated spouses, children, and disabled workers.

Computer-Based Information

Dacey Trust Forms
National Estate Planning Council
180 Church Street
Naugatuck, CT 06770
(800) 242-3642

The Dacey Trust is an inter vivo trust used to pass wealth on to survivors while avoiding probate. This software is in a question-and-answer format and assists the user in creating his or her own living trust. There are two versions: one with the most commonly used forms for $199 and a complete version with all forms for $350.

Home Lawyer
MECA Software
327 Riverside Avenue
Westport, CT 06880
(800) 288-6322

> From Hyatt Legal Services, a software program that creates last wills and testaments, powers of attorney, and other legal documents. The software prompts a series of questions to the user about each document. The cost is $79.95. Version 2.0 was released in 1991 and requires IBM or IBM-compatible hardware.

It's Legal
Parsons Technology, Inc.
375 Collins Road, NE
Cedar Rapids, IA 52402
(800) 779-6000

> This is a menu-driven software package for preparing a number of legal documents, including wills, Living Wills, Durable Powers of Attorney for Health Care, general and special powers of attorney, and complaint letters to vendors and attorneys general. The cost is $69. Version 2.0 was released in 1991 and requires IBM or IBM-compatible hardware.

Living TrustBuilder
Jian Tools for Sales
127 Second Street
Los Altos, CA 94022
(415) 941-9191

> A software package to assist users in creating a living trust. This product addresses issues such as cash flow, life insurance monies, and income taxes. The finished document can be customized to meet the user's need. Version 2.0 was released in 1990 and retails for $199.

Mac Personal Class
Quadmation, Inc.
1016 East El Camino Real, Suite 160
Sunnyvale, CA 94087

A personal-information organizer that can assist users in organizing family data such as wills, assets and liabilities, insurance data, funeral and burial information, ownership, real estate, and benefits. Version 2.0 is available for $59.

Personal Lawyer
Bloc Publishing
800 SW 37th Avenue, Suite 765
Coral Gables, FL 33134
(800) 888-2562

Software used to prepare enforceable legal documents such as wills, powers of attorney, and other documents. The program claims to meet the legal requirements of the District of Columbia and all states except Louisiana. Version 1.3 was released in 1989 and is sold for $60. It requires IBM or IBM-compatible hardware.

Personal Lawyer—Wills
Lassen Software, Inc.
5923 Clark Road, Suite F
Paradise, CA 95969
(916) 877-0408

An interactive software package to create a last will and testament. The program asks questions, analyzes the answers, and formulates the next appropriate question. A will that is unique to the individual's needs is created. It claims to be legal in every state except Louisiana. This software can be used with Apple, IBM, and IBM-compatible hardware. Version 2.0 was released in 1984 and is sold for $79.95.

WillMaker
Nolo Press
950 Parker Street
Berkeley, CA 94710
(415) 549-1976

Using plain English, this software assists users in drafting their own wills. All steps are easily understandable. Version 4.0 was released in 1988 and sells for $37. It can be used on Apple, Commodore, IBM, and IBM-compatible hardware.

General

Books and Articles

Myers, Teresa Schwab. *How To Keep Control of Your Life after 60: A Guide for Your Legal, Medical and Financial Well-Being.* Lexington, MA: Lexington Books, 1989. 448p. ISBN 0-669-19456-5.

> A guide to all legal issues that affect the older person. This book advises older adults and families on maintaining control over their lives, even when someone has a debilitating illness. The author discusses in plain English such legal documents as trusts, Living Wills, powers of attorney, Medigap, and long-term care insurance. The book also reviews patients' rights, Medicare and Medicaid, discharge policies, legal competence, and other issues. Contains 35 appendices.

Strauss, Peter J., Robert Wolf, and Dana Shilling. *Aging and the Law.* Chicago: Commerce Clearing House, 1990. 892p. $135 with supplement. Item no. 4892.

> Written for attorneys who specialize in the practice of law relating to the elderly, this lengthy volume cites pertinent federal and state statutes, regulations, and case law about nursing homes, home care, Medicare and Social Security, financial planning, death and dying, and intergenerational equity. Although primarily written for attorneys, it's an invaluable source for anyone interested in the legal issues surrounding aging.

Computer-Based Information

Ageline
National Gerontology Resources Center
1909 K Street, NW
Washington, DC 20049
(202) 728-4895

> Ageline is the database of the American Association of Retired Persons (AARP). It contains extracts from sociological and psychological books on the process of aging. The database could be of interest to aging-related organizations, academic institutions, government agencies, and the general public.

Glossary

Actuarial tables   Mortality tables developed by insurance companies to estimate the length of life for a male or female at any given age.

Advance Medical Directive   A document, recognized by both the medical and legal communities, that describes what type of medical care an individual chooses to use and refuse. It may or may not name a health care agent.

Agent   A person who is empowered to act for another, usually by being named in a legal document.

Alternative container   A container used for immediate burials and direct cremations. It is often made of hard cardboard, particle board, or pine.

Appraisal   A process to determine the value of a person's estate at the time of that person's death.

Autopsy   The examination of a body to determine the cause of death.

Bequest   A gift of personal property in a will.

Best interests   A legal standard in which an individual is called on to make decisions for another in the latter's best interest, based on standard views and practices in the medical community.

Body donation   A means of final disposition, in which the remains of the deceased are donated to a medical or dental school.

Brain death   A legal definition stating that death occurs when a person is certified to have no electrical activity in the brain, determined both by clinical observation and by electroencephalograms.

Casket   A container of metal or wood for the remains of the deceased.

Codicil   An amendment to a will.

Columbarium   A building with niches or spaces for urns containing cremated remains.

Comatose   A medical term used to describe a patient experiencing a deep and prolonged state of unconsciousness due to an illness or injury.

Community property   A legal standard used in eight states, and to some extent in Wisconsin, in which marriage is considered to be an economic partnership and all property acquired during a marriage is jointly owned.

Co-sign   To take responsibility with another party (e.g., a spouse) for a debt.

Courtesy credit card   A credit card granted to a spouse for her/his use when the credit account is solely in the name of the other partner.

Creditor   A person to whom the deceased owes a debt.

Cremains or cremated remains   The pulverized bone fragments of the body that remain after cremation, popularly referred to as the ashes of the deceased.

Cremation   A means of final disposition in which the body is incinerated.

Crematorium or crematory   A facility where a body is cremated.

Crypt   A space in a mausoleum encasing the remains of the deceased.

Death taxes   Estate and inheritance taxes.

Deceased   The person who died, sometimes called the decedent.

Direct cremation   A process in which a deceased person's remains are cremated without embalming or services with the body present.

Durable Power of Attorney   A legal document giving power to someone to act as the agent of another.

Durable Power of Attorney for Health Care   A power of attorney that relates to decisions about medical treatment, such as when to use or refuse medical treatment. It may include provisions about hospice or nursing home placement and other matters.

Embalming   A process of draining the body of fluids and inserting chemicals to retard decay. Embalming is used with a traditional funeral or for public health reasons.

Equal Credit Opportunity Act   A federal law prohibiting discrimination based on age, sex, race, and other factors in granting credit.

Estate   Personal and real property held by the deceased at the time of death.

Estate income tax   Taxes due on income earned by the estate in excess of standard exemptions.

Estate tax   A tax levied on the estate of the deceased; estate taxes may be required by both federal and state agencies.

Freedom-of-choice laws   State laws that designate which next of kin may decide funeral planning and organ donation questions.

Funeral director   A person licensed in every state (except Colorado) to arrange or prearrange or provide other services related to a funeral.

Funeral Rule   A rule issued by the Federal Trade Commission that requires funeral homes to disclose prices and prohibits certain practices in funeral sales and services.

Garden plot   Grave sites that have no above-ground markers.

Grave liner   A product used to prevent ground settlement with in-ground burials. A liner is made of a hard synthetic material, usually concrete.

Grief   The internal feelings a person experiences as the result of a major loss.

Guardian   A person legally placed in charge of making decisions for someone who is incapable of managing his or her own affairs.

Heir   A person named to inherit property under a will.

Holographic will   An unwitnessed will written in longhand. Half of the states recognize these wills as valid.

Immediate burial   A process in which a body is interred directly without embalming or any kind of service with the remains present.

Incapacitated   The term used to describe individuals who are unable or unfit to make decisions for themselves. It is usually used to describe a temporary situation.

Incompetent   The legal term used to describe individuals who are not able to make decisions for themselves. It is often used to describe a condition considered to be permanent, but also can be used to define a temporary condition.

Inheritance tax   A tax imposed on an heir who is receiving property from the deceased.

Interment   Burial in the ground.

Intestate   Dying without a will. In this case, the estate is distributed according to state law.

Inurnment   Placement of the cremated remains in an urn.

Irrevocable   An agreement that cannot be canceled.

Lawn crypt   A below-ground mausoleum.

Living trust   A trust created to avoid probate.

Living Will   A written statement of a patient's wishes in regard to medical treatments and life-sustaining procedures should the person become terminally ill.

Mausoleum   A large or small building containing crypts.

Mechanical respiration   The use of medical equipment that simulates normal breathing.

Memorial park   A cemetery limited to garden plots or burial sites with no above-ground markers.

Memorialization   A term used to describe the installation of a marker or memorial to honor the deceased.

Mourning   The external expression or manifestation of grief.

Nonprobate property   Property not subject to the probate process, such as life insurance policies.

Nutrition and hydration   The use of intravenous tubes to supply nutrition and fluids to a patient who is unable to eat or drink. In some cases and some states, this is considered a life-support procedure.

Oral will   A will given orally to one or more persons. These wills are recognized as valid in 20 states.

Organ donation   Donating organs and tissues after death for transplant or other use by living people.

Outer burial container   A grave liner or vault used in cemeteries to prevent ground settlement with an in-ground burial.

Perpetual care   A service that maintains cemetery grounds forever.

Persistent vegetative state   The medical term used to describe a patient who is comatose or unresponsive to external stimuli and who has little or no hope of recovery.

Personal property Personal items such as home furnishings, heirlooms, collections, jewelry, and so on.

Personal representative A person named in a will or appointed by a court to administer an estate in probate; also called the P.R., executor/executrix, and administrator/administratrix.

Prearrangement Arranging a funeral or burial in advance of the death. It is often formalized with an agreement to deliver specific goods and services.

Pre-need plan Paying for a funeral in advance.

Preplanning Planning a funeral in advance of need.

Probate The legal process of gathering and distributing the assets of the deceased.

Probate property Property subject to the probate process.

Real property Personal homes, unimproved land, and rent-producing property.

Remains The body of the deceased.

Revocable An agreement that can be canceled.

Right of survivorship The ability to pass property automatically to a co-owner; also called tenancy of the whole.

Right to die The movement, and the individual belief, that a person has the right to refuse or terminate medical treatment that prolongs life when there is little or no hope of recovery from a terminal illness.

Self-proving will A will executed according to state law, witnessed and notarized at the time it is written.

Separate property laws A legal standard used in 41 states, by which property is owned separately by each partner in a marriage unless there is a joint ownership agreement.

Small estate administration   Simplified probate procedures that require little court supervision; also called summary administration.

Substitute judgment   The legal standard in which an individual is asked to make decisions for another based on the individual's knowledge and understanding of the other person's wishes.

Supervised administration   Formal estate administration procedures requiring probate court approvals at major steps in the process.

Traditional funeral   A series of rituals and practices honoring the deceased. These include embalming the body, an open casket presentation, and services at a house of worship and a cemetery.

Trust   A legal relationship in which one party holds property on behalf of another.

Tube feeding   The use of intravenous tubes for supplying nutrition to medical patients who are unable to eat.

Uniform donor card   A document, which may be legally binding, that bestows anatomical gifts after death.

Urn   A container used to hold the cremated remains, or ashes, of a body.

Vault   A structure used to line a grave to prevent ground settlement. Vaults are normally made of steel-reinforced concrete and lined with metal or asphalt.

Ventilators   A medical device that simulates the breathing process for a patient who is unable to breathe unaided.

Viewing   A common funeral practice allowing friends and relatives to see the deceased.

Will   A written document representing the instructions of the deceased for the distribution of the estate.

Will substitute   Joint ownership of property, life insurance, and other items that designate a beneficiary but bypass probate.

Appendixes

Appendix A

Letter of Instruction

A Letter of Instruction is a list of everything a person owns and owes. It's left behind to help survivors sort out the final details after the person's death.

Letter of Instruction

Money You Can Expect

From my employer: _____
               (person to contact, department, phone)

_____
(life insurance)   *(profit sharing)*

_____
(accident insurance)   *(pension plan)*

_____
(other benefits)

From insurance companies: _____
                      (total amount)

From Social Security: _____
               (lump sum plus monthly benefits)

From the Veterans Administration: _____
                    (you must inform the VA)

From other sources: _____

Updated _____
     (date)

First Things To Do

1. Call _____ to help.
     (friend or relative)

2. Notify my employer (or former employer). _____
                               (name, phone number)

3. Make arrangements with funeral home. See page _____ of this document.
4. Request at least 10 copies of the death certificate. Usually the funeral director will get them.
5. Call my lawyer. _____
(name, phone number)
6. Contact local Social Security Office.
7. Get and process my insurance policies.
8. Notify bank that holds my home mortgage.

Location of Personal Papers
Last will and testament: _____
Birth and baptismal certificates: _____
Communion and confirmation certificates: _____
School diplomas: _____
Marriage certificate: _____
Military records: _____
Naturalization papers: _____
Other (adoption, divorce, etc.): _____

Savings Accounts and Certificates
Bank: _____
Address: _____
Name(s) on account: _____
Account number: _____
Kind of account: _____
Repeat to cover all accounts of husband and wife. Canceled checks are in:
_____
(name, location of bank)

Social Security
Name: _____
Number: _____
Location of card: _____
File a claim immediately to avoid losing any benefit checks.
Call the local Social Security office for an appointment. The personnel will tell you what to bring. _____
(phone)

Safe Deposit Box
Bank: _____
Address: _____
Name(s) on account: _____ Number: _____
Location of key: _____
List of contents: _____

House, Condominium, or Co-op
Names on deed: _____
Address: _____

Lot: _____ Block: _____ On map called: _____
Other descriptions needed: _____
Lawyer at closing: _____
               (name)   *(address)*
Location of statement of closing, policy or title insurance, deed, land
survey, etc: _____
Mortgage held by: _____
                     (bank)
Amount of original mortgage: _____
Date taken out: _____
Amount owed now: _____
Method of payment: _____
Location of payment book or payment statements: _____
_____

Life insurance on mortgage? yes _____   no _____
Veteran's exemption claim
Location of documentation: _____
Annual amount: _____
Contact local tax assessor for further documentation.
Property taxes on home
Amount: _____
Location of receipts: _____
Cost of house
Initial buying price: _____
Purchase closing fee: _____
Other costs to buy (real estate agent, legal, taxes, etc.): _____
_____

Improvements as of

_____ , _____
(date)   *(total)*
Itemized house improvements
Improvement: _____ Cost: _____ Date: _____
Location of bills: _____
If renting, is there a lease? yes _____   no _____
Lease location: _____ Expires:_____
                                         (date)
Landlord: _____

Doctors
Doctors: _____
           (name, address, phone, whose doctor)
Dentists: _____
Pediatrician: _____
Children's dentist: _____

Relatives and Friends To Inform
List names, addresses, phone numbers:

_____
_____
_____

Personal Effects
I would like certain people to be given these personal effects.
Item   Person

_____
_____
_____

Special Wishes

_____
_____
_____

Cemetery and Funeral Arrangements
Cemetery plot
Location: _____
When purchased: _____
Deed number: _____
Location of deed: _____
Other information: _____
(pre-need arrangement, perpetual care, etc.)
Facts for funeral director; survivor should bring this information and
cemetery deed to funeral director.
My full name: _____
Residence: _____
Phone: _____
Marital status: _____ Spouse: _____
Date of birth: _____ Birthplace: _____
Father's name and birthplace: _____
Mother's maiden name and birthplace: _____
Length of residence in state: _____ in United States_____
Military service: yes _____ no _____ When: _____
(Bring veteran's discharge papers if possible.)
Social Security number: _____
Occupation: _____
Life insurance: Bring policy if proceeds will be used for funeral expenses.

Funeral Preferences
My choice of funeral home: _____
Type of funeral preferred: _____
Prearrangement agreement: yes _____   no _____
Where filed: _____
Pre-need agreement: yes _____   no _____
Where filed: _____

Other personal preferences or desires: _____
_____
_____

Life Insurance
Location of all policies; to collect benefits, a copy of the death certificate
must be sent to each company.
Policy: _____
    (amount)
Whose life is insured: _____
Insurance company: _____
Company address: _____
Kind of policy: _____ Policy number: _____
Beneficiaries: _____
Issue date: _____ Maturity Date: _____
How paid out: _____
Other options on payout: _____
Other special facts: _____
Repeat information above for each policy.
For _____
    (amount)
in veteran's insurance, call local Department of Veterans Affairs
office: _____
    (phone number)

Other Insurance
Accident
Company: _____
Address: _____
Policy number: _____
Beneficiary: _____
Coverage: _____
Location of policy: _____
Agent, if any: _____
Car, Home, and Household
Give information below for each policy.
Coverage: _____
Company: _____
Address: _____
Policy number: _____
Location of policy: _____
Term (when to renew): _____
Agent, if any: _____
Medical
Coverage: _____
Company: _____
Address: _____

Policy number: _____

Location of policy: _____

Through employer or other group: _____

Agent, if any: _____

Repeat for all other insurance policies

Mortgage Insurance

Company: _____

Policy number: _____

Location of policy: _____

Vehicles

Year, make, and model: _____

Body type: _____

License number: _____

Color: _____

Identification number: _____

Location of papers: _____

(title, registration)

Repeat for each car.

Credit Cards

All credit cards in my name should be canceled or converted to

_____'s name.

Company: _____ Phone: _____

Address: _____

Name on card: _____ Number: _____

Location of card: _____

Repeat for each card.

Loans Outstanding (other than mortgages)

Bank: _____

Address: _____

Name on loan: _____

Account number: _____

Monthly payment: _____

Location of papers, including payment book: _____

Collateral, if any: _____

Life insurance on loan? yes _____   no _____

Repeat for all loans.

Investments

(Repeat for each investment.)

Stocks

Company: _____

Name on certificate(s): _____

Number of shares: _____

Certificate numbers(s): _____

Purchase price and date: _____

Location of certificate(s): _____

Bonds/Notes/Bills

Issuer: _____

Issued to: _____

      (owner)

Face amount: _____ Bond number: _____

Purchase price and date: _____

Maturity date: _____

Location of certificate(s): _____

Mutual Funds

Company: _____

Name of account: _____

Number of shares or units: _____

Location of statements or certificates: _____

Other investments (U.S. Savings Bonds, etc.)

For each investment, list amount invested, to whom issued, issuer, maturity date and other applicable data, location of certificates, and other vital papers.

Income Tax Returns

Location of all previous returns (federal, state, local):

_____

My tax preparer: _____

      (name, address, phone)

Check: Are estimated quarterly taxes due?

Important Warranties and Receipts

Item(s): _____

_____

(warranty location)   *(receipt location)*

_____

Appendix B

Funeral and Cemetery Regulatory Information, Right-To-Die Laws, and Schools for Body Donations

Alabama

A. Regulatory Information

1. *Funeral directors are regulated by:*
   Alabama Board of Funeral Service
   100 Commerce Street, Suite 804
   Montgomery, AL 36130
   (205) 261-4049

   The board consists of seven members, all licensed funeral directors.

2. *Cemeteries are regulated by:*
   Registration Services
   Vital Statistics Division
   434 Monroe Street
   Montgomery, AL 36130
   (205) 242-5042

3. *Alabama has neither a funeral trust law nor a cemetery pre-need trust law.*

   Insurance-funded pre-need contracts are regulated to some extent by:
   Insurance Commissioner
   135 South Union Street, Suite 181
   Montgomery, AL 36130
   (205) 269-3550

B. Right-To-Die Laws
In Alabama, right-to-die issues are addressed in: Alabama Natural Death Act [1981], Ala. Code Sections 22-8A-1–10 (1984)

C. Schools for Body Donations
Alabama Anatomical Board
Department of Anatomy
College of Medicine
University of South Alabama
Mobile, AL 36688
(205) 460-6490 (weekdays, 8 A.M.–5 P.M.)

University of Alabama
Anatomy Department
University Station
Birmingham, AL 35294
(205) 934-4494

Alaska

A. Regulatory Information

1. *Funeral directors are regulated by:*
   State of Alaska Division of Occupational Licensing
   Mortuary Science Section
   P.O. Box D-Lic
   Juneau, AK 99811
   (907) 465-2580
      Alaska has no state funeral board.
2. *There is no state cemetery board.*
3. *State law does not designate a specific agency to regulate pre-need sales in Alaska.* The Department of Commerce licenses funeral directors, but a license is not required to sell pre-need plans. The state of Alaska requires 100 percent trusting of all funds that have been deposited. The amount of earnings that becomes part of the trust is not specified. When the trust is revocable, the consumer may withdraw any or all funds. However, the funeral provider can withhold 15 percent.
      Alaska has no pre-need law for cemetery purchases.
      Insurance-funded pre-need contracts are regulated to some extent by:
   Director of Insurance
   P.O. Box D
   Juneau, AK 99811
   (907) 465-2515

B. Right-To-Die Laws
In Alaska, right-to-die issues are addressed in: Alaska Rights of Terminally Ill Act [1986], Alaska Stat. Sections 18-12-010–100 (1986)
Alaska Statutory Form Power of Attorney Act [1988], Alaska Stat. Sections 13-26-332–353 (H.B. 491 signed June 6, 1988)

C. Schools for Body Donations
Alaska has no medical schools. Nearby states may be checked for their requirements.

Arizona

A. Regulatory Information

1. *Funeral directors and embalmers are regulated by:*
Arizona State Board of Funeral Directors and Embalmers
1645 West Jefferson, Room 410
Phoenix, AZ 85007
(602) 542-3095
    The board consists of seven members—four licensed funeral directors and three consumers.
2. *Cemeteries are regulated by:*
Commissioner of Real Estate
202 East Earll Drive, Suite 400
Phoenix, AZ 85012
(602) 279-2909
3. *Funeral pre-need contracts are regulated by the State Board of Funeral Directors and the Banking Commission.* Pre-need plans can only be sold by individuals who hold a permit or license. The state of Arizona requires 85 percent trusting of all funds that have been deposited.
    Additionally, 90 percent of the income becomes part of the trust, and the funeral director can retain 10 percent per year and any bank charges as a service fee. The consumer may withdraw all funds within three days and up to 85 percent plus all accrued interest after three days if the full amount has been paid.
    Arizona has no pre-need law for cemetery purchases.
    The Banking Commission can be contacted at:
Superintendent of Banks
3225 North Central, Suite 815
Phoenix, AZ 85012
(602) 255-4421
(800) 544-0708 (toll-free in Arizona)
    Insurance-funded pre-need contracts are regulated to some extent by:
Director of Insurance
3030 North Third Street, Suite 1100
Phoenix, AZ 85012
(602) 255-5400

B. Right-To-Die Laws
In Arizona, right-to-die issues are addressed in: Arizona Medical Treatment Decision Act [1985], Ariz. Rev. Stat. Ann. Sections 36-3201–3210 (1986)

Arizona Powers of Attorney Act [1974], Ariz. Rev. Stat. Ann. Sections 14-5501–5502 (Supp. 1989), as interpreted by Rasmussen v. Fleming, 154 Ariz. 207, 741 P.2d 674 (1987)

C. Schools for Body Donations
University of Arizona
College of Medicine
Department of Anatomy
1501 North Campbell Avenue
Tucson, AZ 85724
(602) 626-6084
(602) 626-6443 (after 5 P.M.)

Arkansas

A. Regulatory Information

1. *Funeral directors and embalmers are regulated by:*
Arkansas State Board of Embalmers and Funeral Directors
400 Harrison, Suite 203
Batesville, AR 72501
(501) 698-2072
   The board consists of seven members—five licensed funeral directors and two consumers. One of the consumer members is a senior citizen representative.

2. *Cemeteries are regulated by:*
Arkansas State Cemetery Board
Heritage West Building
201 East Markham, Third Floor
Little Rock, AR 72201

3. *Funeral and cemetery pre-need contracts are regulated by the state Securities Department.* Pre-need plans can only be sold by individuals who hold a permit or license. The state of Arkansas requires 100 percent trusting of all funds that have been deposited, and 100 percent of the earnings become part of the trust. If the contract is revocable, the customer can withdraw up to 85 percent of the funds and 15 percent can be retained by the funeral director.
   The state securities commissioner can be contacted at:
Arkansas Securities Department
Heritage West Building
201 East Markham
Little Rock, AR 72201
(501) 324-9260
   Insurance-funded pre-need contracts are regulated to some extent by:
Insurance Commissioner
400 University Tower Building
Little Rock, AR 72204
(501) 371-1325

B. Right-To-Die Laws

In Arkansas, right-to-die issues are addressed in: Arkansas Rights of the Terminally Ill or Permanently Unconscious Act [1987], Ark. Code Ann. Sections 20-17-201–218 (Supp. 1987)

In addition, the state of Arkansas has a statute authorizing surrogate decision making entitled: Arkansas Rights of the Terminally Ill or Permanently Unconscious Act, Section 20-17-214

C. Schools for Body Donations

University of Arkansas
Department of Anatomy
School of Medicine
Little Rock, AR 72205-7199
(501) 661-5180
(501) 661-5000

California

A. Regulatory Information

1. *Funeral directors are regulated by:*
   California Board of Funeral Directors and Embalmers
   1020 N Street, Room 418
   Sacramento, CA 95814
   (916) 455-2413
   The board consists of five members—two licensed funeral directors and three consumers.
2. *Religious cemeteries and very small cemeteries are exempt from regulatory oversight. All other cemeteries are regulated by:*
   California Cemetery Board
   1434 Howe Avenue, Suite 88
   Sacramento, CA 95825
   (916) 920-6078
3. *Funeral pre-need contracts are also regulated by the Funeral Directors and Embalmers Board.* The state of California requires 100 percent trusting of all funds that have been deposited. The consumer may withdraw any or all funds from revocable plans at their option. However, a 10 percent revocation fee may be charged. A maximum of 4 percent of the original value of the trust can be deducted from earnings on an annual basis by the funeral director.

   California requires that 100 percent of the retail value of cemetery goods and services be trusted unless constructive delivery is taken. Constructive delivery means the merchandise has been manufactured and stored, and a certificate of ownership has been issued. This is the equivalent of actual delivery and bypasses trusting requirements.

Insurance-funded pre-need contracts are regulated to some extent by:
Commissioner of Insurance
100 Van Ness Avenue
San Francisco, CA 94102
(415) 557-3245 (San Francisco)
(213) 736-2551 (Los Angeles)
(800) 233-9045 (toll-free in California)

B. Right-To-Die Laws

In California, right-to-die issues are addressed in: California Natural Death Act [1976], Cal. Health & Safety Code Sections 7185–7195 (West Supp. 1989)
California Statutory Form Durable Power of Attorney for Health Care Act [1984, 1985, 1988], Cal. Civil Code Sections 2430–2444 (West Supp. 1990)

C. Schools for Body Donations

Los Angeles College of Chiropractic
16200 East Amber Valley Drive
P.O. Box 1166
Whittier, CA 90609
(213) 947-8755

University of California, Davis
Department of Human Anatomy
Davis, CA 95616
(916) 752-2100

University of California, San Diego
School of Medicine
La Jolla, CA 92093
(619) 534-4536

University of California, San Francisco
School of Medicine
San Francisco, CA 94143
(415) 476-1981

University of California, Los Angeles
Department of Anatomy
Los Angeles, CA 90024
(213) 825-9563

University of Southern California
School of Medicine
1333 San Pablo Street
Los Angeles, CA 90033
(213) 222-0231

College of Osteopathic Medicine of the Pacific
309 Pomona Mall East
Pomona, CA 91766
(714) 623-6116
(714) 433-5717 (evenings and weekends)

Stanford University
School of Medicine
Division of Human Anatomy
Stanford, CA 94305
(415) 723-2404
(415) 723-2300 (after 5 P.M.)

Colorado

A. Regulatory Information

1. *Funeral directors are not regulated. Colorado is the only state that doesn't license funeral directors or embalmers.*
2. *Cemeteries are regulated by:*
Financial Affairs Section
Division of Insurance
303 West Colfax Avenue
Denver, CO 80204
(303) 620-4647
3. *Funeral pre-need contracts are also regulated by the Insurance Division.* Pre-need plans can only be sold by individuals who hold a permit or license. The state of Colorado requires that 85 percent of all payments be deposited in trust. Up to 15 percent of the contract plus 100 percent of the interest must remain in the trust. The consumer may withdraw 85 percent of payments from a revocable contract and 100 percent at death.

   Colorado requires that 85 percent of all funds received for cemetery pre-need contracts must be trusted unless constructive delivery is taken. Constructive delivery means the merchandise has been manufactured and stored, and a certificate of ownership has been issued. This is the equivalent of actual delivery and bypasses trusting requirements.

   Insurance-funded pre-need contracts are also regulated to some extent by:
Division of Insurance
303 West Colfax Avenue, Suite 500
Denver, CO 80204
(303) 620-4647

B. Right-To-Die Laws
In Colorado, right-to-die issues are addressed in: Colorado Medical Treatment Decision Act [1985, 1989], Colo. Rev. Stat. Sections 15-18-101–113 (H.B. 1036 signed March 29, 1989)

Colorado Powers of Attorney Act [1963], Colo. Rev. Stat. Sections 15-14-501–502 (1987), as interpreted by in re Rodas, no. 86PR139 (Colo. Dist. Ct. Mesa County Jan. 22, 1987, as modified, April 3, 1987) (Buss, J.)

C. Schools for Body Donations
University of Colorado
Anatomical Board
4200 East 9th Street
Denver, CO 80262
(303) 394-8554
(303) 399-1211 (after working hours)

Connecticut

A. Regulatory Information

1. *Funeral directors and embalmers are regulated by two agencies:*
Connecticut Board of Examiners of Embalmers and Funeral Directors
150 Washington Street
Hartford, CT 06106
(203) 566-1039
(203) 566-4068

Connecticut Department of Health
150 Washington Street
Hartford, CT 06106
(203) 566-1483

The board consists of five members—three licensed funeral directors and two consumers.

2. *There is no state cemetery board.*
3. *Funeral pre-need plans can only be sold by individuals who hold a funeral director's license.* The state of Connecticut requires 100 percent trusting of all funds that have been deposited, and 100 percent of all earnings must be deposited to the account or paid to the customer, minus administrative expenses. The consumer may withdraw 100 percent of the funds less the origination fee, not to exceed 5 percent of the trust.

Connecticut has no pre-need law for cemetery purchases.

Insurance-funded pre-need contracts are not permitted at this time.
Insurance Commissioner
165 Capitol Avenue
Hartford, CT 06106
(203) 297-3800

B. Right-To-Die Laws
In Connecticut, right-to-die issues are addressed in: Connecticut Removal of Life Support Systems Act [1985], Conn. Gen. Stat. Sections 19a-570–575 (Supp. 1989)

In addition, Connecticut has a statute authorizing surrogate decision making entitled: Connecticut Removal of Life Support Systems Act, Conn. Gen. Stat. Section 19a-571.

C. Schools for Body Donations
University of Connecticut
School of Medicine
Farmington, CT 06032
(203) 679-2117
(203) 223-4340

Yale University
School of Medicine
New Haven, CT 06520
(203) 785-2813

Delaware

A. Regulatory Information

1. *Funeral directors are regulated by:*
Delaware State Board of Funeral Service Practitioners
P.O. Box 1401
Margaret O'Neill Building
Dover, DE 19903
(302) 739-4522
   The board consists of seven members, two of whom are not connected with funeral service.

2. *There is no state cemetery board.*

3. *Funeral pre-need contracts are regulated by the state bank commissioner.* Pre-need plans can only be sold by individuals who hold a permit or license. The state of Delaware requires that 100 percent of all trust funds be deposited, and 100 percent of all earnings must be deposited to the account or paid to the consumer. Consumers may withdraw any or all funds from revocable plans at their option.
   Delaware has no pre-need law for cemetery purchases.
   The state bank commissioner can be contacted at:
State Bank Commissioner
555 East Loockerman Street, Suite 210
Dover, DE 19901
(302) 739-4235
   Insurance-funded pre-need contracts are regulated to some extent by:
Insurance Commissioner
841 Silver Lake Boulevard
Dover, DE 19901
(302) 736-4251

B. Right-To-Die Laws

In Delaware, right-to-die issues are addressed in: Delaware Death with Dignity Act [1982, 1983], Del. Code Ann. Tit. 16, Sections 2501–2509 (1983)

C. Schools for Body Donations

The state of Delaware has no medical schools. The nearest state should be checked for those considering body donation.

District of Columbia

A. Regulatory Information

1. *Funeral directors and embalmers are regulated by:*
   Department of Consumer and Regulatory Affairs
   Board of Funeral Directors and Embalmers
   P.O. Box 37200
   Washington, DC 20001
   (202) 727-7468
       The board consists of five members—three licensed funeral directors, one consumer member, and one chief medical examiner.
2. *There is no cemetery board.*
3. *The District of Columbia has neither a funeral trust law nor a cemetery pre-need trust law.*
       Insurance-funded pre-need contracts are regulated to some extent by:
   Superintendent of Insurance
   614 H Street, NW
   North Potomac Building, Suite 516
   Washington, DC 20001
   (202) 727-7424

B. Right-To-Die Laws

In the District of Columbia, right-to-die issues are addressed in: District of Columbia Natural Death Act of 1981 [1982], D.C. Code Ann. Sections 6-2421–2430 (Supp. 1988)
District of Columbia Health-Care Decisions Act [1988], D.C. Code Ann. Sections 21-2201–2213 (1989)
    In addition, the District of Columbia has a statute authorizing surrogate decision making entitled: District of Columbia, Health Care Decisions Act of 1988, Section 11

C. Schools for Body Donations

George Washington University
Department of Anatomy
2300 I Street, NW
Washington, DC 20037
(202) 676-3511
(202) 676-3125

Georgetown University
School of Medicine and Dentistry
Department of Anatomy
3900 Reservoir Road, NW
Washington, DC 20007
(202) 625-2271 (weekdays 8:30 A.M.–5 P.M.)

Howard University
College of Medicine
Department of Anatomy
Washington, DC 20059
(202) 636-6655
(202) 636-6556

Florida

A. Regulatory Information

1. *Funeral directors are regulated by:*
   Department of Professional Regulation
   State Board of Funeral Directors/Examiners
   1940 North Monroe Street
   Tallahassee, FL 32399-0754
   (904) 488-8690
   The board consists of seven members—five licensed funeral directors and two consumers.

2. *Cemeteries are regulated by:*
   Office of the Comptroller
   Department of Banking and Finance
   Division of Finance
   The Capitol
   202 Blount Street
   Tallahassee, FL 32399-0350
   (904) 487-4283

3. *Funeral pre-need contracts are regulated by the Department of Insurance.* Pre-need plans can only be sold by individuals who hold a permit or license. Under Chapter 639.11, the state of Florida requires that at least 70 percent of all funds received be trusted. The earnings are available for withdrawal by the funeral home. The funeral home must report as income to the IRS 100 percent of the money received from the consumer.

   However, under Chapter 639.149, at least 90 percent of consumer funds are trusted. The principal in trust is tax-deferred to the funeral home until the contract is canceled or fulfilled. At that time, the trustee may release the earnings. When canceled, the contract proceeds are returned to the purchaser according to the terms of the contract, which may be 70–100 percent refunded; on fulfillment the proceeds are disbursed to the funeral establishment.

Generally, the funeral establishment or the certificate holder has up to 30 days to deposit the required funds in trust, and 30 days to return the funds to a purchaser who cancels the contract.

Florida requires that 110 percent of the cost of merchandise and services for cemetery pre-need contracts be trusted unless constructive delivery is taken or a bond or letter of credit is issued. Constructive delivery means the merchandise has been manufactured and stored, and a certificate of ownership has been issued. This is the equivalent of actual delivery and bypasses trusting requirements.

Insurance-funded pre-need contracts are also regulated to some extent by:

Insurance Commissioner
Plaza Level Eleven
The Capitol
Tallahassee, FL 32399-0300
(904) 488-3440
(800) 342-2762 (toll-free in Florida)

B. Right-To-Die Laws

In Florida, right-to-die issues are addressed in: Florida Life-Prolonging Procedure Act [1984, 1985, 1990], Fla. Stat. Ann. Sections 765.01–765.15 (H.B. 513 enacted without signature June 30, 1990)
Florida Durable Power of Attorney Act [1974, 1977, 1983, 1988, 1990], Fla. Stat. Ann. Section 709.08 (S.B. 748 signed July 2, 1990)
Health Care Surrogate Act (S.B. 748 signed July 2, 1990)

In addition, the state of Florida has a statute authorizing surrogate decision making entitled: Florida Life Prolonging Procedure Act, Fla. Stat. Ann. Section 765.07

C. Schools for Body Donations

Florida State Anatomical Board
1 Hills Miller Health Center
Box J-235
Gainesville, FL 32610
(904) 392-3588

The state of Florida requires that the family of the deceased pay for transportation and embalming before body donation.

Georgia

A. Regulatory Information

1. Funeral directors are regulated by:
Georgia State Examining Boards
166 Pryor Street, SW
Atlanta, GA 30303
(404) 656-3933

The board consists of seven members appointed by the governor, one of whom is a consumer member.

2. *Cemeteries are regulated by:*
Office of the Secretary of State
Business Services and Regulations Division
West Tower, Suite 802
2 Martin Luther King Jr. Drive
Atlanta, GA 30334
(404) 656-3079

3. *Funeral pre-need contracts are regulated by the insurance commissioner.* Pre-need plans can only be sold by individuals who hold a permit or license. The state of Georgia requires that 100 percent of all trust funds be deposited, and 100 percent of all earnings must be deposited to the account or paid to the consumer. Consumers may withdraw any or all funds from revocable plans at their option.

Georgia requires that 35 percent of the sales price for cemetery merchandise and 100 percent of the sales price for cemetery services must be trusted. Constructive delivery, a bond, or proof of financial responsibility can bypass the need for trusting. Constructive delivery means the merchandise has been manufactured and stored, and a certificate of ownership has been issued. This is the equivalent of actual delivery and bypasses trusting requirements.

Insurance-funded pre-need is prohibited in the state of Georgia.

B. Right-To-Die Laws
In Georgia, right-to-die issues are addressed in: Georgia Living Wills Act [1984, 1986, 1987, 1989], Ga. Code Ann. Sections 31-32-1–12 (1985 & Supp. 1989)
Georgia Durable Power of Attorney for Health Care Act [1990], Ga. Code Sections 31-36-1–36 (H.B. 999 signed April 11, 1990).

C. Schools for Body Donations
Emory University
School of Medicine
Atlanta, GA 30322
(404) 727-6242

Morehouse School of Medicine
720 Westview Drive, SW
Atlanta, GA 30310
(404) 752-1560 (weekdays)
(404) 752-1500 (all other times)

Medical College of Georgia
Anatomy Department
Augusta, GA 30912
(404) 721-3731

Mercer University
School of Medicine
1550 College Street
Macon, GA 31207
(912) 744-2555
(912) 474-2308

Hawaii

A. Regulatory Information

1. *Funeral directors are regulated by:*
State of Hawaii Department of Health
Sanitation Branch
1250 Punchbowl Street
Honolulu, HI 96813
(808) 548-6478
    Hawaii has no state funeral board. Funeral directors are regulated by the Professional and Vocational Licensing Division of the Department of Commerce and Consumer Affairs.

2. *Cemeteries are regulated by:*
Cemetery and Pre-Need Funeral Authority Program
Department of Commerce and Consumer Affairs
P.O. Box 3469
Honolulu, HI 96801
(808) 586-2690

3. *Funeral and cemetery pre-need contracts are regulated by the Department of Commerce and Consumer Affairs.* Pre-need plans can only be sold by individuals who hold a permit or license. The state of Hawaii requires that 70 percent of all trust funds be deposited. The interest earned in trust accounts goes to the pre-need sales authority, but based on an annual study the trust officer may require that interest be added to the principal. Generally the funds are held in a trust. The consumer can withdraw the interest.
Cemetery and Pre-Need Funeral Authority Program
Department of Commerce and Consumer Affairs
P.O. Box 3469
Honolulu, HI 96801
(808) 586-2690
    Insurance-funded pre-need contracts are regulated to some extent by:
Insurance Commissioner
P.O. Box 3614
Honolulu, HI 96811
(808) 548-5450

B. **Right-To-Die Laws**

In Hawaii, right-to-die issues are addressed in: Hawaii Medical Treatment Decisions Act [1986], Hawaii Rev. Stat. Sections 327D-1–27 (Supp. 1988)

Hawaii Uniform Durable Power of Attorney Act [1989], Hawaii Rev. Stat. Sections 551D-1–7 (Supp. 1989)

Health care decisions are authorized by Medical Treatment Decisions Act, Hawaii Rev. Stat. Section 237D-2 (Supp. 1988).

In addition, the state of Hawaii has a statute authorizing surrogate decision making entitled: Hawaii Medical Treatment Decisions Act, Hawaii Rev. Stat. Section 327D-21, as interpreted by in re Guardianship of Crabtree, no. 86-0031 (Hawaii Fam. Ct. 1st Cir. April 26, 1990) (Heeley, J.)

C. **Schools for Body Donations**

University of Hawaii
Department of Anatomy
1960 East-West Road, T311
Honolulu, HI 96822
(808) 948-7132
(808) 941-4734 (Island Wide Mortuary Service)

Idaho

A. **Regulatory Information**

1. *Funeral directors are regulated by:*
   Idaho State Board of Morticians
   Bureau of Occupational Licenses
   2417 Bank Drive, Room 312
   Boise, ID 83705
   (208) 334-3233

   The board consists of three members, all of whom are licensed funeral directors. There are no consumer members.

2. *Cemeteries are regulated by:*
   Department of Finance
   Securities Bureau
   700 West State Street
   Statehouse Mail
   Boise, ID 83720-2700
   (208) 334-3684

3. *Funeral pre-need contracts are regulated by the State Board of Morticians.* A certificate of authority is required to sell pre-need plans. The state of Idaho requires that 85 percent of all trust funds be deposited, and 100 percent of all earnings must be deposited to the account to be used for the payment of taxes or other costs as allowed by law, or paid

to the consumer. The consumer may withdraw any or all funds unless the plan is irrevocable.

Idaho has no pre-need law for cemetery purchases.

Insurance-funded pre-need contracts are regulated to some extent by:
Idaho Insurance Department
500 South Tenth Street
Boise, ID 83720
(208) 334-2250

B. Right-To-Die Laws

In Idaho, right-to-die issues are addressed in: Idaho Natural Death Act [1977, 1986, 1988], Idaho Code Sections 39-4501–4509 (1985 & Supp. 1989)

C. Schools for Body Donations

The state of Idaho has no medical schools. The nearest state should be checked by those considering body donation.

Illinois

A. Regulatory Information

1. *Funeral directors and embalmers are regulated by:*
Funeral Directors and Embalmers Licensing and Disciplinary Boards
Illinois Department of Professional Regulation
320 West Washington Street, 3rd Floor
Springfield, IL 62786
(217) 782-8556

The board consists of seven members who are licensed funeral directors and one consumer member.

2. *Cemeteries are regulated by:*
Office of the Comptroller
State of Illinois Center, Suite 15-500
Chicago, IL 60601
(312) 814-5918

3. *Funeral pre-need contracts are regulated by the comptroller.* Pre-need plans can only be sold by individuals who hold a permit or license. The state of Illinois requires 95 percent trusting of all funds that have been deposited on services and caskets, and 95 percent of all earnings must be deposited to the account or paid to the consumer. Vaults must be trusted at 85 percent. The consumer may withdraw the amount in the trust account less 25 percent or $300, whichever is less.

Illinois requires that 50 percent of the sales price of cemetery merchandise (except vaults and urns) and services must be trusted. Additionally, 95 percent of the purchase price of urns and 85 percent of the purchase price of vaults must be trusted. There are provisions for constructive delivery or installation of merchandise which bypass trusting requirements. Constructive delivery means the merchandise has been manufactured and stored, and a certificate of ownership has been issued. This is the equivalent of actual delivery and bypasses trusting requirements.

Office of the Comptroller
State of Illinois Center, Suite 15-500
Chicago, IL 60601
(312) 814-5918

Insurance-funded pre-need contracts are regulated to some extent by:
Department of Insurance
320 West Washington Street, 4th Floor
Springfield, IL 62767
(217) 782-4515
(217) 524-4872

B. Right-To-Die Laws

In Illinois, right-to-die issues are addressed in: Illinois Living Will Act [1984, 1988], Ill. Ann. Stat. ch. 110½, Sections 701–710 (Smith-Hurd Supp. 1989)

Illinois Powers of Attorney for Health Care Act [1987, 1988], Ill. Ann. Stat. ch. 110½, Sections 804-1–11 (Smith-Hurd Supp. 1989)

C. Schools for Body Donations

Anatomical Gift Association
2240 West Fillmore
Chicago, IL 60612
(312) 733-5283

Indiana

A. Regulatory Information

1. *Funeral directors are regulated by:*
   Indiana Board of Funeral and Cemetery Service
   1021 State Office Building
   100 North Senate Avenue
   Indianapolis, IN 46204
   (317) 232-2890

   The board consists of 11 members—4 licensed funeral directors, 4 individuals active in the cemetery industry, 2 consumer members, and the secretary of the state Board of Health.

2. *Cemeteries are regulated by the same board as funeral directors.*
   Indiana Board of Funeral and Cemetery Service
   1021 State Office Building
   100 North Senate Avenue
   Indianapolis, IN 46204
   (317) 232-2890

3. *Funeral and cemetery pre-need contracts are regulated by the Board of Funeral and Cemetery Service.* All pre-need sellers must register with the state board. Indiana requires 100 percent of all trust funds be deposited to the account, and 100 percent of all earnings must be deposited to the account or paid to the consumer. All contracts are irrevocable, with the amount in excess of the funeral expenses going to the estate. All contracts are also guaranteed-price contracts. Trusting is not required if prepaid services are delivered no more than one year after the date of the final payment.

Insurance-funded pre-need contracts are regulated to some extent by:
Commissioner of Insurance
311 West Washington Street, Suite 300
Indianapolis, IN 46204
(317) 232-2385
(800) 622-4461 (toll-free in Indiana)

B. **Right-To-Die Laws**
In Indiana, right-to-die issues are addressed in: Indiana Living Wills and Life-Prolonging Procedures Act [1985], Ind. Code Ann. Sections 16-8-11-1–22 (Burns Supp. 1989)

C. **Schools for Body Donations**
Indiana State Anatomical Board
Medical Science Building, Room 258
635 Barnhill Drive
Indianapolis, IN 46223
(317) 274-7450
(317) 892-4242

Iowa

A. **Regulatory Information**

1. *Funeral directors are regulated by:*
Board of Mortuary Science Examiners
Iowa Department of Public Health
Lucas State Office Building
Des Moines, IA 50319-0075
(515) 281-4401

The board consists of five members—three licensed funeral directors and two consumer members.

2. *Cemeteries are regulated by:*
Insurance Division
Department of Commerce
Lucas State Office Building
Des Moines, IA 50319
(515) 281-4440

3. *Funeral pre-need contracts are regulated by the Insurance Commission.* Pre-need plans can only be sold by individuals who hold a permit or license. The state of Iowa requires that 80 percent of all trust funds be deposited. The cancellation or default charge varies per funeral home per contract; it must be reasonable and defensible in court.

Iowa requires that 80 percent of all payments made for cemetery merchandise and services must be trusted. Constructive delivery or a surety bond can substitute for trusting requirements. Constructive delivery means the merchandise has been manufactured and stored, and a certificate of ownership has been issued. This is the equivalent of actual delivery and bypasses trusting requirements.

Insurance-funded pre-need contracts are also regulated by:
Supervisor
Regulated Industries Unit, Securities Bureau
Insurance Division, Department of Commerce
Lucas State Office Building, Second Floor
Des Moines, IA 50319
(515) 281-4441

B. Right-To-Die Laws

In Iowa, right-to-die issues are addressed in: Iowa Life-Sustaining Procedures Act [1985, 1987], Iowa Code Ann. Sections 144A.1–A.11 (1989) Iowa Power of Attorney Act [1975], Iowa Code Sections 633.705–633.706 (Supp. 1989)

Health care decisions are authorized by Iowa Life-Sustaining Procedures Act, Section 144A.7(a) (1989).

In addition, the state of Iowa has a statute authorizing surrogate decision making entitled: Iowa Life-Sustaining Procedures Act, Iowa Code Ann. Section 144A.7

C. Schools for Body Donations

Palmer College of Chiropractic
Department of Anatomy
1000 Brady Street
Davenport, IA 52803
(319) 326-9692 (8 A.M.–5 P.M. weekdays)
(319) 355-4433

University of Osteopathic Medicine and Health Science
3200 Grand Avenue
Des Moines, IA 50312
(515) 271-1481 (8 A.M.–4:30 P.M.)
(515) 271-1400

University of Iowa
Department of Anatomy, BSB
Iowa City, IA 52242
(319) 353-5905
(319) 356-1616 (after 5 P.M.)

Kansas

A. Regulatory Information

1. *Funeral directors and embalmers are regulated by:*
   Kansas State Board of Mortuary Arts
   1200 South Kansas, Suite 2
   Topeka, KS 66612-1331
   (913) 296-2980

   The board consists of five members—three licensed funeral directors and two consumers.

2. *Cemeteries are regulated by:*
   Office of Secretary of State
   Capitol Building
   Topeka, KS 66612
   (913) 296-2236

3. *The secretary of state and the board regulate funeral pre-need contracts.*
   Kansas requires that 100 percent of all trust funds be deposited, and 100 percent of all earnings must be deposited to the account or paid to the consumer. Consumers may withdraw any or all funds from revocable plans at their option. In irrevocable contracts, 100 percent of the funds, up to $2,000, remains the consumer's property but must be used toward the funeral.

   Kansas requires that 110 percent of the wholesale cost of cemetery merchandise, after the seller has retained 35 percent of the purchase price, must be trusted. Services are not covered by this law. The Office of Secretary of State oversees cemetery pre-need accounts. Constructive delivery can bypass trusting requirements. Constructive delivery means the merchandise has been manufactured and stored, and a certificate of ownership has been issued. This is the equivalent of actual delivery.

   Insurance-funded pre-need sales are regulated to some extent by:
   Commissioner of Insurance
   420 SW 9th Street
   Topeka, KS 66612
   (913) 296-7801
   (800) 432-2484 (toll-free in Kansas)

B. Right-To-Die Laws

In Kansas, right-to-die issues are addressed in: Kansas Natural Death Act [1979], Kan. Stat. Ann. Sections 65-28,101–28,109 (1985)
Kansas Durable Power of Attorney for Health Care Act [1989], (H.B. 2009 signed April 7, 1989).

C. Schools for Body Donations

University of Kansas
Department of Anatomy
Medical Center
39th and Rainbow
Kansas City, KS 66103
(913) 558-7000
(913) 588-5000

Kentucky

A. Regulatory Information

1. *Funeral directors and embalmers are regulated by:*
   State Board of Embalmers and Funeral Directors
   210 East 4th Street, Cagel Building
   P.O. Box 335
   Beaver Dam, KY 42320
   (502) 274-4515
   The board consists of five members—four licensed funeral directors and one consumer member.

2. *Cemeteries are regulated by:*
   Office of the Attorney General
   Consumer Protection Division
   209 St. Clair Street
   Frankfort, KY 40601
   (502) 564-2203

3. *Funeral pre-need contracts are regulated by the attorney general.* Pre-need plans can only be sold by individuals who hold a permit or license. The state of Kentucky requires that 100 percent of all trust funds be deposited, and 100 percent of all earnings must be deposited to the account or paid to the consumer. The consumer may withdraw any or all funds at their option.

   Kentucky requires that 100 percent of payments for vaults, caskets, and services should be trusted and 40 percent of payments for other cemetery merchandise must be trusted. Constructive delivery can bypass trusting requirements. Constructive delivery means the merchandise has been manufactured and stored, and a certificate of ownership has been issued. This is the equivalent of actual delivery.

   Insurance-funded pre-need contracts are regulated to some extent by:
   Insurance Commissioner
   229 West Main Street
   P.O. Box 517
   Frankfort, KY 40602
   (502) 564-3630

B. Right-To-Die Laws

In Kentucky, right-to-die issues are addressed in: Kentucky Living Will Act [1990], 1990 Ky. Acts, ch. 122 (H.B. 113 signed March 23, 1990) Kentucky Health Care Surrogate Act [1990], 1990 Ky. Acts, ch. 123 (S.B. 88 signed March 23, 1990)

C. Schools for Body Donations

University of Kentucky
Department of Anatomy
University Medical Center
Lexington, KY 40536
(606) 233-5276
(606) 233-5811 (after 5 P.M.)

University of Louisville
Health Science Center
Department of Anatomy
Louisville, KY 40292
(502) 588-5744
(502) 368-3396 (after 5 P.M.)

Louisiana

A. Regulatory Information

1. *Funeral directors and embalmers are regulated by:*
State Board of Embalmers and Funeral Directors
3500 Causeway Boulevard
North Executive Towers, Suite 1232
P.O. Box 8757
Metairie, LA 70011
(504) 838-5109
   The board consists of seven members—three licensed funeral directors, three embalmers, and one senior citizen consumer member.

2. *Cemeteries are regulated by:*
Louisiana Cemetery Board
2901 Ridgelake Drive, Suite 212
Metairie, LA 70002
(504) 838-5267

3. *Funeral pre-need contracts are regulated by the State Board of Funeral Directors and Embalmers.* Pre-need plans can only be sold by licensed funeral establishments or those licensed to sell funeral insurance only. The state of Louisiana requires that 100 percent of all trust funds be deposited, and 100 percent of all earnings must be deposited to the account or paid to the consumer. Consumers may withdraw any or all funds at their option.

   Louisiana requires that 50 percent of gross receipts, less sales taxes, for cemetery merchandise and services must be trusted. Constructive delivery can bypass trusting requirements. Constructive delivery means the merchandise has been manufactured and stored, and a certificate of ownership has been issued. This is the equivalent of actual delivery.

   Insurance-funded pre-need contracts are regulated to some extent by:
Commissioner of Insurance
P.O. Box 94214
Baton Rouge, LA 70804
(504) 342-5328

B. Right-To-Die Laws

In Louisiana, right-to-die issues are addressed in: Louisiana Life-Sustaining Procedures Act [1984, 1985], La. Rev. Stat. Ann. Sections 40:1299.58.1–.10 (West Supp. 1989)

In addition, the state of Louisiana has a statute authorizing surrogate decision making entitled: Louisiana Declarations Concerning Life-Sustaining Procedures Act, La. Rev. Stat. Ann. Section 40:1299.58.5

C. Schools for Body Donations
Department of Health and Human Resources
Anatomical Services
1901 Perdido Street
New Orleans, LA 70112-1393

New Orleans area:
Anatomy Department
Louisiana State University
(504) 568-5012

Anatomy Department
Tulane University
1430 Tulane Avenue
New Orleans, LA 70112
(504) 588-5255 (daytime)
(504) 861-0383 or (504) 522-1441 (J.T. Willie Funeral Home)

Shreveport area:
Anatomy Department
Louisiana State University
(318) 226-3312 (daytime)
(318) 226-3369 (LSU Security Office)

Maine

A. Regulatory Information

1. *Funeral directors are regulated by:*
Maine State Board of Funeral Services
State House Station 35
Augusta, ME 04333
(207) 582-8723
   The board consists of seven members—six licensed funeral directors and one consumer member.
2. *There is no state cemetery board.*
3. *Funeral pre-need contracts are also regulated by the State Board of Funeral Service.* The state of Maine does not require a permit or license to sell pre-need plans. The state does require that 100 percent of all trust funds be deposited, and 100 percent of all earnings must be deposited to the account or paid to the consumer. Consumers may withdraw any or all funds at their option if the contract is revocable.
   Maine has no pre-need law for cemetery purchases.
   Insurance-funded pre-need contracts are regulated to some extent by:

Superintendent of Insurance
State House Station 34
Augusta, ME 04333
(207) 582-8707

B. **Right-To-Die Laws**
In Maine, right-to-die issues are addressed in: Maine Powers of Attorney Act [1986], Me. Rev. Stat. Tit. 18-A, Section 5-501 (Supp. 1989)

In addition, the state of Maine has a statute authorizing surrogate decision making entitled: Maine Uniform Rights of the Terminally Ill Act [1985, 1990], Me. Rev. Stat. Tit. 18-A, Sections 5-701–714 (H.B. 1497 signed April 17, 1990)

C. **Schools for Body Donations**
University of New England
College of Osteopathic Medicine
11 Hills Beach Road
Biddeford, ME 04005
(207) 283-0171, ext. 202/206
(207) 284-8870

Maryland

A. **Regulatory Information**

1. *Funeral directors are regulated by:*
State Board of Morticians
4201 Patterson Avenue
Baltimore, MD 21215
(301) 764-4792
(301) 764-5987 (FAX)

The board consists of 12 members—10 licensed funeral directors and 2 consumer members.

2. *Cemeteries are regulated by:*
Office of the Secretary of State
State House
Annapolis, MD 21401
(301) 974-5531

3. *Funeral pre-need contracts are regulated by the State Board of Morticians.* Pre-need plans can be sold by licensed funeral directors or morticians only. The state of Maryland requires that 100 percent of all trust funds be deposited, and 100 percent of all earnings must be deposited to the account or paid to the consumer. Consumers may withdraw any or all funds at their option.

Maryland requires that 55 percent of the retail price for cemetery merchandise and services must be trusted, after the receipt of the first

50 percent by the vendor. Constructive delivery can bypass trusting requirements. Constructive delivery means the merchandise has been manufactured and stored, and a certificate of ownership has been issued. This is the equivalent of actual delivery.

Insurance-funded pre-need contracts are prohibited in the state of Maryland.

B. Right-To-Die Laws

In Maryland, right-to-die issues are addressed in: Maryland Life-Sustaining Procedures Act [1985, 1986, 1987], Md. Health-General Code Ann. Sections 5-601–614 (Supp. 1988)

Maryland Durable Power of Attorney Act [1969, 1974], Md. Est. & Trust Code Ann. Sections 13-601–603 (1974), as interpreted by 73 Opinions of the Attorney General [Opinion No. 88-046 (October 17, 1988)]

C. Schools for Body Donations

State Anatomy Board
Department of Health and Mental Hygiene
655 West Baltimore Street
Bressler Research Building, Room B-026
Baltimore, MD 21201
(301) 547-1222

Massachusetts

A. Regulatory Information

1. *Funeral directors and embalmers are regulated by:*
Board of Registration in Embalming and Funeral Service
Saltonstall Building, Room 1519
100 Cambridge Street
Boston, MA 02202
(617) 727-1718
(617) 727-7369

The board consists of five members—four licensed funeral directors and one consumer member.

2. *There is no state cemetery board.*

3. *Funeral pre-need contracts are regulated by the State Board of Funeral Directors.* Only registered, licensed, or certified funeral directors are able to sell pre-need plans. The state of Massachusetts requires that 100 percent of all trust funds be deposited, and 100 percent of all earnings must be deposited to the account or paid to the consumer. The consumer may withdraw 100 percent of the principal but cannot collect interest unless the contract is irrevocable.

Massachusetts has no pre-need law for cemetery purchases.

Insurance-funded pre-need contracts are regulated to some extent by:

Commissioner of Insurance
280 Friend Street
Boston, MA 02114
(617) 727-7189, ext. 300

B. Right-To-Die Laws
The state of Massachusetts has not passed any legislation dealing with the right-to-die issue.

C. Schools for Body Donations
Boston University School of Medicine
80 East Concord Street
Boston, MA 02118
(617) 638-4245
(617) 638-4144 (after 5 P.M.)

Harvard Medical School
25 Shattuck Street
Boston, MA 02115
(617) 732-1735
(617) 732-1111 (after 5 P.M.)

Tufts University School of Medicine
136 Harrison Avenue
Boston, MA 02111
(617) 956-6685
(617) 956-6610 (after 5 P.M.)

University of Massachusetts Medical School
55 Lake Avenue North
Worcester, MA 01605-2397
(617) 856-2460

Michigan

A. Regulatory Information

1. Funeral directors are regulated by:
Michigan Board of Mortuary Science
Department of Licensing and Regulation
P.O. Box 30018
Lansing, MI 48909
(517) 373-3877
(517) 373-3105
   The board consists of nine members—six licensed funeral directors and three public representatives.
2. Cemeteries are regulated by:

Cemetery Commissioner
Department of Licensing and Regulation
P.O. Box 30018
Lansing, MI 48909
(517) 373-0505

3. *Funeral pre-need contracts are regulated by the Department of Licensing and Regulation.* Pre-need plans can only be sold by businesses or persons who are registered with the department. The state of Michigan requires that 100 percent of all trust funds be deposited, and 100 percent of all earnings must be deposited to the account or paid to the consumer. The consumer may cancel and receive 90–100 percent, depending on the terms of the contract.

Michigan requires that 130 percent of the wholesale price of vaults and memorials must be trusted. There are no trusting requirements for cemetery services. Constructive delivery can bypass trusting requirements. Constructive delivery means the merchandise has been manufactured and stored, and a certificate of ownership has been issued. This is the equivalent of actual delivery.

Insurance-funded pre-need contracts are regulated to some extent by:
Commissioner of Insurance
Insurance Bureau
P.O. Box 30220
Lansing, MI 48909
(517) 373-9273

B. Right-To-Die Laws
Proposed legislation is pending in Michigan regarding the right-to-die issue.

C. Schools for Body Donations
University of Michigan Medical School
Department of Anatomy and Cell Biology
Medical Science II Building
Ann Arbor, MI 48109
(313) 764-4359 (8 A.M.–5 P.M. weekdays)
(313) 764-1817 (person on call)

Wayne State University Medical School
Department of Anatomy
540 East Canfield
Detroit, MI 48201
(313) 577-1188
(313) 577-1198 (nights)

Michigan State University
College of Human Medicine
East Lansing, MI 48823
(517) 355-1855

Minnesota

A. Regulatory Information

1. *Funeral directors are regulated by:*
   Minnesota Mortuary Science Advisory Council
   Minnesota Department of Health
   717 Delaware Street, SE
   Minneapolis, MN 55440
   (612) 623-5491

   The Mortuary Science Advisory Council consists of five members. Two members are licensed in mortuary science in Minnesota, two are public members representing the state, and one is a full-time academic staff member from the course in mortuary science at the University of Minnesota.

2. *There is no state cemetery board, although there is some county regulation of cemeteries.*

3. *There is no single agency regulating pre-need sales in Minnesota.* However, the Minnesota Department of Health receives reports on all funeral trust funds deposited in Minnesota and conducts an audit of such trust funds upon cause. Minnesota is a 100 percent trust state, meaning that 100 percent of the principal and 100 percent of the interest remains in trust until the death of the individual for whose benefit the trust has been established.

   Either a revocable or irrevocable trust can be established; in the latter case, the individual may not withdraw funds in the trust. Any funeral home may be made a trustee. However, a funeral home, employee, or director of a funeral home may not be named beneficiary on any policy, nor can a funeral home or a funeral director, directly or indirectly, receive any compensation upon the sale of a life insurance policy to be used for pre-need funding.

   Minnesota has no pre-need law for cemetery purchases.

   Insurance-funded pre-need contracts are regulated to some extent by:
   Commissioner of Insurance
   500 Metro Square Building
   St. Paul, MN 55101
   (612) 296-2594

B. Right-To-Die Laws
In Minnesota, right-to-die issues are addressed in:
Minnesota Adult Health Care Decisions Act [1989], Minn. Stat. Sections 145B.01–.17 (Supp. 1990)

C. Schools for Body Donations
University of Minnesota
Bequest Program
4-135 Jackson Hall
321 Church Street
Minnesota, MN 55455
(612) 625-1111

Mayo Clinic Foundation
Rochester, MN 55901
(507) 284-2511

Mississippi

A. Regulatory Information

1. *Funeral directors are regulated by:*
State Board of Funeral Service
802 North State Street, Suite 401
Executive Building
Jackson, MS 39202
(601) 355-4636
   The board consists of seven members—three funeral service licensees, three funeral director licensees, and one consumer member.

2. *There is no state cemetery board.*

3. *Funeral and cemetery pre-need contracts are regulated by the state attorney general.* A permit or license is not required to sell pre-need plans. The state of Mississippi requires that 50 percent of all trust funds be deposited, and 50 percent of all earnings must be deposited to the account or paid to the consumer. The consumer may withdraw 100 percent of the interest if the contract is revocable. Terms may vary, depending on the contractual agreement.
   Insurance-funded pre-need contracts are regulated to some extent by:
Commissioner of Insurance
1804 Walter Sillers Building
Jackson, MS 39201
(601) 359-3569

B. Right-To-Die Laws
In Mississippi, right-to-die issues are addressed in:
Mississippi Withdrawal of Life-Saving Mechanisms Act [1984], Miss. Code. Ann. Sections 41-41-101–121 (Supp. 1988)
Mississippi Durable Power of Attorney for Health Care Act [1990], (S.B. 2599 signed April 9, 1990)

C. Schools for Body Donations
University of Mississippi
Medical Center
Jackson, MS 39216
(601) 984-1000

Missouri

A. Regulatory Information

1. *Funeral directors and embalmers are regulated by:*

State Board of Embalmers and Funeral Directors
P.O. Box 423
Jefferson City, MO 65102
(314) 751-0813
    The board consists of six members—five licensed funeral directors and one consumer member.
2. *There is no state cemetery board.*
3. *Funeral pre-need contracts are regulated by the State Board of Embalmers and Funeral Directors.* Sellers and/or providers of pre-need plans must register with the board. The state of Missouri requires that 80 percent of all pre-need trust funds be deposited. The amount of earnings that becomes part of the trust varies. If the funds are deposited into a joint account, then 100 percent must be deposited. The consumer may withdraw the amount deposited in the trust if the contract is revocable. The total amount is refunded if the policy is canceled within 30 days.

    Missouri requires that 80 percent of the face value of the pre-need contract be deposited into trust. Cemetery services are not covered by Missouri law.

    Any insurance-funded portion of a pre-need contract is regulated by:
Director of Insurance
301 West High Street, Room 630
P.O. Box 690
Jefferson City, MO 65102
(314) 751-2451

B. Right-To-Die Laws
In Missouri, right-to-die issues are addressed in:
Missouri Life Support Declarations Act [1985], Mo. Ann. Stat. Sections 459.010–.055 (Vernon Supp. 1989)

C. Schools for Body Donations
Logan College of Chiropractic
1851 Schoettler Road
P.O. Box 100
Chesterfield, MO 63017
(314) 227-2100, ext. 135
(314) 962-0271

University of Missouri, Columbia
Department of Anatomy
School of Medicine
Columbia, MO 65212
(314) 882-2288

University of Missouri, Kansas City
Department of Anatomy
2411 Holmes Street
Kansas City, MO 64108
(816) 276-1984
(816) 474-8831

Kirksville College of Osteopathic Medicine
800 West Jefferson
Kirksville, MO 63501
(816) 626-2468

St. Louis University
School of Medicine
Department of Anatomy
1402 South Grand Boulevard
St. Louis, MO 63104
(314) 577-8271
(314) 577-8078 (night)

Washington University
Department of Anatomy
4566 Scott Avenue
St. Louis, MO 63110
(314) 362-3597

Montana

A. Regulatory Information

1. *Funeral directors are regulated by:*
Board of Morticians
1424 9th Avenue
Helena, MT 59620-0407
(406) 444-5433
   The board consists of five members—four licensed funeral directors and one consumer member.
2. *There is no state cemetery board.*
3. *Funeral and cemetery pre-need contracts are regulated by the Banking Commission.* A permit or license is not required to sell pre-need plans. Montana requires that 100 percent of all trust funds be deposited, and 100 percent of all earnings must be deposited to the account or paid to the consumer. The consumer may withdraw any or all funds upon mutual consent.
   The Banking Commission can be contacted at:
Commissioner
Financial Institutions
1520 East Sixth Avenue, Room 50
Helena, MT 59620-0542
(406) 444-2091
   Insurance-funded pre-need contracts are regulated to some extent by:
Commissioner of Insurance
126 North Sanders
Mitchell Building, Room 270
Helena, MT 59620
(800) 332-6148 (toll-free in Montana)

Montana Living Will Act [1985, 1989], Mont. Code Ann. Sections 50-9-101–104, 111, and 201–206 (1987)

C. Schools for Body Donations
The state of Montana has no medical schools. The nearest state should be checked by those considering body donation.

Nebraska

A. Regulatory Information

1. *Funeral directors are regulated by:*
   State Board of Embalmers and Funeral Directors
   Bureau of Examining Boards
   P.O. Box 95007
   Lincoln, NE 68509-5007
   (402) 471-2115
   The board consists of four members—three licensed funeral directors and one consumer member.

2. *Cemeteries are regulated by:*
   Department of Insurance
   Terminal Building
   941 O Street, Suite 400
   Lincoln, NE 68509
   (402) 471-2201

3. *Both trust-funded and insurance-funded funeral and cemetery pre-need contracts are regulated by the Insurance Department.* Pre-need plans can only be sold by individuals who hold a permit or license. The state of Nebraska requires that 85 percent of all trust funds be deposited. Up to 15 percent can be retained by the seller as a service charge.
   Department of Insurance
   Terminal Building
   941 O Street, Suite 400
   Lincoln, NE 68509
   (402) 471-2201

B. Right-To-Die Laws
At the time of data collection, Nebraska had no statutes governing the right to die.

C. Schools for Body Donations
Anatomical Board
State of Nebraska
Creighton University and University of Nebraska Schools of Medicine
42nd and Dewey Avenue
Omaha, NE 68105
(402) 280-2914 (Creighton)
(402) 559-2839 (University of Nebraska)
(402) 559-6249
(402) 331-2839

Nevada

A. Regulatory Information

1. *Funeral directors and embalmers are regulated by:*
Nevada State Board of Embalmers and Funeral Directors
P.O. Box 2462
Reno, NV 89505
(702) 323-3312
c/o Walton's Sierra Directors
875 West 2nd Street
Reno, NV 89503
(702) 323-7189

   The board consists of three members—two licensed funeral directors and one consumer member.

2. *Cemeteries are regulated by:*
Department of Commerce
Insurance Division
1665 Hot Springs Road
Carson City, NV 89710
(702) 687-4270

3. *Both trust-funded and insurance-funded pre-need contracts are regulated by the Insurance Division.* Pre-need plans can only be sold by individuals who hold a permit or license. The state of Nevada requires that 75 percent of all trust funds be deposited. There is no set amount of income which becomes part of the trust. The consumer may withdraw 100 percent of the 75 percent of the contract that is placed in the trust.

   Nevada requires that 100 percent of the retail price for cemetery merchandise and services, minus commissions, be trusted. Constructive delivery can bypass trusting requirements. Constructive delivery means the merchandise has been manufactured and stored, and a certificate of ownership has been issued. This is the equivalent of actual delivery.

   Insurance-funded pre-need contracts are regulated to some extent by:
Department of Commerce
Insurance Division
1665 Hot Springs Road
Carson City, NV 89710
(702) 687-4270
(800) 992-0900, ext. 4270 (toll-free in Nevada)

B. Right-To-Die Laws

In Nevada, right-to-die issues are addressed in:
Nevada Withholding or Withdrawal of Life-Sustaining Procedures Act [1977, 1985, 1987], Nev. Rev. Stat. Sections 449.540–.690 (1986 & Supp. 1988)
Nevada Durable Power of Attorney for Health Care Act [1987], Nev. Rev. Stat. Ann. Sections 449.800–.860 (Supp. 1989)

C. Schools for Body Donations
University of Nevada
Department of Anatomy
School of Medicine
Reno, NV 89557
(702) 784-6113
(702) 784-6169

New Hampshire

A. Regulatory Information

1. *Funeral directors and embalmers are regulated by:*
Board of Registration of Funeral Directors and Embalmers
Health and Human Service Building
6 Hazen Drive
Concord, NH 03001-6527
(603) 271-4651
   The board consists of five members—four licensed funeral directors
   and one consumer member.
2. *There is no state cemetery board.*
3. *No specific authority has been named to regulate pre-need sales in New
   Hampshire.* A license is required for licensed funeral directors to sell
   pre-need plans. The state requires that 100 percent of all trust funds be
   deposited, and 100 percent of all earnings must be deposited to the
   account or paid to the consumer. The consumer may withdraw any or
   all of the funds except where the contract is irrevocable.
   New Hampshire has no pre-need law for cemetery purchases.
   Insurance-funded pre-need contracts are regulated to some extent by:
Insurance Commissioner
169 Manchester Street
Concord, NH 03301
(603) 271-2261
(800) 852-3416 (toll-free in New Hampshire)

B. Right-To-Die Laws
In New Hampshire, right-to-die issues are addressed in:
New Hampshire Terminal Care Document Act [1985], N.H. Rev. Stat.
Ann. Sections 137-H:1–H:16 (Supp. 1988)

C. Schools for Body Donations
Dartmouth Medical School
Department of Anatomy
Hanover, NH 03756
(603) 646-7636 (8 A.M.–4 P.M.)
(603) 646-5000 (after 4 P.M., Hitchcock Medical Center)

New Jersey

A. Regulatory Information

1. *Funeral directors are regulated by:*
State Board of Mortuary Science of New Jersey
1207 Raymond Boulevard, 6th Floor
Newark, NJ 07102
(201) 648-2532/2533
   The board consists of eight members—five licensed funeral directors, two public members, and one state agency representative.

2. *Cemeteries are regulated by:*
Cemetery Board
CN 040
Trenton, NJ 08625
(609) 292-5892

3. *Trust-funded pre-need funeral contracts are regulated by the attorney general and the Department of Banking.* The state of New Jersey does not require a permit or license to sell pre-need plans. The state does require that 100 percent of all trust funds be deposited, and 100 percent of all earnings must be deposited to the account or paid to the consumer. The consumer may withdraw any or all funds at their option.
   New Jersey has no pre-need law for cemetery purchases.
   Insurance-funded pre-need contracts are regulated to some extent by:
Commissioner
Department of Insurance
CN325-20 West State Street
Trenton, NJ 08625
(609) 292-5363

B. Right-To-Die Laws

In New Jersey, right-to-die issues are addressed in:
New Jersey Act [1972], N.J. Stat. Ann. Section 46:2B-8 (Supp. 1989), as interpreted in re Peter, 108 N.J. 365, 529 A.2d 419 (1987)

C. Schools for Body Donations

Fairleigh Dickinson University
College of Dental Medicine
140 University Plaza Drive
Hackensack, NJ 07601
(201) 692-2577/2571 (9 A.M.–5 P.M.)
(201) 748-0240

University of Medicine and Dentistry of New Jersey
Robert Wood Johnson Medical School
Rutgers Pathology and Anatomy Association
P.O. Box 101
Piscataway, NJ 08854
(201) 463-4580

New Mexico

A. Regulatory Information

1. *Funeral directors are regulated by:*
New Mexico Board of Thanatopractice
725 St. Michaels Drive
P.O. Box 25101
Santa Fe, NM 87504
(505) 827-7177
   The board consists of five members—three licensed funeral directors, one consumer member, and one representative of the health care field or direct disposal firm.
2. *Cemeteries owned by a church or a municipality are not regulated.*
For-profit perpetual-care cemeteries are regulated by:
Financial Institutions Division
Regulations and Licensing
Cemeteries Division
P.O. Box 25101
Santa Fe, NM 87504
(505) 827-7100
3. *Funeral directors may not accept pre-need trust funds.* However, a funeral director may sell insurance-funded pre-need plans if he holds a valid insurance agent's license.
   New Mexico has no pre-need law for cemetery purchases.
   Insurance-funded pre-need contracts are regulated to some extent by:
Superintendent of Insurance
PERA Building, Room 428
P.O. Drawer 1269
Santa Fe, NM 87504
(505) 827-4500

B. Right-To-Die Laws
In New Mexico, right-to-die issues are addressed in:
New Mexico Right To Die Act [1977, 1984], N.M. Stat. Ann. Sections 24-7-1–11 (1986)
New Mexico Act (providing for the appointment of a conservator or other protective orders) [1989], N.M. Stat. Ann. Sections 45-5-501–502 (H.B. 510 signed April 5, 1989)
   In addition, the state of New Mexico has a statute authorizing surrogate decision making entitled:
New Mexico Right To Die Act, N.M. Stat. Ann. Section 24-7-8.1

C. Schools for Body Donations
University of New Mexico
Department of Anatomy
Albuquerque, NM 87131
(505) 277-5555
(505) 277-3053 (medical investigator)

New York

A. Regulatory Information

1. *Funeral directors are regulated by:*
Bureau of Funeral Directing Regulation
Department of Health
Corning Tower Building
Room 765, Empire State Plaza
Albany, NY 12237
(518) 453-1989

   There is also an advisory board consisting of 10 members—6 licensed funeral directors and 4 consumer members.

2. *Cemeteries are regulated by:*
Division of Cemeteries
Department of State
270 Broadway, Room 754
New York, NY 10007
(212) 587-5713

3. *Pre-funded funeral agreements are regulated by the attorney general.* The state of New York does not require a permit or license to sell pre-need plans. The state does require that 100 percent of all trust funds be deposited, and 100 percent of all earnings must be deposited to the account or paid to the consumer. Consumers may withdraw any or all funds at their option.

   New York has no pre-need law for cemetery purchases.

   Life insurance designed to fund funeral expenses only, or with the funeral director or an agent as beneficiary, is not authorized in New York.

B. Right-To-Die Laws

In New York, right-to-die issues are addressed in:
New York Health Care Agents and Proxies Act, S.B. 6176-A (signed July 22, 1990)

C. Schools for Body Donations

Union University
Albany Medical College
Albany, NY 12208
(518) 445-5379/5375
(518) 445-3125

Yeshiva University
Albert Einstein College of Medicine
Bronx, NY 10461
(718) 340-5378

State University of New York
Health Science Center at Brooklyn
450 Clarkson Avenue
Brooklyn, NY 11203
(718) 270-1014/2379
(718) 227-1402 (any time)

State University of New York
Department of Anatomical Sciences
Buffalo, NY 14214
(716) 831-2912
(716) 834-8128 (other times)

Columbia University
College of Physicians and Surgeons
630 West 168th Street
New York, NY 10032
(212) 305-3451

Cornell University Medical College
Department of Cell Biology and Anatomy
1300 York Avenue
New York, NY 10021
(212) 472-6400

New York University
School of Medicine
New York, NY 10016
(212) 340-5360

University of Rochester
601 Elmwood Avenue
School of Medicine
Rochester, NY 14642
(315) 275-2272

State University of New York
School of Medicine
Stony Brook, NY 11794
(516) 444-3111
(516) 599-0041

State University of New York
Health Science Center at Syracuse
Department of Anatomy and Cell Biology
766 Irving Avenue
Syracuse, NY 13210
(315) 473-5120
(315) 473-5280

Mt. Sinai Medical Center
One Gustave Levy Place
New York, NY 10029
(212) 241-7057

North Carolina

A. Regulatory Information

1. *Funeral directors are regulated by:*
   North Carolina State Board of Mortuary Science
   412 North Wilmington Street
   Raleigh, NC 27601
   (919) 733-9380
   The board consists of seven members—six licensed funeral directors or embalmers and one consumer member.

2. *Cemeteries are regulated by the North Carolina Cemetery Commission, which can be contacted at:*
   North Carolina Cemetery Commission
   430 North Salisbury Street
   Raleigh, NC 27611
   (919) 733-4915

3. *Funeral pre-need contracts are regulated by the Banking Commission.*
   Pre-need plans can only be sold by individuals who hold a funeral director's license. The state of North Carolina requires that 100 percent of all trust funds be deposited, except only 90 percent must be deposited where the contract price is guaranteed. The state requires that 100 percent of all earnings be deposited to the account or paid to the consumer. Consumers may withdraw any or all funds at their option. On a guaranteed contract, the interest on the 10 percent that may be retained is nonrefundable.
   The Banking Commission can be contacted at:
   Commissioner of Banks
   P.O. Box 29512
   Raleigh, NC 27626-0512
   (919) 733-3016
   North Carolina requires that 60 percent of the retail price for cemetery merchandise and services must be trusted. A surety bond can bypass trusting requirements.
   Insurance-funded pre-need contracts are regulated to some extent by:
   Commissioner of Insurance
   Dobbs Building
   P.O. Box 26387
   Raleigh, NC 27611
   (919) 733-7343

B. Right-To-Die Laws
In North Carolina, right-to-die issues are addressed in:
North Carolina Right to Natural Death Act [1977, 1979, 1981, 1983], N.C. Gen. Stat. Sections 90-320–322 (1985)
North Carolina Power of Attorney Act [1983], N.C. Stat. Sections 32A-8–14 (1987)

In addition, the state of North Carolina has a statute authorizing surrogate decision making entitled:

North Carolina Right to Natural Death Act, N.C. Gen. Stat. Ann. Section 90-322

C. Schools for Body Donations

University of North Carolina
314 Berry Hill Hall, 219-H
Chapel Hill, NC 27514
(919) 966-1134 (8:30 A.M.–4:30 P.M.)

Duke University
School of Medicine
Durham, NC 27710
(919) 684-4124
(919) 684-8111 (after 5 P.M.)

East Carolina University
School of Medicine
Department of Anatomy
Greenville, NC 27834
(919) 757-2849
(919) 757-2246

Wake Forest University
Bowman-Gray School of Medicine
Winston-Salem, NC 27103
(919) 748-4368

North Dakota

A. Regulatory Information

1. *Funeral directors are regulated by:*
   North Dakota Board of Funeral Service
   Box 633
   Devils Lake, ND 58301
   (701) 662-2511
   The board consists of three members, all of whom are licensed funeral directors. The state medical officer serves as well.
2. *There is no state cemetery board.*
3. *Funeral and cemetery pre-need contracts are regulated by the commissioner of securities.* The state of North Dakota does not require a permit or license to sell pre-need plans. The state does require that 100 percent of all trust funds be deposited for funeral merchandise and 50 percent be deposited for cemetery merchandise. In addition, 100 percent of all earnings must be deposited to the account or paid to the

consumer. Consumers may withdraw any or all funds at their option. The commissioner of securities can be contacted at:
Securities Commissioner
State Capitol Building
600 East Boulevard Avenue
Bismarck, ND 58501
(701) 224-2910
   Insurance-funded pre-need contracts are regulated to some extent by:
Commissioner of Insurance
Capitol Building, 5th Floor
600 East Boulevard Avenue
Bismarck, ND 58505-0320
(701) 224-2440
(800) 247-0560 (toll-free in North Dakota)

B. Right-To-Die Laws
In North Dakota, right-to-die issues are addressed in:
North Dakota Rights of the Terminally Ill Act [1989], N.D. Cent. Code Sections 23-06.4-01–14 (Supp. 1989)

C. Schools for Body Donations
University of North Dakota
Department of Anatomy
Medical Science South
Grand Forks, ND 58202
(701) 777-2101 (8 A.M.–4:30 P.M. weekdays)
(701) 772-7444
(701) 775-5047
(701) 772-0484

Ohio

A. Regulatory Information

1. *Funeral directors and embalmers are regulated by:*
Board of Embalmers and Funeral Directors of Ohio
77 South High Street, 16th Floor
Columbus, OH 43266-0313
(614) 466-4252
   The board consists of five members—four licensed funeral directors and one consumer member.
2. *There is no state cemetery board.*
3. *Funeral pre-need contracts are also regulated by the Board of Embalmers and Funeral Directors of Ohio.* Pre-need plans can only be sold by individuals who hold a permit or license. The state of Ohio requires that 100 percent of all trust funds be deposited; only 90 percent must be deposited where the contract price is guaranteed. The

amount of earnings that becomes part of the trust is 100 percent, or 80 percent where the contract price is guaranteed.

The consumer may withdraw 100 percent of the funds if the contract is canceled within 7 days. After 15 days, 100 percent of the trust and earnings must be returned if there is no guaranteed price. Where the contract is guaranteed, 90 percent of the contract price and 80 percent of the interest must be returned.

Ohio requires that 60 percent of all payments made for vaults be trusted. There are no trusting requirements for other cemetery merchandise and services.

Insurance-funded pre-need contracts are regulated to some extent by:
Director of Insurance
2100 Stella Court
Columbus, OH 43266
(614) 644-2651
(800) 282-4658 (toll-free in Ohio, Policyholder Services)
(800) 843-8356 (toll-free in Ohio, Fraud Division)

B. Right-To-Die Laws
In Ohio, right-to-die issues are addressed in:
Ohio Power of Attorney Act [1989], Ohio Rev. Code Ann. Sections 1337.11–.17 (Anderson 1989)

C. Schools for Body Donations
Ohio University
College of Osteopathic Medicine
Athens, OH 45701
(614) 593-1800 (8 A.M.–5 P.M. weekdays)
(614) 594-2416

University of Cincinnati
College of Medicine
231 Bethesda Avenue, ML 521
Cincinnati, OH 45267
(513) 872-5674 (8:30 A.M.–5 P.M. weekdays)
(513) 872-5612 (Hamilton County Coroner's Office)

Case Western Reserve University
School of Medicine
Department of Anatomy
2119 Abington Road
Cleveland, OH 44106
(216) 368-3430
(216) 221-9330

Ohio State University
College of Medicine
Department of Anatomy
333 West 10th Avenue
Columbus, OH 43210
(614) 292-4831

University Hospital Morgue
Wright State University
North Dayton, OH 45431
(513) 873-3066

Northeastern Ohio Universities
College of Medicine
Rootstown, OH 44272
(216) 325-2511

Medical College of Ohio
3000 Arlington Avenue
Toledo, OH 43614
(419) 381-4109

Oklahoma

A. Regulatory Information

1. *Funeral directors and embalmers are regulated by:*
   Oklahoma State Board of Embalmers and Funeral Directors
   4545 Lincoln Boulevard, Suite 175
   Oklahoma City, OK 73105
   (405) 525-0158/0159
   The board consists of seven members—five licensed funeral directors and two consumer members.

2. *Cemeteries are regulated by:*
   Oklahoma State Banking Department
   4100 Lincoln Boulevard
   Oklahoma City, OK 73105
   (405) 521-2782

3. *Both trust-funded and insurance-funded pre-need funeral contracts are regulated by the Insurance Commission.* Pre-need plans can only be sold by individuals who hold a permit or license. The state of Oklahoma requires that 90 percent of all trust funds be deposited. The amount of earnings that becomes part of the trust is 100 percent less expenses, not to exceed 1.375 percent per year. Consumers may withdraw 100 percent of the amount paid into the trust fund plus any accumulated interest, less 1.375 percent per year.

   Oklahoma requires that 65 percent of the retail price of a vault be trusted, after the vendor has retained 35 percent. Other cemetery merchandise must be trusted at 110 percent of wholesale cost after the vendor has retained 35 percent of the purchase price. There are no trusting requirements for services. Constructive delivery can bypass trusting requirements. Constructive delivery means the merchandise has been manufactured and stored, and a certificate of ownership has been issued. This is the equivalent of actual delivery.

Insurance Commission
P.O. Box 53408
Oklahoma City, OK 73152
(405) 521-2828
(800) 522-0071 (toll-free in Oklahoma)

B. Right-To-Die Laws
In Oklahoma, right-to-die issues are addressed in:
Oklahoma Natural Death Act [1985, 1987, 1990], Okla. Stat. Ann. Tit. 63, Sections 3101–3111 (H.B. 1482 signed May 25, 1990)
Oklahoma Hydration & Nutrition for Incompetent Patients Act [1987, 1990], Okla. Stat. Ann. Tit. 63, Sections 3080.1–.2 (H.B. 1482 signed May 25, 1990)

C. Schools for Body Donations
Oklahoma University
Health Sciences Center
P.O. Box 26901
Oklahoma City, OK 73190
(405) 271-2424
(405) 271-6666

Oklahoma College of Osteopathic Medicine
1111 West 17th
Tulsa, OK 74107
(918) 582-1972

Oregon

A. Regulatory Information
1. *Funeral directors and cemeteries are regulated by:*
State Mortuary and Cemetery Board
1400 SW Fifth Avenue, Room 505
P.O. Box 231
Portland, OR 97201
(503) 229-5681
The board consists of nine members—six licensed funeral directors and three consumer members. One of the consumer members must be a member of a senior citizen organization.
2. *Cemeteries are also regulated by:*
State Mortuary and Cemetery Board
1400 SW Fifth Avenue, Room 505
P.O. Box 231
Portland, OR 97201
(503) 229-5681
3. *Funeral and cemetery pre-need contracts are regulated by the Secretary of State.* Pre-need plans can only be sold by individuals who hold a permit

or license. The state of Oregon requires that 90 percent of all trust funds be deposited where the contract is guaranteed and 100 percent where the contract is not guaranteed. The state also requires that 100 percent of all trust funds be deposited to the account or paid to the consumer. Consumers may withdraw any or all funds at their option.

Constructive delivery can bypass trusting requirements. Constructive delivery means the merchandise has been manufactured and stored, and a certificate of ownership has been issued. This is the equivalent of actual delivery.

Insurance-funded pre-need contracts are regulated to some extent by:
Insurance Commissioner
21 Labor and Industries Building
Salem, OR 97310
(503) 378-4271

B. Right-To-Die Laws
In Oregon, right-to-die issues are addressed in:
Oregon Rights with Respect to Terminal Illness Act [1977, 1983], Or. Rev. Stat. Sections 97.050–.090 (1984)
Oregon Durable Power of Attorney for Health Care Act [1989], Ore. Rev. Stat. Sections 127.505–.585 (1989)

In addition, Oregon has a statute authorizing surrogate decision making entitled:
Oregon Rights with Respects to Terminal Illness Act, Or. Rev. Stat. Section 97.083

C. Schools for Body Donations
Oregon Health Science University
School of Medicine
3181 SW Sam Jackson Park Road
Portland, OR 97201
(503) 225-7811

Pennsylvania

A. Regulatory Information

1. *Funeral directors are regulated by:*
Board of Funeral Directors
P.O. Box 2649
Harrisburg, PA 17105-2649
(717) 783-1253

The board consists of seven members—five licensed funeral directors and two consumer members.

2. *Cemeteries are regulated by:*

Commissioner
Pennsylvania State Real Estate Commission
382 Old Chairton Road
Pittsburgh, PA 15236
(717) 783-7200

3. *Funeral pre-need contracts are also regulated by the State Board of Funeral Directors.* The state does not require a permit or license to sell pre-need plans. Pennsylvania requires that 100 percent of all trust funds be deposited. Consumers may withdraw any or all funds from revocable plans at their option.

Pennsylvania requires that 70 percent of the retail sales price for cemetery merchandise and services be trusted. Constructive delivery can bypass trusting requirements. Constructive delivery means the merchandise has been manufactured and stored, and a certificate of ownership has been issued. This is the equivalent of actual delivery.

Insurance-funded pre-need contracts are regulated to some extent by:
Insurance Commissioner
Strawberry Square, 13th Floor
Harrisburg, PA 17120
(717) 787-5173

B. Right-To-Die Laws
In Pennsylvania, right-to-die issues are addressed in:
Pennsylvania Durable Powers of Attorney Act [1982], Pa. Stat. Ann. Tit. 20, Sections 5604–5607 (Supp. 1989)

C. Schools for Body Donations
Human Gifts Registry
130 South 9th Street
Philadelphia, PA 19107
(215) 922-4440

Rhode Island

A. Regulatory Information
1. *Funeral directors and embalmers are regulated by:*
Board of Examiners in Embalming and Funeral Directing
Division of Professional Regulation
Department of Health
Cannon Building, Room 104
75 Davis Street
Providence, RI 02908
(401) 277-2827

The board consists of five members—three licensed funeral directors and two consumer members.

2. *There is no state cemetery board.*

3. *Funeral pre-need contracts are regulated by the Division of Professional Regulation.* A permit or license is not required to sell pre-need plans. The state of Rhode Island requires that 100 percent of all trust funds be deposited, and 100 percent of all earnings must be deposited to the account or paid to the consumer. Consumers may withdraw any or all funds at their option.

   Rhode Island has no pre-need law for cemetery purchases.

   Insurance-funded pre-need contracts are regulated to some extent by:
   Insurance Commissioner
   233 Richmond Street
   Providence, RI 02903
   (401) 277-2246

B. Right-To-Die Laws
In Rhode Island, right-to-die issues are addressed in:
Rhode Island Health Care Power of Attorney Act [1986, 1989], R.I. Gen. Laws Sections 23-4.10-1–.10-2 (1989)

C. Schools for Body Donations
Brown University
Division of Biology and Medicine
Providence, RI 02912
(401) 863-3355
(401) 863-1000 (after 5 P.M.)

South Carolina

A. Regulatory Information

1. *Funeral directors are regulated by:*
   South Carolina State Board of Funeral Service
   P.O. Box 305
   424 Calhoun Street
   Johnston, SC 29832
   (803) 275-3832
      The board consists of 11 members—9 licensed funeral directors and 2 consumer members.

2. *Cemeteries are regulated by the South Carolina State Cemetery Board, which can be contacted at:*
   State Cemetery Board
   Secretary of State
   P.O. Box 11350
   Columbia, SC 29211
   (803) 734-2174

3. *Funeral pre-need contracts are regulated by the State Board of Bank Control.* Pre-need plans can only be sold by licensed funeral directors who hold a license to do so. The state of South Carolina requires that 100 percent of all trust funds be deposited, and 100 percent of all earnings must be deposited to the account. Consumers may withdraw any or all funds at their option if the account is revocable. The consumer may enter an irrevocable contract, which is transferable. Both nonguaranteed-price and guaranteed-price (inflation-proof) contracts are available.

The State Board of Bank Control can be contacted at:

Commissioner of Banking
1026 Sumter Street, Room 217
Columbia, SC 29201
(803) 734-1050

South Carolina requires that 100 percent of the actual cost for cemetery merchandise must be trusted. Cemetery services are not covered. Constructive delivery can bypass trusting requirements. Constructive delivery means the merchandise has been manufactured and stored, and a certificate of ownership has been issued. This is the equivalent of actual delivery.

South Carolina law prohibits the sale of insurance to fund a preneed contract for specific funeral services and merchandise. Funeral personnel cannot be licensed to sell insurance, and insurance personnel cannot hold a funeral director's license. Under South Carolina pre-need law, only general advertising of pre-need funeral contracts is allowed. No door-to-door or unsolicited telephone selling is allowed.

B. Right-To-Die Laws

In South Carolina, right-to-die issues are addressed in:
South Carolina Death with Dignity Act [1986, 1988], S.C. Code Ann. Sections 44-77-10–160 (Law. Co-op Supp. 1988)
South Carolina Powers of Attorney Act [1986, 1990], S.C. Code Ann. Sections 62-5-501–502 (H.B. 4444 signed May 14, 1990)

C. Schools for Body Donations

Medical University of South Carolina
Department of Anatomy
171 Ashley Avenue
Charleston, SC 29425
(803) 792-3521, ext. 211

University of South Carolina
School of Medicine
Department of Anatomy
Columbia, SC 29208
(803) 733-3369
(803) 777-7000

South Dakota

A. Regulatory Information

1. *Funeral directors are regulated by:*
South Dakota State Funeral Board
P.O. Box 1115
Pierre, SD 57501
(605) 224-6281
   The board consists of seven members—five licensed funeral directors and two consumer members.

2. *There is no state cemetery board.*

3. *Funeral pre-need contracts are regulated by the State Board of Funeral Service.* Pre-need plans can only be sold by individuals who hold a permit or license. The state of South Dakota requires 85 percent trusting where the contract is guaranteed and 100 percent trusting where the contract is not guaranteed. It requires that 100 percent of all earnings must be deposited to the account or paid to the consumer. Revocable trusts can be canceled if 30 days' written notice is given.
   South Dakota has no pre-need law for cemetery purchases.
   Insurance-funded pre-need contracts are regulated to some extent by:
Director of Insurance
Insurance Building
910 East Sioux Avenue
Pierre, SD 57501-3940
(605) 773-3563

B. Right-To-Die Laws

In South Dakota, right-to-die issues are addressed in:
South Dakota Durable Powers of Attorney Act [1977, 1979, 1990], S.D. Codified Laws Ann. Sections 59-7-2.1–4 (H.B. 1233 signed February 24, 1990)

C. Schools for Body Donations

University of South Dakota
Office of Dean
School of Medicine
Vermillion, SD 57069
(605) 677-5431
(605) 677-5141
(605) 624-3932

Tennessee

A. Regulatory Information

1. *Funeral directors and embalmers are regulated by:*

Board of Funeral Directors and Embalmers
Volunteer Plaza, 2nd Floor
500 James Robertson Parkway
Nashville, TN 37219
(615) 741-2378
   The board consists of five members—four licensed funeral directors and one consumer member.

2. *Cemeteries are regulated by:*
Director
Burial Services Section
Department of Commerce and Industry
500 James Robertson Parkway, 2nd Floor
Nashville, TN 37243-1145
(615) 741-5062

3. *Funeral pre-need contracts are regulated by the Commissioner of Commerce and Industry.* Pre-need plans can only be sold by individuals who hold a permit or license. The state of Tennessee requires that 100 percent of all trust funds be deposited, and 100 percent of all earnings less the trustee fee must be deposited to the account or paid to the consumer. Consumers may withdraw any or all funds from revocable plans at their option.

   Tennessee requires that 120 percent of the wholesale cost of cemetery merchandise and services must be trusted. Vaults are not sold by cemeterians in Tennessee. They can only be sold by funeral directors. Constructive delivery can bypass trusting requirements. Constructive delivery means the merchandise has been manufactured and stored, and a certificate of ownership has been issued. This is the equivalent of actual delivery.

   Insurance-funded pre-need contracts are regulated to some extent by:
Commissioner of Insurance
500 James Robertson Parkway
Nashville, TN 37219
(615) 741-2241
(800) 342-4029 (toll-free in Tennessee)

B. Right-To-Die Laws

In Tennessee, right-to-die issues are addressed in:
Tennessee Right to Natural Death Act [1985], Tenn. Code Ann. Sections 32-11-101–110 (Supp. 1988)
Tennessee Durable Power of Attorney for Health Care [1990], Tenn. Code Ann. Tit. 34, Ch. 6 (H.B. 2345 signed April 9, 1990)

C. Schools for Body Donations

East Tennessee State University
Department of Anatomy
P.O. Box 19960A
Johnson City, TN 38614
(615) 929-6241 (8 A.M.–5 P.M.)
(615) 929-4480

University of Tennessee
Department of Anatomy
875 Monroe Avenue
Memphis, TN 38163
(901) 528-5965 (days)
(901) 528-5500

Meharry Medical College
1005 Todd Boulevard
Nashville, TN 37208
(615) 327-6000

Vanderbilt University
School of Medicine
113 Light Hall
Nashville, TN 37232
(615) 322-7948

Texas

A. Regulatory Information

1. *Funeral directors are regulated by:*
   Texas Funeral Service Commission
   8100 Cameron Road
   Building B, Suite 550
   Austin, TX 78753
   (512) 834-9992
      The board consists of nine members—five licensed funeral directors and four consumer members.
2. *Cemeteries are regulated by:*
   Banking Commissioner
   2601 North Lamar Boulevard
   Austin, TX 78705
   (512) 459-4105
3. *Funeral pre-need contracts are regulated by the Banking Commission.* Pre-need plans can only be sold by individuals who hold a permit or license. The state of Texas requires that 90 percent of all trust funds be deposited, and 100 percent of all earnings less the trust expense must be deposited to the account or paid to the consumer. The consumer may withdraw all payments that are held in the trust except for the interest.
      The Banking Commission can be contacted at:
   Banking Commissioner
   2601 North Lamar Boulevard
   Austin, TX 78705
   (512) 479-1200
      Texas requires that 90 percent of all funds collected for vaults and cemetery services must be trusted. There are no trusting requirements for other cemetery merchandise.

Insurance-funded pre-need contracts are regulated to some extent by the Banking Commission and by:
Claims and Compliance Division
State Board of Insurance
1110 San Jacinto Boulevard
Austin, TX 78701
(512) 463-6501
(800) 252-3439 (toll-free in Texas, complaints only)

B. Right-To-Die Laws

In Texas, right-to-die issues are addressed in:
Texas Natural Death Act [1977, 1979, 1983, 1985], Tex. Rev. Civ. Stat. Ann. Art. 4590h (Vernon Supp. 1989)
Texas Durable Power of Attorney for Health Care Act [1989], Tex. Rev. Civ. Stat. Tit. 71, Ch. 20, Art. 4590h (Vernon 1989)

In addition, Texas has a statute authorizing surrogate decision making entitled:
Texas Natural Death Act, Tex. Rev. Civ. Stat. Ann. Art. 4590h Section 4(c)

C. Schools for Body Donations

Texas A&M University
Department of Anatomy
Medical Science Building
Medical College
College Station, TX 77843
(409) 845-4914
(409) 822-1571

University of Texas
Health Science Center
Southwestern Medical School
5323 Harry Hines Boulevard
Dallas, TX 75235
(214) 688-2232
(214) 688-2221

North Texas State University
College of Osteopathic Medicine
Camp Bowie at Montgomery
Ft. Worth, TX 76107
(817) 735-2210

University of Texas
Medical Branch at Galveston
Galveston, TX 77550
(409) 761-1293
(409) 761-1011

Baylor College of Medicine
Department of Cell Biology
Texas Medical Center
Houston, TX 77030
(713) 799-4930
(713) 449-6511 (Brookside Funeral Home)

University of Texas Medical School
Health Science Center
Department of Neurobiology and Anatomy
P.O. Box 20708
Houston, TX 77225
(713) 792-5703
(713) 449-6511 (Brookside Funeral Home)

Texas Tech University
School of Medicine
Lubbock, TX 79430
(806) 743-2700 (Monday through Friday)
(806) 743-3111

Texas Chiropractic College
5912 Spencer Highway
Pasadena, TX 77505
(713) 487-1170

University of Texas
Health Science Center
7703 Floyd Curls Drive
San Antonio, TX 78284-7762
(512) 691-6533

Utah

A. **Regulatory Information**

1. *Funeral directors are regulated by:*
   State Funeral Service Examiners Board
   Division of Occupational and Professional Licensing
   160 East 300 S
   P.O. Box 45802
   Salt Lake City, UT 84145
   (801) 530-6628
      The board consists of five members—four licensed funeral directors
   and one consumer member.
2. *There is no state cemetery board.*
3. *Funeral pre-need contracts are regulated by the Department of Business Regulation.* Pre-need plans can only be sold by individuals who
   hold a permit or license. The state of Utah requires that 75 percent of

all trust funds be deposited, and 100 percent of all earnings must be deposited to the account or paid to the consumer. The consumer may withdraw 60 percent of the trust plus any interest accrued.

Utah has no pre-need law for cemetery purchases.

Insurance-funded pre-need contracts are regulated to some extent by:
Commissioner of Insurance
P.O. Box 45803
Salt Lake City, UT 84145
(801) 530-6400

B. Right-To-Die Laws
In Utah, right-to-die issues are addressed in:
Utah Personal Choice and Living Will Act [1985, 1988], Utah Code Ann. Sections 75-2-1101–1118 (Supp. 1988)

In addition, the state of Utah has a statute authorizing surrogate decision making titled:
Utah Personal Choice and Living Will Act, Utah Code Ann. Section 75-2-1105 (2)

C. Schools for Body Donations
University of Utah
Department of Anatomy
50 North Medical Drive
Salt Lake City, UT 84132
(801) 581-6728 (8 A.M.–5 P.M. weekdays)
(801) 581-2121

Vermont

A. Regulatory Information

1. *Funeral directors are regulated by:*
Division of Licensing and Registration
Board of Funeral Service
109 State Street, Pavilion Office Building
Montpelier, VT 05602
(802) 828-2390
   The board consists of three members, all of whom are licensed funeral directors.
2. *There is no state cemetery board.*
3. *The state of Vermont has no pre-need law for funeral directors or cemeteries.*
   Insurance-funded pre-need contracts are regulated to some extent by:
Commissioner of Insurance
State Office Building
Montpelier, VT 05602
(802) 828-3301

B. **Right-To-Die Laws**
In Vermont, right-to-die issues are addressed in:
Vermont Terminal Care Document Act [1982], Vt. Stat. Ann. Tit. 18, Section 5251, and Tit. 13, Section 1801 (1987)
Vermont Durable Powers of Attorney for Health Care Act [1987], Vt. Stat. Ann. Tit. 14, Ch. 121, Sections 3451–3467 (Supp. 1988)

C. **Schools for Body Donations**
University of Vermont
Department of Anatomy
Burlington, VT 05405
(802) 656-2230 (8 A.M.–5 P.M. weekdays)
(802) 656-2230

Virginia

A. **Regulatory Information**

1. *Funeral directors and embalmers are regulated by:*
Commonwealth of Virginia
Department of Health Professions
Virginia Board of Funeral Directors and Embalmers
1601 Rolling Hills Drive, Surry Building
Richmond, VA 23229-5005
(804) 662-9907
(804) 662-9941

    The board consists of nine members—seven licensed funeral directors and two consumer members.

2. *There is no state cemetery board.*

3. *Funeral pre-need contracts are also regulated by the Board of Funeral Directors and Embalmers.* Pre-need plans can only be sold by individuals who hold a permit or license. The state of Virginia requires that 100 percent of all trust funds be deposited, and 100 percent of all earnings must be deposited to the account or paid to the consumer. Consumers may withdraw any or all funds plus interest at their option.

    Virginia requires that 40 percent of the retail price for cemetery merchandise and services must be trusted. Constructive delivery can bypass trusting requirements. Constructive delivery means the merchandise has been manufactured and stored, and a certificate of ownership has been issued. This is the equivalent of actual delivery.

    Insurance-funded pre-need contracts are regulated to some extent by:
Commissioner of Insurance
Virginia State Corporation Commission
700 Jefferson Building
P.O. Box 1157
Richmond, VA 23209
(804) 786-3741
(804) 225-3806
(800) 552-7945 (toll-free in Virginia)

B. Right-To-Die Laws

In Virginia, right-to-die issues are addressed in:

Virginia Natural Death Act [1983, 1988, 1989], Va. Code Sections 54.1-2981–2992 (1988), Amended (1991)

Virginia Durable Power of Attorney Act [1954, 1968, 1987], Va. Code Sections 11-9.1–9.4 (1988)

Health care decisions are authorized by Va. Code Section 37.1-134.4 (1990), Substituted Consent Act (1989, 1990, 1991).

In addition, the state of Virginia has a statute authorizing surrogate decision making entitled:

Virginia Natural Death Act, Va. Code Section 54:1-2986 (1988)

Va. Code Section 37.1-134.4 (Supp. 1989)

C. Schools for Body Donations

State Anatomical Program—Body Donations
Department of Health
James Madison Building
Richmond, VA 23219
(804) 786-3174

Washington

A. Regulatory Information

1. *Funeral directors are regulated by:*

Washington Funeral and Cemetery Boards
Division of Professional Licensing
P.O. Box 9012
Olympia, WA 98504-8001
(206) 586-4905

The board consists of five members—four licensed funeral directors and one consumer member.

2. *Cemeteries are regulated by:*

Washington Funeral and Cemetery Boards
Division of Professional Licensing
P.O. Box 9012
Olympia, WA 98504-8001
(206) 586-4905

The Washington Cemetery Board consists of six members—three industry members, one accountant, one attorney, and one at-large member.

3. *Funeral pre-need contracts are regulated by the Department of Licensing.* Pre-need plans can only be sold by individuals who hold a permit or license. The state of Washington requires that 85 percent of all trust funds be deposited, and 100 percent of all earnings must be deposited to the account or paid to the consumer. Consumers may withdraw any

or all funds, which includes the 85 percent entrusted and the 15 percent held plus interest, at their option.

Washington requires that at least 50 percent of the contract price for cemetery merchandise and services must be trusted. Constructive delivery can bypass trusting requirements. Constructive delivery means the merchandise has been manufactured and stored, and a certificate of ownership has been issued. This is the equivalent of actual delivery.

Insurance-funded pre-need contracts are regulated to some extent by:
Insurance Commissioner
Insurance Building AQ21
Olympia, WA 98504
(206) 753-7301
(800) 562-6900 (toll-free in Washington)

B. Right-To-Die Laws

In Washington, right-to-die issues are addressed in:
Washington Natural Death Act [1979], Wash. Rev. Code. Ann. Sections 70.122.010–.905 (Supp. 1989)
Washington Durable Power of Attorney–Health Care Decisions Act [1989], Wash. Rev. Code Ann. 11.94.010 (H.B. 1952 signed May 3, 1989)

C. Schools for Body Donations

University of Washington
Department of Biological Structure
SM-20
Seattle, WA 98195
(206) 543-1860
(206) 548-3300

West Virginia

A. Regulatory Information

1. *Funeral directors and embalmers are regulated by:*
West Virginia Board of Funeral Directors and Embalmers
812 Quarrier Street, 4th Floor
Charleston, WV 25301
(304) 348-0302/0303
The board consists of seven members—six licensed funeral directors and one consumer member.

2. *There is no state cemetery board.*

3. *Funeral pre-need contracts are regulated by the attorney general.* Pre-need plans can only be sold by individuals who hold a permit or license. The state of West Virginia requires that 90 percent of all trust funds be deposited. At the time of need, if the cost of the funeral is greater than the original amount, the funeral home may withhold the interest needed to

cover these costs. The balance of the interest goes to the estate. Consumers may withdraw 90 percent of all funds plus interest at their option.

West Virginia has no pre-need law for cemetery purchases.

Insurance-funded pre-need contracts are regulated to some extent by:
Insurance Commissioner
2019 Washington Street, East
Charleston, WV 25305
(304) 348-3394
(800) 642-9004 (toll-free in West Virginia)

B. Right-To-Die Laws

In West Virginia, right-to-die issues are addressed in:
West Virginia Natural Death Act [1984], W. Va. Code Sections 16-30-1–10 (1985)
West Virginia Medical Power of Attorney Act [1990], W. Va. Code Sections 16-30a-1–20 (H.B. 4197 signed March 15, 1990)

C. Schools for Body Donations

Marshall University
School of Medicine
Department of Anatomy
Huntington, WV 25704
(304) 429-6788
(304) 525-8121

West Virginia School of Osteopathic Medicine
400 North Lee Street
Lewisburg, WV 24901
(304) 645-6270

West Virginia University
School of Medicine
4052 BSB, WVU Medical Center
Morgantown, WV 26506
(304) 293-6322
(304) 293-0111

Wisconsin

A. Regulatory Information

1. Funeral directors are regulated by:
Wisconsin Funeral Directors Examining Board
1400 East Washington Avenue
P.O. Box 8935
Madison, WI 53708
(608) 266-1574

The board consists of six members—four licensed funeral directors and two consumers. Additionally, the board regulates funeral homes through establishment permits.

2. *There is no state cemetery board.*

3. *The Funeral Directors Board also regulates funeral pre-need contracts.* The state of Wisconsin requires 100 percent trusting of all funds that have been deposited. Consumers may withdraw any or all funds from revocable plans at their option.

Cemetery pre-need sellers must be registered and are subject to reporting and auditing requirements. Wisconsin requires that at least 40 percent of each principal payment for cemetery merchandise and services be trusted. However, for vaults, 100 percent of the retail price must be trusted. Constructive delivery, excluding vaults, can bypass trusting requirements. Constructive delivery means the merchandise has been manufactured and stored, and a certificate of ownership has been issued. This is the equivalent of actual delivery.

Insurance-funded pre-need contracts are regulated to some extent by:
Commissioner of Insurance
P.O. Box 7873
Madison, WI 53707
(608) 266-3585
(800) 236-8517 (toll-free in Wisconsin)

B. Right-To-Die Laws
In Wisconsin, right-to-die issues are addressed in:
Wisconsin Natural Death Act [1984, 1986, 1988], Wisc. Stat. Ann. Sections 154.01–.15 (West 1989)
Wisconsin Power of Attorney for Health Care Act [1990], 1989 Wisc. Act 200 (H.B. 305 signed April 12, 1990)

C. Schools for Body Donations
University of Wisconsin
Medical School
Department of Anatomy
1300 University Avenue
Madison, WI 53706
(608) 262-2888 (Monday through Friday, 8 A.M.–4:30 P.M.)
(608) 262-2800
(608) 262-2122

Medical College of Wisconsin
Department of Anatomy
8701 Watertown Plank Road
P.O. Box 26509
Milwaukee, WI 53226
(414) 257-8621

Wyoming

A. Regulatory Information

1. *Funeral directors are regulated by:*
Wyoming State Board of Embalming
P.O. Box 349
Worland, WY 82401
(307) 347-4028
   The board consists of five members, including the secretary of the State Board of Health. None of the members are consumers.
2. *There is no state cemetery board.*
3. *Wyoming licenses sellers of funeral and cemetery pre-need plans.* In addition, pre-need contract sellers must be bonded. Wyoming requires that 100 percent of trust funds be deposited in an approved depository. Funeral goods and services must be guaranteed in terms of price and similarity in quality sold at the time of need. All contract forms and withdrawal forms must be approved prior to use. No funds may be withdrawn without written approval of the Insurance Department.
   Insurance-funded pre-need is prohibited in the state of Wyoming.

B. Right-To-Die Laws
In Wyoming, right-to-die issues are addressed in:
Wyoming Act [1984, 1985, 1987], Wyo. Stat. Sections 33-22-01–109 (1988)

C. Schools for Body Donations
The state of Wyoming has no medical schools. The nearest state should be checked by those considering body donation.

Index

DATE DUE

OCT 28 2009